Sociology on Film

Sociology on Film

Postwar Hollywood's Prestige Commodity

CHRIS CAGLE

Rutgers University Press

New Brunswick, New Jersey, and London

Library of Congress Cataloging-in-Publication Data
Names: Cagle, Chris, 1974– author.
Title: Sociology on film : postwar Hollywood's prestige commodity / Chris Cagle.
Description: New Brunswick, New Jersey : Rutgers University Press, 2016. | Includes bibliographical references and index.
Identifiers: LCCN 2016012329 | ISBN 9780813576947 (hardcover : alk. paper) | ISBN 9780813576930 (pbk. : alk. paper) | ISBN 9780813576954 (e-book (epub)) | ISBN 9780813576961 (e-book (web pdf))
Subjects: LCSH: Social problems in motion pictures. | Motion pictures—Social aspects—United States. | Motion pictures—United States—History—20th century.
Classification: LCC PN1995.9.S62 C34 2016 | DDC 791.43/6556—dc23
LC record available at https://lccn.loc.gov/2016012329

A British Cataloging-in-Publication record for this book is available from the British Library.

www.rutgersuniversitypress.org

Manufactured in the United States of America

For my late mother

Contents

Acknowledgments

I would like to express my gratitude for the guidance, support, and input that I have received while writing this book. The seed of this project was planted when I first watched *Gentleman's Agreement* in Chuck Maland's American film class at the University of Tennessee. Chuck's interest in the social problem film was infectious and stayed with me long after college. My other dissertation readers, Phil Rosen and Mary Ann Doane, were and are the intellectual models I aspire to. I have benefited from the friendship and advice from graduate school colleagues at Brown, and this book would not have come to be were it not for Karl Schoonover and Rosalind Galt, from whom I have learned so much. Chris Holmlund as mentor and friend has always challenged me intellectually and offered conversation and counsel, as the occasion requires. Nora Alter has been a valued advocate and a guide in the writing process. A big credit goes to Leslie Mitchner at Rutgers University Press for nurturing this project from the proposal phase to a workable book. It has been a dream of a process thanks to her.

I am grateful to Temple University, where I have had the luck of a collegial department in Film and Media Arts. The university's research support helped me with conference travel and time off for writing. Jenifer Baldwin and Brian Boling of Paley Library provided me with material crucial for this project. My research on the film industry drew from the resources of the University of Southern California Doheny Library's Special Collections in Cinema and Television, the Margaret Herrick Library at the

Academy of Motion Picture Arts and Sciences, and the UCLA Library's Special Collections. Ned Comstock at the Doheny Library and Barbara Hall at the Herrick Library were especially helpful.

An earlier version of chapter 1 was published as "Two Modes of Prestige Film," *Screen* 38, no. 3 (Autumn 2007), published by Oxford Journals on behalf of the University of Glasgow. Chapter 2 uses portions of two essays: "The Postwar Cinematic South: Realism and the Politics of Liberal Consensus," in *American Cinema and the Southern Imaginary*, edited by Deborah Barker and Kathryn McKee (Athens: University of Georgia Press, 2011), and "*Knock on Any Door:* Realist Form and Popularized Social Science," in *Lonely Places, Dangerous Ground: Nicholas Ray in American Cinema*, edited by Steven Rybin and Will Scheibel (Albany, NY: SUNY Press, 2014). Grateful acknowledgment is made to the editors and the publishers.

In addition to those listed above, many colleagues have read and commented on portions of this book: Oliver Gaycken, Ellen Scott, Patrick Keating, Jennie Hirsch, Franklin Cason Jr., Bob Rehak, Rebecca Wingfield, Gabe Wettach, Elena Gorfinkel, and Francine Latil. My colleagues at Temple and in the Philadelphia area have provided intellectual stimulation, including (but not only) Jeff Rush, Suzanne Gauch, Allan Barber, Elisabeth Subrin, Dan Friedlaender, Tim Corrigan, Patty White, Karen Beckman, Peter Decherney, Meta Mazaj, Michael Dwyer, and Kathleen Rowe Karlyn. Rita Kozen has helped me in so many moments of my time at Temple. My students, too many to name, have pushed me to think about film differently and for that I am grateful. Most of all, I owe a special debt to the book's reviewers for pushing the book's writing and argument in a productive direction.

Thank you to friends; in addition to those above, Diana King, Paul Harrill, Whit Hendon, Joe Fallon, and Wally Pansing have played a continued supporting role. I could not begin to repay my family, particularly my sisters, Jan Cagle and Kathy Marker, for all they have given me. And last but not least, I express gratitude to my partner, Chris Devine, for the patience of a saint.

Sociology on Film

Introduction

A glance at the Academy Award Best Picture nominations from the years immediately following World War II reveals a pattern of films with topical subject matter: *The Lost Weekend* (Billy Wilder, 1945), a "gritty" exposé of the problems of alcoholism; *The Best Years of Our Lives* (William Wyler, 1946), a triptych of the problems facing returning veterans; *Gentleman's Agreement* (Elia Kazan, 1947), an indictment of anti-Semitism; *The Snake Pit* (Anatole Litvak, 1948), a plea for more humane mental health care; and *Pinky* (Elia Kazan, 1949), a melodrama about racial passing in the South.[1] These films performed well at the box office and were often the movies that studios touted in their publicity. Their success touched off a cycle of films that continued into the 1950s and 1960s, notably with the films of producer-director Stanley Kramer, including *The Defiant Ones* (1958) and *Guess Who's Coming to Dinner* (1967). At the time, popular press critics and movie producers alike called these "social problem films," and that label has stuck.

Film historians and critics have treated the social problem film as something between a fad and a full-fledged genre. Scare quotes are common, as in Robert Ray's assessment that "the result [of Hollywood's search for realism] was the 'problem picture' that earnestly portrayed veterans' struggles to adapt to homecoming . . . cruelties caused by racial prejudice . . . or the sufferings of maltreated patients."[2] Genre theorists frequently stress that a genre is not a thing in itself but rather a critical label at best identifying formulas and patterns in film narrative.[3] Social problem films do not circulate as self-consciously as musicals, Westerns, or horror films and therefore seem to lack coherence as a category. Nonetheless, Charles Maland's provisional definition of the social problem film offers a good starting point: "a narrative feature whose central narrative concern or conflict relates to or includes the presentation of a social problem." He adds, "The social problem has a contemporary setting . . . and is generally animated by a humane concern for the victim(s) of or crusader(s) against the socal problem and, often, by an implicit assumption that the problem can be treated or even eliminated through well-intentioned liberal social reform."[4] To Maland's definition could be added two additional traits: problem films frequently have a didactic tone and an affective appeal at odds with their putatively objective storytelling.

A prime example of the postwar problem film would be *Gentleman's Agreement.* Directed by Elia Kazan and produced by 20th Century–Fox, the film follows a journalist, Phil Green (Gregory Peck), and his difficulties in writing an exposé on anti-Semitism. He resists the assignment, believing that the story has been done and that it will suffer from a "facts and figures" approach, until he devises a plan to pass as Jewish in order to write about the experience. He gets his story but is unprepared for the extent of anti-Semitism in the upper-middle-class world of New York City and its suburbs, and his crusade against injustice strains his relationship with his fiancée, Kathy (Dorothy McGuire). The film demonstrates how the postwar problem film combines an overt theme of social or political change with some formal markers of didactic address to the spectator. For instance, in one scene Phil explains to his son, Tommy (Dean Stockwell), what anti-Semitism is and why religion is a separate matter from national identity. "One thing's your country, see, like America," he says, "like America, or France or Germany or Russia, all of it. . . . But the other thing is religion, like the Jewish, or the Catholic or the Protestant religions. . . . Don't get mixed up about it . . . 'cause some people are mixed up." Phil's words about the problems of anti-Semitism double for the film's position, and the editing reinforces the dialogue's didacticism. As the scene holds disproportionately on shots with Phil in a frontal composition, the viewer shares Tommy's position, watching Phil deliver his monologue. In essence, Phil is talking at the viewer.

Thematically, *Gentleman's Agreement* suggests that incremental change arises from interpersonal relationships as much as it does from narrowly political action. The screenplay draws close parallels between ethnic

FIGURE 1 *Gentleman's Agreement*: the postwar prestige style.

conflict and three interpersonal spheres: Kathy and her friends; Phil and his Jewish friend, Dave (John Garfield); and Tommy and his schoolmates. At the same time, the film depicts class and institutions as social entities; the realist mise-en-scène of New York City, the Midtown corporate office, and the garden suburb all emphasize the "gentleman's agreement" as an *haute bourgeois* phenomenon. The film's aesthetics and theme both point to a sense of a sociological dimension to the phenomenon of anti-Semitism.

As fiction cinema, *Gentleman's Agreement* is many steps removed from sociology proper, but it bears a significant resemblance in spirit to contemporary sociological studies like *The Authoritarian Personality*.[5] Like these studies, the film assesses the psychology of bigotry but also understands psychology as emerging from group dynamics. *Gentleman's Agreement*, too, depicts primary and secondary groups as the terrain for racial prejudice. Phil Green's ruse to pass as Jewish in order to research his exposé depends on subjecting the office place of *Smith's Weekly* to a sociological experiment (he passes with the magazine's employees, too, to gauge their reaction). This action parallels the story of Phil's secretary, Elaine Wales, who had conducted a résumé experiment (complete with a control group) by applying for jobs with two résumés, one with a Jewish and the other a Gentile name. Meanwhile, the main narrative conflict between Phil and Kathy, and between Dave and Kathy, springs from the different ways the characters recognize that one's immediate peer group, whether neighborhood, high society, or (in the case of Tommy) school, actively replicates prejudicial attitudes. In short, *Gentleman's Agreement*, like other social problem films, invokes the social in its otherwise personalized narrative.

This convergence of Hollywood and sociological ideas bears examination. Sociology had been established in the United States since the late nineteenth century, but the field developed the attributes of an established academic field only during the first half of the twentieth century, culminating in a postwar boom. Springing from sociology's growth as a discipline, the subfield of social problem sociology emerged, too, gaining its own journal, *Social Problems*, in 1950. The notion of a "sociological" and eventually (by the 1940s) "social problem" film came to define what would become, at least among film scholars and some critics, a genre. The connection between the "social" of the social problem film and sociology's concept of the social might at first view seem tenuous. Indeed, to date, while film historians have made valuable discursive readings of 1940s cinema generally and of earlier (1910s and 1930s) social problem films, few have paid sustained attention to the ideas of 1940s and postwar sociology.

However, this critical period of growth and intellectual firmament in U.S.-based sociology fostered Hollywood's desire, at least in certain quarters, to inscribe sociology on film. Rather than simply depict social issues, social problem films in the 1940s acted as a type of popular social science. They drew inspiration from the school of functionalism then in vogue in American sociology and cited prominent sociological works. Borrowing, too, from the aligned cultural fields of journalism and literature, they created an aesthetic form suitable for expressing abstract relations between members of a national body. Much as Alfred Hitchcock and film noir directors popularized psychoanalysis by developing a specifically cinematic expression of Freudian ideas, social problem films found aesthetic forms suitable for the ascendant field of sociology.

Some critics have demonstrated how 1920s and especially 1930s cinema specialized in portrayals of the masses, whether in crowd scenes or in the "mass ornament" of Busby Berkeley musicals.[6] These depictions were important and influential figurations of a national collectivity, but the 1940s' invention of the social shied away from collectivity per se in favor of invisible determination. The Hollywood problem film sought a cinematic means of representing the more abstract conception of the social in lieu of the visualized collective. In *Gentleman's Agreement*, for example, anti-Semitism is the accumulation of myriad interpersonal interactions, not confrontations between groups visualized collectively.

The sociological impulse was not without pitfalls, and sociologists, historians, and cultural critics in more recent decades have criticized postwar sociology for its complicity with dominant power structures and the bureaucratic operation of the state. In the instance of race, postwar functionalist sociology became associated with a dominant (white) liberal view of racial politics, through its impact on influential policy documents like the Moynihan Report.[7] This policy work has a mixed heritage, on the one hand lending intellectual support to Lyndon Johnson's Great Society attempts at poverty amelioration while, on the other, pathologizing African American culture and feeding into post-1970 counterreaction.[8] Complicating this matter, important African American sociologists like E. Franklin Frazier, Kenneth Clark, and Mamie Clark contributed to scholarship amenable to the dominant, functionalist vein, and within its context functionalism did provide an antiracist critique of both Jim Crow and nationwide racism.

Social problem films, too, have a complex legacy. Leftist and left-leaning filmmakers wrote, directed, produced, or otherwise contributed to many of the social problem films, and the anti-Communist hunt in the form of the House Un-American Activities Committee (HUAC) and the subsequent blacklist targeted social problem content, citing films such as the popular *The Best Year of Our Lives* as examples of un-Americanism.[9] At the same time, social problem films' themes and character-centered narratives have meant the genre has been associated with reformist liberalism rather than a more far-reaching leftism. One foundational and early study of the genre coauthored by Peter Roffman and Jim Purdy captures this ambivalence perfectly by showing both sympathy with the problem film's attempt to avoid escapist narrative and concern that the genre acts as a safety valve, tying up messy social contradictions.[10] Similarly, the race problem cycle reflected a progress in civil rights consciousness but one constrained within the worldview of a white, liberal spectator. Ellen Scott's study of racial censorship presents a compelling case that even liberal problem films like

No Way Out (Joseph Mankiewicz, 1950) were compromised by their treatment of black bodies and black problems as spectacle for a white audience.[11] Whether through the lens of race or class, the necessities of industry economics, self-regulation, and audience ideology imposed political compromises and constrained the social problem films.

The social problem film was as ideological as its critics have contended, but this picture is not complete. In the formulation of Jürgen Habermas, social science discourse may be ideology but not merely ideology.[12] We now have sufficient historical distance on the postwar era to diagnose the cultural undercurrents of the period. As useful as poststructuralist discursive reading can be, it has the unfortunate effect of always putting the present-day scholar in the position of historical superiority over those of the past. Much of the most recent wave of revisionist film history aims to think about prior intellectual moments differently. Such scholarship has taken up the history of what Charles Acland and Haidee Wasson call "useful cinema," the cinema designed for institutional and educational purposes, and has treated the intellectual history of earlier waves of film studies not primarily as an occasion for ideological dismissal but as a genealogy of half-forgotten work.[13] Similarly, Karl Schoonover casts the contemporary debates around humanistic spectatorship as central to the postwar reception of fiction cinema, from Hollywood to Italian neorealism.[14] Without discounting how postwar critics and thinkers participated in an ideology, we can recognize how complex the intellectual and popular discourses of the postwar period could be and how they do not always conform to the retrospective caricature of political containment that subsequent decades often have of them.

Additionally, as useful as the traditional accounts are, they miss how complex a genre the social problem films could be. Rather than a side development, problem films were a central part of the refashioning that Hollywood would undergo after World War II. In the context of the film industry of the 1940s, postwar social problem films were a form of popular sociology marrying contemporary developments in American sociology to the new type of prestige filmmaking. Although the "prestige film" can be a loose term, throughout the studio years it was generally a production category with higher budgets, better production values, and more sophisticated subject matter. The social problem films were disproportionately represented among the postwar prestige films.

The sociological aspirations of these films were not mere naive gestures or labeling conventions. Movie producers referred to "sociological films," and filmmakers cited sociological studies. These changes came in addition to the application of social science research to film-going itself, whether in George Gallup's marketing research or in media-effects studies.[15] From the narratives of the films to their critical reception and the proclamations of the filmmakers, there was a shared sense that these movies had a new way of depicting the social body and diagnosing its pathologies. The meaning of the term "social" evolved from the Progressive era to the middle of the twentieth century and, with it, the social problem film's response to a growing discipline of American sociology. However much prestige films popularized sociology, Hollywood still embraced important aspects of sociological thought.

As a translator of social science into popular culture, the social problem film had a hybrid aesthetic. On the one hand, problem films belong to a canon of politicized filmmaking aligned with political leftism and a combination of film noir and postwar documentary-tinged realism. Accordingly, Bill Nichols identifies Hollywood's social problem films as part of a "discourse of sobriety" that also characterized documentary film, public policy, and rationalist culture more broadly.[16] On the other hand, many of the problem films were adapted from best-selling novels and had as much in common with melodramas like *Cass Timberlane* (George Sidney, 1947) and *The Green Years* (Victor Saville, 1946) as they did with the noir films and *films gris* favored by blacklist historians. Far from sober, they are punctuated by moments of stylistic excess, extreme pathos, and heated conflict between characters. Their aesthetic was a peculiar form of realism that synthesized documentary and sentimentality, the social scientific and the novelistic. Recent scholarship has argued that postwar neorealist and European art cinema were never fully divorced from a more traditionally generic appeal.[17] A similar dynamic was at play in the taste hierarchies that Hollywood inhabited in the middle of the twentieth century, and the "feminine" genres of the melodrama and the literary adaptation were more closely connected to the "masculine" genres of noir and the social problem film than critics have acknowledged. As such, the "official" realms of public policy and public debate intersected with what Miriam Hansen has called the vernacular modernism of cinema and literature.[18] The postwar prestige films' affective dimension was a paradoxical component of their realist rhetoric.

The Social Problem Discourse

Even outside of its use as a genre label, the term "social problem" demarcates an idea with a variable and at times vague meaning, yet the concept of the social problem is as central to the postwar problem films as the question of historical knowledge is to the history film. One can treat this social problem analysis as social science and see the representation and analysis of social phenomena and as worthy in aim or in result. Undoubtedly, this was the position of the genre's proponents at the height of its postwar popularity. To take the example of *The Snake Pit*, the narrative is structured around the personal challenges facing one mental health patient, Virginia Cunningham (Olivia de Havilland).[19] Many of the key conflicts therefore center on her delusional anxiety around other men, including her husband, and her uncertainty in trusting her doctor, Dr. Kix (Leo Genn). Additionally, however, other conflicts in the films—especially those between Dr. Kix and the hospital board—point to social problem dimensions of the personal problem. The film's theme stresses the need for new therapeutic measures, including Freudian psychotherapy and electric shock treatment. These measures face resistance for reasons of budgetary expediency, suggesting a second theme calling for policy measures, including increased state funding of mental hospitals and lower patient-doctor ratios. Director Anatole Litvak claimed the film sought "to reassure the public that mental disorder is an illness which can be cured, and to direct attention to the facilities now available in our institutions."[20] Even accepting Hollywood's sweeping approach to its messages, these themes can be more or less correct—or more or less desirable than their scientific or policy alternatives.

While postwar filmmakers and critics often valued then-recent developments in social science, many sociologists and critical theorists in the intervening years have often viewed the popular sociology and academic sociology of the postwar years as especially ideological, tied into either the interests of the state or a conformist social order. In this view, social problem analysis legitimizes a particular power relationship. To return to the example of *The Snake Pit*, Leslie Fishbein views the film's psychiatric model as a type of social control and concludes that "while *The Snake Pit* won public acclaim for its realistic treatment of the theme of mental illness, its more central concern was a crisis in modern womanhood which popularized Freudianism had promised to solve by its parallel equation of femininity and mental health."[21] For a similar reason, John Hill posits a "social problem discourse" in his study of British problem films of the 1950s. Because these films about juvenile delinquency or race relations end up articulating an order based on white, middle-class values, Hill views social problem definition as a matter of power:

> A social problem is the product of discourse rather than the property of any particular condition in itself. What then becomes accepted as a social problem is not in any way inevitable but a consequence of the ability to have any particular definition legitimated, be it via the media, or other "accredited agencies." . . . To this extent, the "social problems" so defined are not so much the problems of "society" as a whole as the "problems" of those who enjoy the ability to universalize their particular point of view as the point of view of all in society.[22]

Hill's notion of a social problem discourse stresses, in Marxian fashion, the power relations underlying social legitimation. As Charles Maland notes, this idea very often aligns with a left critique of problem films' specific "answers" and with a belief that reformism deflects attention from larger systemic problems.[23]

In connecting social problem analysis to political ideology, critics like Fishbein and Hill follow a historical wave of reflexivity and self-critique within sociology itself. Maland mentions Lee Rainwater's work, but Howard Becker's labeling theory of deviance or Erving Goffman's study of mental institutions as a battle of social performance equally calls social problem definition into question.[24] By the mid-1960s, these interventions in the field had changed social problem sociology. Becker's 1966 social problem sociology textbook presents the social problem as an epistemological prism dependent on social position:

> Consider race relations. Although clearly an area of major social concern, it is not clear what the "problem" is. For the Negro and for many white citizens as well, the problem is how to achieve as rapidly as possible the full participation of the Negro in American society. For other whites the problem is different: the possible loss of social advantages they have long enjoyed at the expense of Negroes. For many politicians and for some social scientists the problem is the tension and violence of a situation in which Negroes demand rights that Whites are unwilling to grant. For professionals—social workers and

educators, among others—the problem is to undo the harm done by generations of segregation and discrimination so that the Negro will be equipped to take advantage of his rights. This does not exhaust the list.[25]

Statements like these treat the social problem as a construction and thus parallel cultural-construction readings of the social problem film of the sort that semiotic-textual readings use.

The nominative form of the term "the social" can designate a historically specific intellectual understanding of the unit of sociological analysis. The political theorist Jacques Donzelot adds to this nominative usage an institutional critique.[26] By "the social" and "the social question" Donzelot refers to matters of class power that in English might be labeled "political" matters. In Gilles Deleuze's summary of Donzelot, "*the* social refers to a *particular sector* in which quite diverse problems and special cases can be grouped together, a sector comprising specific institutions and an entire body of qualified personnel ('social' assistants, 'social' workers)."[27] In fact, the French usage of the nominative version of the social is closer to the understanding of "social problems" that Progressives—and Progressive-era cinema—invoked in the term than to the later understanding that the postwar problem films invoked. At the same time, Donzelot treats the term as a historical discourse and argues for a central role of Emile Durkheim in shifting French society to conceive of the "social" differently. His analysis suggests how the intellectual discourse abetted the political institutions of the modern state.

Liberalism, Leftism, and the Blacklist

At various points, problem films have formed a primary site of government censorship of cinema, with the social problem discourse as justification for film censorship in general. The transitional cinema period (before the emergence of the classical studio system) saw intense debates about cinema's effect on society. Lee Grieveson connects the social science discourse of the 1900s and 1910s to juridical efforts to control and regulate cinema, often in favor of upper-middle-class sensibility against that of working-class and African American audiences.[28] Grieveson, like William Uricchio and Roberta Pearson, sees the transitional cinema as a period of possibility, an alternative public sphere in Miriam Hansen's formulation, that the social problem discourse and classical cinema shut down.[29] Ellen Scott's study of racial censorship has demonstrated that the problem film was central to many of the censorship debates in the 1930s, 1940s, and 1950s, and the representations of the race problem pictures like *Pinky* or *No Way Out* emerged in large part from the censorship battles internal to the film industry and between the film industry and outside political bodies.[30]

Liberalism as a political movement was rapidly changing in these years, though. As Edward Buscombe argues in his analysis of Frank Capra's social comedy *American Madness* (1932), "No studio in the 1930s would have tolerated Communist movies, or anything very close to that. . . . But within these parameters considerable diversity was possible."[31] Buscombe is referring to the New Deal, which changed the nature of American liberalism, at least as historians use the term. A new political coalition championed an enlarged role for the state, an increased role for labor, and new forms of mixed economy.[32] After World War II, these elements would inform the liberal consensus that Godfrey Hodgson and other historians have characterized as narrowing down the political spectrum in the postwar years.[33] Even if the United States never had invigorated public sectors on the level that European mixed economies did, in the aftermath of its war economy a "Keynesian compact" emerged in which both capital and labor accepted that, in Claus Offe's summary, "each class must 'take the role of the other.'"[34] This acceptance was not automatic or without political struggle, and both the Taft-Hartley Act and the general movement of McCarthyism curtailed union gains and suppressed political protest. Despite these setbacks, though, elite opinion and political party policy converged toward a combination of anti-Communism, enlarged government, and some modest measures of the welfare state and welfare capitalism.[35] If the postwar years saw a political containment of the more left and radical potentialities of the New Deal, they were also a time in which many New Deal tenets were solidified and furthered.

One group to fare badly in the new liberal consensus was the political left, particularly Hollywood's left. The prominence and visibility of problem films prompted a wave of anti-Communism directed at the film industry, and in turn the genre bore the brunt of the blacklist. The historiography on HUAC and the blacklist gives a narrative in which political battles embroiled studios and punished writers, directors, and producers of social problem films.[36] A film like *Crossfire* (Edward Dmytryk, 1947), a noir police procedural about an anti-Semitic hate crime, can make the case for the problem film as a leftist, not liberal, genre. Its narrative traces the efforts of both police and a diffident soldier to find the person who committed a hate crime murder of a Jewish man. The detective's (Robert Young) final revelation of the killer's motive becomes a soliloquy about the virulence of hate. By playing down the sociological middle-class milieu of films like *Gentleman's Agreement* or *Snake Pit*, *Crossfire* offers a narrative about anti-Semitism as well as something else: domestic fascism. Many in the postwar American left, that is, feared the forces of reaction, and rhetorically cast racism and prejudice as just incarnations of a broader reactionary turn in American politics. *Crossfire*'s left-progressive producer Adrian Scott was convinced that anti-Semitism was part of an emerging fascism in the United States.[37] Alongside a more straightforward liberal message about racial tolerance, therefore, the film is also a subtle allegory of Fair Deal politics. The year 1947 was a crisis point of the Truman administration's attempt to steer the continued course of New Deal liberalism, particularly labor rights and full employment policy, through a resistant Congress and an organized political opposition by reinvigorated business interests.[38]

For this reason, *Crossfire* is aligned not only with the liberal problem film but also with a cycle of realist noirs that the film historian Thom Andersen has called *film gris*.[39] These films often featured proletarian heroes, urban settings, allegorical narratives, B-budget noir stylistics, and action-oriented narratives. A disproportionate number of blacklist victims were connected to *films gris* and B-budget problem films, including Adrian Scott, Edward Dmytryk, Abraham Polonsky, and Joseph Losey. The history of their tenure at the studios, particularly RKO, suggests their attempts to find a place for counterhegemonic politics within the studio system.[40]

At face value, canonical histories capture much of the problem film's significance, particularly given the genre's finite heyday and its prominent role in the blacklist crisis. However, blacklist historiography needs to be challenged on several counts. Most immediately, the problem film mentality reached far beyond the short list of blacklisted films. Indeed, it affected studios that specialized in topical material, like 20th Century–Fox and RKO, as well at those that did not, like MGM and Columbia. Moreover, it emerged from radicalized artists (the Adrian Scott unit at RKO), industry liberals (Walter Wanger and Dore Schary), and a cautious Republican producer (Darryl F. Zanuck at 20th Century–Fox).

These films appealed to multiple constituencies, who often saw different attributes. In *Crossfire*, an extreme version of anomie (bigotry as a pathology) is also a version of social and class conflict (fascism starts at home—the implicit rallying cry against the Fair Deal's opponents). RKO producer Dore Schary privileged the former, while the Adrian Scott unit privileged the latter.[41] Postwar films combined liberal thematic directness with left-wing allegorical resonance. Across the genre, these films could read as melodramas about individual problems or as social analysis. From a certain left critique, the liberalism of these films denies a proper social analysis.[42] However, midcentury liberalism differed as much from classic, individualistic liberalism as it did from socialism. This difference corresponds to a hermeneutic problem, since problem films were seen as both liberal and left in their politics.

Middlebrow Aesthetics of Popular Sociology

Critical ambivalence around the social problem films emerges in large part from their status as popular science. Much as the historical film can be understood as a type of popular history, problem films were more popular sociology than academic social science. For many historians of science, "popular science" is an umbrella term that encompasses two processes: vernacular science and popularization.[43] Vernacular science is scientific knowledge created by those outside of elite scientific communities. Cultural studies and sociology-of-science approaches focus on vernacular science as part of a conventionalist account that views science as part of a process of social hegemony.[44] Popularization, on the other hand, refers to the circulation of scientific knowledge among laypeople and in popular culture. The process of popularization often relies on the specialized labors of scientific experts and popular culture interpreters.[45] Historians of science have been divided between those who view popularization as merely a process of translating and disseminating expertise and those who see a dynamic interchange between expert and public.[46] "Rather than treating elite science as something simply to be accepted or rejected," Roger Cooter and Stephen Pumfrey write in favor of an interchange model, "a more sophisticated reading would have the 'lower orders' treating the products of elite culture as resources which are appropriated and reconstituted."[47]

Some combination of diffusion and dynamic-interchange models applies to Hollywood's popularization of American developments in sociology. By most understandings of the term, movies did not qualify as vernacular science. Instead, they translated and adapted ideas from the academy. Sociology in fact was gaining autonomy as a discipline in this period and rising in stature and influence within wider publics.[48] Whereas academic social science still had more indirect than direct influence on American culture, journalism and other arenas of the public sphere spread and adapted understanding of social problem sociology. Seemingly a one-way vector of ideas emanated from the academy, through the intermediary of applied fields like policy and journalism, and finally to a popular entertainment culture. However, Hollywood's role as interpreter influenced the ideas about the social perhaps as much as it transmitted them. Particularly in the 1940s, as sociological terms and concepts became widespread among an educated public, academic sociology was in an implicit dialogue with its publics.

Moreover, as an entertainment medium and an art, Hollywood cinema added the the problem of aestheticization to the normal anxieties around social science popularization. Unlike nonfiction translations of social scientific knowledge, narrative films imposed their own logic and had to function first and foremost as dramatic works that could serve as entertainment commodities. As John Guillory describes the middlebrow so succinctly, "Middlebrow culture is the ambivalent mediation of high culture within the field of the mass cultural."[49] Social problem films differed from previous prestige films that adapted canonical masterpieces of literature or accepted historical works. Rather, they were middlebrow on two counts, first by aligning themselves with other strains of high culture—social science, policy, and journalism—and second by adapting novels that occupied a middlebrow cultural position themselves. Novels like *The Lost Weekend* (Charles R. Jackson, 1944) and *Gentleman's Agreement* (Laura Z. Hobson, 1947) were neither high modernist literature nor popular genre fiction. As published literature in a realist vein, these novels had a cachet that Hollywood did not and that the studios were eager to borrow, at least at times. This disposition was behind the ultimate critical rejection of the social problem film. As Andrew Sarris, a prominent critic of the genre, quipped about one of its key producer-directors, "If Stanley Kramer had not existed, he would have had to have been invented as the most extreme example of thesis or message cinema."[50]

All the same, the middlebrow disposition of the films is not the whole story. Some scholars have questioned the very term "middlebrow," arguing that the word has a built-in classism.[51] There are good reasons to retain the term, since it designates a relational aesthetic category, but the skeptics are right to remind us that to diagnose the middlebrow is to invoke a position of cultural superiority. The historical middlebrow is culturally safe since it is not our middlebrow but a distant one, yet film scholarship on classical Hollywood still overwhelmingly privileges auteurs or low genres. In the late 1940s, especially, prestige films and other middlebrow genres compared favorably in number to film noirs, musicals, and Westerns; however, many of these middlebrow works barely receive any critical attention.

The social problem film thrived in the nexus of middle-class and middlebrow culture, between a broad audience and the logic of aesthetic differentiation relation. Put less abstractly, social problem films and other prestige films could be both middlebrow culture and a self-critical commentary on middle-class life. To take central films in the genre, *The Best Years of Our Lives, Gentleman's Agreement, The Lost Weekend,* and *The Snake Pit* all interrogated middle-class (bourgeois or petit bourgeois) culture, both confirming some of its ideology and challenging other aspects. During the postwar period, after all, cultural critics began to diagnose middlebrow culture in a widespread manner, with Russell Lynes's 1949 high/middle/low typology preceding the now more famous writing of Dwight Macdonald.[52] The middle of the twentieth century brought a rapid expansion of the white-collar classes, including the professional-managerial class, and the ascendancy of the new classes colored their ideological disposition toward a new, less hidebound kind of middlebrow.[53] Social problem films therefore occupied a paradoxical position: mass culture geared toward a mass audience but speaking to the class ethos of certain audience factions.

A Social Fields Explanation

Specific logics of autonomous social fields provide a useful model for how popularization maintained some specificity of the underlying social science while aligning the discourse toward new ends. This conception of the social field draws extensively from the work of Pierre Bourdieu and the field theory of sociologists inspired by Bourdieu.[54] The social field refers to a range of objective social relations that structure the disposition of individuals who inhabit or traverse it—and is in turn structured by them. Bourdieu defines these social fields, first by their particular quantity and mix of economic and cultural capital, and second by their autonomy (or lack thereof) from other fields.[55] In the case of social problem sociology, key social fields are responsible for social problem definition: a social scientific field responsible for an expert definition; a political field responsible for an applied definition; a journalistic field responsible for a popularized definition; and a mass citizenry comprised of multiple fields and capable of responding to social problem definitions in the form of political acclaim. For the social problem film, this simplified model would add the film industry (a field of cultural production) and would assign the mass citizenry the additional role as mass audience.

Each field has its own history and its own internal logic. Sociology developed into a mature discipline with the dominance of functionalism, a school of thought derived from Emile Durkheim's sociology. Liberal consensus characterized the political sphere. This consensus had as an ultimate cause the Keynesian welfare state and mass public sphere formations of competitive party democracy and as a proximate cause the political party coalitions and issue battles of the late 1940s and early 1950s.[56] The economics of the film industry changed rapidly with antitrust enforcement of the *Paramount* ruling and with shifting market conditions domestically and abroad. The film audience, by some measures, became an increasingly middlebrow audience willing to elevate cinema culturally and artistically.

Despite the autonomous history of these arenas, there were important overlaps between the various fields concerned with the "social" in the postwar United States. Each of the following chapters provides a partial explanation for why the social problem film changed from the 1930s to the postwar years and why the genre gained such prominence in Hollywood's output after World War II. Chapter 1, "Two Modes of Prestige Film," argues that social problem films were a central catalyst in the industry's shift in approach to "serious" filmmaking. An interplay between industry economics and critical reception pushed Hollywood toward midbudget, realist prestige films, different in style than the prestige films dominant in the 1930s. Chapter 2, "Hollywood as Popular Sociology," traces 1940s social problem films to the intellectual foundations of American sociology. While topical films had often faced the "sociological" label, the nature of sociology itself had shifted over time. Functionalist approaches to sociology pushed Hollywood to conceive of social problems less as problems *to* society than as problems *of* society—and to frame "society" less as a collective mass and more as an abstract relation of the individual to a diffuse social body. Chapter 3, "Hollywood and the Public Sphere," argues that a desire to participate in the mass public sphere prompted Hollywood to look to popular sociology. The chapter gives an account of two comparisons that Hollywood studios envisioned for themselves in the 1940s: analogies between cinema and journalism and those between Hollywood and documentary film. Chapter 4, "A Genre Out of Cycles," traces the solidification of a social problem genre around the discourse of the social, arguing that the film industry began to converge in its conception of the genre only as the abstract sense of the social began to predominate. Chapter 5, "Realist Melodrama," points to an overlooked source of social problem narrative and style: what the literary historian Gordon Hutner calls "middle-class novels"—best-selling, nongenre novels that addressed contemporary concerns and combined a distinctly American literary realism with sentimental tone.[57] As Hollywood adapted and mimicked these novels, studio cinematographers worked to find a correlative realist visual style.

Behind these features was the interplay between an intellectual and an industrial logic. Intellectually, sociology developed a core sense of the social that spread through a process of popularization. Industrially, economic conditions led to the inclusion of popular sociology in the aesthetic formulas of prestige cinema. The problem film offers a study in historical and social convergence. Leftist writers converged in their interests with liberal producers or conservative studio heads. Highbrow magazines had similar critical opinions as mass-market newsweeklies. Those making films were aware of the critical reception championing certain Hollywood films as art. Scriptwriters and directors cited academic sociologists in their understanding of social pathology and of public opinion formation. Too often film histories ignore or assume these convergences. They beg, instead, explanation.

Social problem films about racial conflict differ from those, for example, on alcoholism or mental illness. Each topic has its own history and ideological meaning. Despite these differences, though, the genre shared an underlying assumption about what it meant to make social problem cinema. In order to depict the "social" of the social problem, Hollywood had to search for new aesthetic formulas and new ways to deal with thematic directness in the context of entertainment cinema. Writers, directors, cinematographers, producers, and others wrestled with ways of dealing with social abstraction cinematically. The mass collectivities of 1930s cinema served as a powerful correlative to political challenges of the Great Depression. Hollywood's embrace of sociology in these 1940s films was a more fitful process but no less vital.

1

Two Modes of Prestige Film

In gauging the changes that Hollywood underwent during the 1940s, two scenes from "quality" films released two decades apart are exemplary. In the first, *Dodsworth* (William Wyler, 1936), a series of six shots immediately signal classical film narration and elevated production values. Sam Dodsworth's (Walter Huston) entrance into an ocean liner dining room consists of an elaborate tracking shot interwoven with the crossing paths of extras behind his forward motion, then a low-angle deep-space composition that morphs into a subtle crane shot of Dodsworth, before Major Lockert (David Niven) joins him. The effect is to assert a narrational presence in excess of the characters, a point of view outside the action that, even if it does not tell the story in a way a third-person omniscient narrator does in literature, connotes a literary voice. Afterward, a low-angle deep-space shot of his wife Fran's (Ruth Chatterton) entrance highlights much of what made the 1930s prestige picture distinctive: the modernist set design to give a sense of solidity and more grandeur than the sound stage sets actually possessed; the populated and fully furnished mise-en-scène; the somewhat experimental yet refined costume design; and the elaborate lighting arrangement keeping the star in full, flattering illumination despite camera and actor movement. Finally, the last

FIGURE 2 *Dodsworth*: literary adaptation and prestige production values.

shot doubles the love triangle theme visually by framing Fran between the two men; this framing will be repeated throughout the film. In sum, both cinematically and thematically, William Wyler and Samuel Goldwyn have given what to them—and to audiences in general—was appropriate treatment of work from a novelist like Sinclair Lewis, with high-culture credentials. "In the years that followed the Second World War," David Thomson offers, "Wyler was Hollywood's idea of a great director—respectable, diligent, tasteful, a servant of stars and box office potential, and a reliable master of big projects."[1] As *Dodsworth* reveals, the same applied before the war. William Wyler was one of the classical Hollywood directors most associated with the prestige film. His projects generally had literary sources, "serious" themes, and lavish production values.

In contrast, *Marty* (Delbert Mann, 1955) resists much of classical Hollywood's "quality" style. In one famous scene, Marty (Ernest Borgnine) and his mother have a dinner conversation about Marty's marriageability. The dining room set is striking in the severity of its low-key lighting and reminiscent of the use B filmmakers historically have made of minimal

FIGURE 3 *Marty*: television style and blocking.

lighting to disguise inexpensive sets.[2] Throughout the scene, fast film stock and heavy single-source overhead lighting leave very little of the room visible, just the table, the characters, and some of a sideboard. Twelve mostly static shots last two-and-a-half minutes; the scene consists of a few long takes containing much of the dialogue (shots 1, 7, and 12 last at least thirty seconds each) and a few shorter shot-countershot alternations done with a multiple-camera setup. The action, that is to say, is blocked and shot much like a television show, not a surprise given that the source was a not a canonical play or a grand historical subject but the anthology television drama program *Goodyear Television Playhouse.* The telecast's director, Delbert Mann, directed the independently produced film, and its writer, Paddy Chayefsky, was known primarily for his writing for anthology programs and for *Marty* specifically. The result was the maintenance of a television aesthetic. As Eric Barnouw argues about the anthology drama,

> To this close-up drama, live television brought an element that had almost vanished from film. . . . Film had long been dominated by its own kinds of

> time, made by splices in the editing room. . . . The manipulation of "film time" offered creative pleasures so beguiling to film makers that they had virtually abolished "real time" from the screen. Its appearance in long stretches of television drama gave a sense of the rediscovery of reality—especially for people whose only drama had been film.[3]

The film version trafficked in this "real time," too: the previous scene, in which Marty calls a woman to ask for a date, is shot in a continuous three-and-a-half-minute take with the camera simply panning to follow Marty's movement or tracking in for emotional punctuation. At an earlier point in Hollywood's history, this live-theater aesthetic would have been read as "cheap" and undesirable. *Marty* had a negative cost of only $400,000, and it is impossible to imagine a feature film so low in budget qualifying as a prestige film in the 1930s. In 1956, however, the film garnered four Academy Awards out of eight nominations and established a precedent for smaller-scale dramas for directors with theatrical and anthology television credentials. Rather than looking for cultural legitimacy in a Broadway play adapting a Nobel Prize–winning author, as *Dodsworth* did, *Marty* inverted the cultural touchstone by looking to a television show itself looking to off-Broadway theater for cultural legitimacy.

The aesthetic difference between these two films registers, in large part, in their diverging conceptions of what "serious" entertainment means and should be. In this area, Hollywood underwent a far-reaching transformation in the postwar years. Newer genres such as the topical political drama, the pseudodocumentary, and eventually the "mature" Broadway adaptations aimed toward thematic, stylistic, and topical importance; location shooting, contemporary settings, and social critique gained a prominent place in American commercial cinema. Beyond this trend in quantity, the postwar years saw a qualitative shift in what counted as serious cinema, since the nature and role of the prestige film changed in Hollywood. When film historians speak of the prestige film in the studio years, they designate a production category surpassing the typical A-film in its budget, treatment, and subject matter. During the postwar years, however, another type of serious film came to prominence, one that can also claim the term "prestige" picture since it speaks to or elicits acclaim from observers inside and outside the film industry. Where the *film industry* defined the prestige picture of the 1930s, *film consumers* defined the new type of prestige film. *Dodsworth* and *Marty*, we can say, represent two modes of prestige film. The industrial mode looked outward, conspicuously, to higher cultural forms to lend Hollywood narratives the aura of respectability. The socially defined mode looked inward, internalizing an aesthetic and mode of perception that were meant to be culturally more elevated. This analytic distinction is also a historical one: over time, the Hollywood prestige film transformed from an overwhelming reliance on the *Dodsworth* mode of prestige cinema to the increasingly internalized middlebrow sensibility of the *Marty* mode. By the time of the emergence of the "New Hollywood" in the 1970s and 1980s, the literary adaptations and historical films favored as prestigious in the classical years had all but disappeared.

Key to this shift was the cycle of social problem films released from 1945 to 1949. Their box-office and critical success led competing studios to produce more message films and, in the process, established a new model for the socially defined prestige film. This transformation was dual. An industrial transformation of the prestige film emerged from the changing conditions of the film industry in the 1940s and particularly after World War II. Meanwhile, a larger cultural legitimization of the cinema created a receptive context that would champion the newer mode of prestige cinema. The social problem films were the site of a mutually influential process in place by the late 1940s: Hollywood's prestige dramas began to incorporate more finely internalized modes of aesthetic judgment just as the popular press critics responsible for legitimization of Hollywood's product took the prestige drama as their main focus. This interplay between internal trends in the film industry and its context as social practice helps explain Hollywood's makeover between the conspicuous cultural touchstone of *Dodsworth* and the quiet respectability of *Marty*—indeed, between Hollywood's classical form and what film scholars identify as postclassical style and content.

Industrial Transformation of the Prestige Film

One overarching factor internal to the film industry was responsible for the emergence of the newer type of prestige film. Starting in 1940 and particularly after 1947, the oligopolistic and vertically integrated arrangement of the industry would undergo reorganization because of antitrust prosecution and rulings. The process stretched two decades, but various stages of its implementation had a more immediate impact. Embedded in the industry's transformation was a transformation of the prestige film. The stability of the cultural marketplace for movies in the 1920s and 1930s was matched by the stability of oligopoly and vertical integration. After World War II, however, the *Paramount* antitrust case upended studio economic arrangements. When combined with new marketplace conditions and more localized economic trends, divorcement set into play ideal conditions for some studios and independent producers to shift modes of prestige film production.

The classical prestige picture had its roots in a stable studio system of content and genre differentiation. As Tino Balio has argued, the prestige picture of the 1930s was not a genre but rather a production category. "A prestige picture is typically a big-budget special based on a pre-sold property," he writes, "often as not a 'classic,' and tailored for top stars." He lists four cycles that dominated the decade's big-budget productions: nineteenth-century European literature; Shakespearean plays; best-selling novels and hit Broadway plays written by Nobel and Pulitzer Prize–winning authors; and biographical and historical subjects.[4] These films were usually two hours or more in their running time and were exhibited on a road-show basis, similar to the legitimate theater, with single features, increased prices, intermissions, and reserved seating. The exhibition treatment, production values, star draw, and overall quality usually made these films the bigger box-office performers of the decade. Just as important, Balio notes, they were the public face defining the studio, both within the industry and among the larger public.

The prestige film of the 1950s shared many of the same characteristics as its 1930s counterparts. If anything, film specials with high-profile premieres and road-show exhibition were now the mainstay of a greatly reduced and entrenched film industry, not occasional productions. Bible epics replicated the spectacle of 1930s historical dramas like *In Old Chicago* (Henry King, 1938) on a grander scale. Literary and historical melodramas like *Raintree County* (Edward Dmytryk, 1957) mimicked *Gone with the Wind* (Victor Fleming, 1939) in its running time, theme, and intermission. Broadway hits by William Inge (*Picnic* [Joshua Logan, 1955]) and Tennessee Williams (*A Streetcar Named Desire* [Elia Kazan, 1951]) got screen adaptations.

Still, at closer examination the postwar prestige film was different. For one thing, legitimate theater had itself changed after the war and now veered away from popular taste and toward a literary realism and "mature" content that suited the highbrow and especially middlebrow tastes of those still attending dramatic theater. More important, the postwar spectacle film was not necessarily the same as a prestigious production. Stanley Kramer's problem films like *The Defiant Ones* still served as exemplars of "serious cinema." Along with *Marty*, other modestly budgeted black-and-white dramas like *On the Waterfront* (Elia Kazan, 1954), *Twelve Angry Men* (Sidney Lumet, 1957), and *Inherit the Wind* (Stanley Kramer, 1960) defined Hollywood at its most literary and intellectual. *From Here to Eternity* (Fred Zinnemann, 1953) surpassed in prestige the box-office juggernaut *The Robe* (Henry Koster, 1953). In the postwar years, the prestige film had split between the popular prestige picture, often an epic spectacle, and the critical prestige picture, including the problem film and the literary melodrama. Two modes of prestige, in essence, sat side by side.

Ultimately, the breakup of the studio's vertical monopoly and horizontal oligopoly put into play secondary changes that fostered the studios' reliance on the critical prestige picture. Most notably, the *Paramount* decision made the distribution market competitive once more: distributors (the studios) still formed an oligopoly, but now exhibitors could begin to purchase films regardless of studio affiliation, without the restrictions of block or blind booking. Michael Conant points out that the process of divorcement was a decade long. After the Supreme Court's ruling in *United States v. Paramount Studios* in 1948, it would take until the end of the 1950s before Loews cinemas divested its ownership of MGM, but already in 1951 Paramount's first-run theaters were booking on a strictly competitive basis.[5] Still other effects were felt earlier: block booking was limited to five feature blocks after the first consent decree in 1940, and the practice ended after the first *Paramount* decree in 1946. In all, divorcement proceeded unevenly, and the lag between the consent decree and final divestment—and the staggering of different studios' divestment—provided fertile ground for the postwar social problem films and new prestige films.

The double feature system of the 1930s and the war years, to begin with, was suddenly subject to instability. For a decade the system had functioned for all three branches of the industry. Brian Taves points to several advantages that B-films held for the studios: they met demand for product, guaranteed cash flow, and "balance[d] a large overhead by using sets, stages, ranches, and contract talent on a nearly continual basis."[6] The fixed rentals of the lower halves of the double bills ultimately hedged against riskier yet potentially more profitable A-films. One can overstate the functional nature of the double feature, since audiences and producers alike frequently chafed at the practice in the 1930s, yet the double feature matched the exhibition market of the Depression years, with its premium on variety and quantity over quality. Generally only first-run downtown theaters could resist the demand for double bills.[7]

The end of block booking mandated by the consent decree did not stop the practice of double features, but it did put more competitive pressure on both the A and B features. The war years were the start of a decade-long shift in budget allotment of the major studios. "Because of the overheated first-run market, the success of reissues, and decree-related selling policies," Thomas Schatz notes, "the majors all but eliminate[d] low-budget productions during the war."[8] Essentially, A-film budgets became less risky and more profitable, so production budgets rose accordingly, fueled additionally by inflation and rising input costs. The limitations of block booking meant that the majors needed A-film quality more and the B-film market hedge less. This situation would become acute in the postwar years, as the ban on block booking would lead to the majors' outright abandonment of their B units. Now that the end of block booking increased demand for higher quality pictures and decreased the demand for the Bs, studios found production costs rising even higher. The postwar market, in fact, was pushing in two directions at once. Studios could not find a market of exhibitors willing to pay what they considered an adequate price for the B product, while parts of the exhibition market, especially the neighborhood and small-town "circuit theaters," were still showing double bills and found it difficult to rent affordable films for the lower half of the bill. By 1949, *Variety* reported that double-bill theaters had difficulty finding nonpercentage-rental pictures when even B-film stalwarts Columbia and Republic announced the plan to cut B production.[9] By the early 1950s, rising production costs and falling profits would effectively implode the double feature system from within.

Paradoxically, the dual feature system's demise particularly impacted the production category by definition never shown in double feature: the prestige film. Aided at first by the strong wartime A-film market, the prestige films of the traditional mold performed quite well for the studios. Spurred by demand, their production costs would rise steadily throughout the decade. Additionally, inflation and the expense of Technicolor pushed the costs of prestige films higher in the postwar years. Industry-wide, the average feature budget in 1942 was \$336,000; that figure rose to \$554,386 in 1945 and to \$665,000 in 1946.[10] The trend was sustainable as attendance was steady or rising, but already in 1947 the exhibition market faced its initial domestic decline and loss of overseas markets to protectionism. Suddenly the worries of industry observers were well-founded.[11] Without a steady income stream from integrated theaters or block-booked B-films, the studios' balance sheets were squeezed and the top end of their output was in crisis. 20th Century–Fox, for instance, produced a few extravagantly budgeted prestige films in the late 1940s. At a time when the cost of studios' A-films ranged from $1 million to $2.5 million, Fox counted on 1946's *The Razor's Edge* (Edmund Goulding, 1946), costing $3.35 million; 1947's *Forever Amber* (Otto Preminger, 1947), costing $6.38 million; and 1948's *Captain from Castile* (Henry King, 1947), costing $4.5 million. Each meant a loss on the balance sheet, with high rental returns ($8 million worldwide for *Amber*, $6 million for *Captain*) that nonetheless failed to recuperate below-the-line costs. As Aubrey Solomon observes on the expensive prestige film, "On the average $1.5 million picture, such returns would be wildly successful, but new extravagance would take its toll on profits."[12] Studios in fact did rein in extravagance, and quickly. Over the next two years, Fox would reduce its typical high-A budget from $2.35 million to almost $1.79 million, a drop echoed across the industry.[13]

One strategy for cutting costs came from the mid-A and near-A market. The social problem film was one obvious success story. Problem films were not entirely new in the late 1940s, but as a prestige genre, their appearance was intermittent, more a hypothetical promise of what serious Hollywood could be than a trend in its achievement. Nonetheless, films like *The Grapes of Wrath* (John Ford, 1940) established the direction that producer Darryl Zanuck, Fox, and the industry in general would go after 1945. William Wyler's independent *The Best Years of Our Lives* shared some stylistic traits with the director's earlier prestige productions but pursued prestige through topical reference rather than presold source material and with a stark, realist aesthetic rather than spectacle. The year before, *The Lost Weekend* had won the Academy Award for Best Picture despite production values that were plain, midbudget, and far removed from *The Grapes of Wrath*'s literary tone and pace. Fox's "race problem" cycle of *Gentleman's Agreement*, *The Snake Pit*, and *Pinky* continued the trend with contemporary milieu, decent but modest production values, and moderate star draw. In fact, Fox found in the midbudgeted A-film social problem picture its most profitable type of film. *Gentleman's Agreement* earned $3.9 million domestically, *The Snake Pit* $4.1 million, and *Pinky* $4.2 million. Even without world rentals, these returns were essentially double the negative costs. Unable to fund profitably lush production values or lavish sets, Fox opted for prestige based on realism in style or content. Poor box-office performance of the spectacle prestige film signaled to the studio that audiences and critics were just as likely to reward the "quality" midbudget drama. Fox's formula was soon copied: Susan Hayward tried to imitate Ray Milland's career success by playing an alcoholic in *Smash-Up: The Story of a Woman* (Stuart Heisler, 1947); normally staid and prestige-focused MGM felt emboldened to adapt *Intruder in the Dust* (Clarence Brown, 1949); and Columbia entered the prestige race with the socially relevant *All the King's Men* (Robert Rossen, 1948).

The postwar problem films were not prestige pictures in the strictest sense of film industry economics: big-budget offerings exhibited on a roadshow basis. Except for *The Best Years of Our Lives*, the initial problem films like *The Lost Weekend* or *Gentleman's Agreement* played as normal A-films, only ones with unexpectedly long runs and strong box office. By other measures, though, they had the marks of the prestige picture. Their advertisements served as the public face of their studios, both in the general press and the trade press. They received disproportionate recognition from the Academy of Motion Picture Arts and Sciences. The popular press championed them, and they tapped into a broad cultural admiration, especially from community groups, clergy, and members of an urban cultural elite.[14] In the new conditions of postwar America, the move to relevant content had guided studios to the new model of the prestige film.

Nowhere was this model clearer than in ambitious Bs that crossed over. RKO's *Crossfire*, for instance, was shot at a negative cost of between $500,000 and $650,000 (a near-A budget in 1947), and grossed four times its cost by becoming a hit in major metropolitan areas, where its run broke local theater records.[15] The film's box-office success prompted *Variety* to write of studios pursuing an aggressive B policy:

> Announcements of the "high end of Bs" have been customarily greeted with a yawn in the trade, but present efforts appear to have a bit more substance than the usual exercise at label-juggling. Such important grossers as 20th Century–Fox's "Boomerang" and RKO's "Crossfire" made it perfectly apparent last year that a B-size budget didn't have to mean a B-sized picture.
>
> . . . Warner Brothers plan is to make the lower-budgeters as exercises for their embryo talent, but Metro and RKO both aim to use generously the

> upper-bracket personnel among producers, writers, directors and players. Dore Schary, RKO production chief who was responsible for the $650,000 "Crossfire," is particularly hot on the idea of making pix at from $400,000 to $600,00 that, by the unusual nature of their story, will compensate for other values that must be shaved to stay within this ceiling. . . .
>
> The type of story is particularly important in the change. The former concept was that minimum cost films must generally be adventure and action yarns. Compare that with Schary's "Boy with Green Hair," now in preparation, which is aimed at fighting prejudice, bearing similarity to this extent to "Crossfire."
>
> Rather than being produced down to audiences who might be expected to see a B in a subsequent-run house, Schary's using the low-budget unit to experiment with mature stories and yarns with social content that can attract the type of audience which just doesn't "go to the movies" but picks its pictures.[16]

The strategy of upgrading B-budgeted films into A-films through problem film material was repeated at RKO, before Schary was ousted,[17] and across the industry. In turn, even A-film problem film producer Fox adopted the upgrading strategy for its low-A *No Way Out*, which would, as Darryl Zanuck's comments on the script indicated, "strive for realism and not extravagance. I visualize this picture in the same category as *Boomerang, Street With No Name* [*13 Rue Madeleine*], and *Call Northside 777*, and while it is in the same milieu as *Gentleman's Agreement* and *The Snake Pit*, it does not, of course, demand such an expensive overall production."[18] Zanuck's comparison points to the distinction the studio made between the problem film and the pseudodocumentary—the A and B genres of postwar realism—and its use of realism as marker of aesthetic distinction. The trend would continue until the final divorcement of MGM from Loews: throughout the 1950s, Dore Schary slated a number of low-budget productions as social problem films, including *Go for Broke!* (Robert Pirosh, 1951) and *Bad Day at Black Rock* (John Sturges, 1955).

These major studio examples do not include the many independent productions that shared the major studios' gambits for prestige. Independent production had been around for some time, usually appended to United Artists' distribution arm. However, the war years encouraged independent production. The emphasis on quality A-films and the first-run market boom led studios to adopt more use of unit production and of independent production, while tax laws encouraged talent to form their own production companies.[19] "Independent" companies proliferated with a wide range of distance from the studios. One key arrangement was the in-house independent, whose freedom brought creative license to use lower-budgeted pictures for a sort of research and development arm for the studio. Meanwhile, by the postwar years, competitive distribution gave truly independent producers entry into the exhibition market.

With their degree of distance from the major and minor studios, independents were able to use social relevance or pseudodocumentary realism to parlay a low-budget film into midbudget prestige and box office. Mark Hellinger, in-house at Universal, turned to pseudodocumentary for *The Naked City* (Jules Dassin, 1948), while Dore Schary's Vanguard Pictures provided the social comedy *The Farmer's Daughter* (H. C. Potter, 1947) for Selznick and RKO. The *films gris* cycle, noir films with a realist milieu and left-leaning message or allegory, displays the range of the new independent relationships: *The Lawless* (Joseph Losey, 1950, Pine-Thomas, in house at Paramount), *Body and Soul* (Robert Rossen, 1947, Enterprise Productions through United Artists), *Give Us This Day/Christ in Concrete* (Edward Dmytryk, 1949, "independent" for poverty row Eagle-Lion), and *Right Cross* (John Sturges, 1950, B-film at MGM).[20] Equally important were the higher-key social problem dramas emerging with the late 1940s "race problem" cycle. Louis de Rochemont's *Lost Boundaries* (Alfred Werker, 1949) managed to combine problem film and pseudodocumentary, and the film's distribution company, Film Classics, was rewarded. The company, in fact, had staked its distribution fee on the film's success. The box-office success and increased prestige of *Lost Boundaries* allowed Film Classics, a small independent distributor specializing in re-releases, to seek better independent productions to increase the money it fronted for independent production projects.[21] Stanley Kramer got a boost from *Home of the Brave* (Mark Robson, 1949), which, like *Lost Boundaries*, was produced for less than $600,000. The number of social problem independents continued and multiplied in the 1950s: the Stanley Kramer films *I Want to Live!* (Robert Wise, 1958) and *Blackboard Jungle* (Richard Brooks, 1955) and the Samuel Fuller films dealing with racial prejudice (notably, *The Crimson Kimono*, 1959) stick out as prominent examples. The example of Walter Wanger's production of *I Want to Live!* shows how independents continued to upgrade low-budget films to A-films for the first-run market by adopting social problem content well into the late 1950s.[22] Afterward, as the Hollywood studio era came upon deep upheaval, the New American

Cinema films and other prestige dramas would supplant the social problem films in their privileged role as prestige films.

Divorcement alone did not bring about the change in the class disposition of prestige cinema. Rather, metaphorically speaking, the industrial changes were a fulcrum or lever that translated broader cultural shifts into the particular decisions of what Hollywood studios produced. That is, filmmakers and producers made the decisions they did partly for idiosyncratic reasons, but always in the context of what audiences responded to and what public discourse circulated about their studios' films. Divorcement helps explain Hollywood's timing in turning toward the socially serious as well as the underlying causes of its new relation to middlebrow taste formations. The prestige film of the 1930s relied on a relatively stagnant hierarchy between cinema and art. The destabilization of that hierarchy had every bit as much to do with the destabilization of the industry as it did with what filmgoers wanted and expected to see.

Cultural Legitimization of Cinema

By its nature, prestige is a social phenomenon. It requires, in C. Wright Mills's pithy summation, "at least two persons: one to claim it, and another to honor the claim."[23] It is one thing for the industry to claim an aesthetically superior and socially edifying product; it is another for viewers and observers to agree with that claim. Understanding the prestige film, then, means not merely tracking its industrial history, but, more broadly, assessing the place of the cinema in what Pierre Bourdieu terms a hierarchy of legitimate culture: "Not all cultural meanings, theatrical presentations, sporting events, recitals of songs, poetry or chamber-music, operettas or operas, are equivalent in dignity and value, and they do not all call for the same approach with the same urgency." He adds:

> In other words, the various systems of expression, from theatre to television, are objectively organized according to a hierarchy independent of individual opinions, which defines cultural legitimacy and its gradations. Faced with meanings situated outside the sphere of legitimate culture, consumers feel they have the right to remain pure consumers, and judge freely; on the other hand, within the field of consecrated culture, they feel measured according to objective norms, and forced to adopt a dedicated, ceremonial and ritualized

> attitude. Thus jazz, cinema and photography do not give rise—because they do not claim it with the same urgency—to the attitude of dedication, which is common coin when one is dealing with works of scholarly culture. Some virtuosos, in a bid for legitimation, transfer to these arts models of behaviour that are current in the realm of traditional culture. But in the absence of an institution to teach them methodically and systematically as constituent parts of legitimate culture, most people experience them in quite a different way, as simple consumers.[24]

For Bourdieu, the "middle arts" like jazz, cinema, and photography fall into a "sphere of the legitimizable" in which formalized aesthetic attitudes begin to take hold, but only variably across the population, and without the institutional legitimacy of the high arts. The history of the prestige film, therefore, is partly a history of the relative importance of "pure consumers" and "virtuosos" in the reception of "quality" films. Over the twentieth century and during the postwar years especially, the cinema underwent an elevation in cultural status, from Bourdieu's sphere of the arbitrary (that of pure consumer) to the sphere of the legitimizable. First, highbrow artists and intellectuals began to view cinema as an art form in its own right, and their cineclubs, criticism, and institutions formed an incipient film culture challenging Hollywood. Subsequently, middlebrow appreciation came to mean not simply Hollywood's citation of high culture but also the filmgoer's distinction between serious, artistic feature cinema and Hollywood's usual product. The shifted relation of cinema to the other arts brought about a shift in a genre, the prestige film, built on a fixed relationship between film and the legitimate arts.

Perhaps the most significant development for the emerging film culture was the development of high-minded film criticism in response to avant-garde filmmaking. David Bordwell has argued that "seventh art" cinephilia emerged from this network of film periodicals, cineclubs, and institutions and that it marked a considerable redefinition of highbrow taste: "The faults of this research program should not lead us to forget how radical it was. For many years after the invention, most well-educated people thought that film could acquire prestige only by aping great works of drama or literature. . . . Nevertheless, the Standard Version fell prey to elite assumptions by expecting film to develop in accord with high-art models."[25] The shift in highbrow sensibility can be measured in the difference separating the *Nation*'s 1913 lampoon of a "Democratic Art" ("To watch one of these exhibitions is like seeing an animated popular magazine without the labor of turning the pages, and like the picture magazine it requires no thought or attention"[26]) and a 1929 *New York Herald Tribune* review of *The Passion of Joan of Arc* (Carl Theodor Dreyer, 1928) as "among the really significant achievements of modern art."[27] Seventh-art film criticism in upscale, "serious" publications like the *New Republic* and the *Nation* and leftist political publications like the *New Masses* championed the avant-garde, disdained most commercial cinema, but nonetheless took seriously the idea that the cinema, including popular cinema, *could* be art.[28]

Increasingly, the highbrow film culture also gained institutional footing. The Museum of Modern Art (MoMA) was instrumental in applying art historical discourse to a popular medium hitherto without history or preservation. The library spoke of periods, of movements and schools of filmmaking, and of aesthetic breakthroughs. It exhibited and distributed programs of films to educational and cultural institutions: "The Development of Narrative," "The Rise of the American Film" and others.[29] Meanwhile, the nonfiction film was following another avenue toward cultural legitimacy. Whereas MoMA's Film Library had been a milestone in the acceptance of film in the artistic and literary fields, government and foundation sponsorship of the documentary movement of the 1930s marked some level of acceptance in the fields of social science and public policy.

Taken together, these developments—the emergence of an aesthetically oriented film criticism and the institutionalization of art historical and social-scientific discourses of cinema—outline a shift in the intellectual field of the interwar years. Previously, highbrow taste factions had dismissed film as frivolous entertainment at best, and culturally undignified at worst, while legitimate social scientific and policy voices saw movies as having an unhealthy influence on society. But whether in response to the importation of foreign avant-garde films, the transition from silent to sound in Hollywood, or the emergence of nonfiction films, certain intellectuals pushed cinema into the sphere of the legitimizable. The effect was to split highbrow response to cinema into two opposed sensibilities: traditionalist disdain for popular culture and reclamation of the aesthetic (or sociologically serious) within the popular art. Bourdieu has described attempts to *épater la bourgeoisie* as "proving the extent of one's power to confer aesthetic status."[30] In many ways the division in American highbrow taste over cinema sprang from a similar gambit by a dominated faction of the bourgeoisie.

The highbrow impulse would flourish in the noncommercial film culture and vibrant avant-garde of the postwar years. In 1947, the largest and most influential of the postwar film societies, Cinema 16, began its successful two-decade run in New York, taking an even more scholastic approach to film exhibition than MoMA and expanding its focus to documentary and nonnarrative films with no chance for commercial exhibition. The American avant-garde, too, was blossoming on both coasts. Even if many of the avant-garde films of the 1940s and 1950s were quasi-narrative in comparison to the structural-materialist films that would come in the 1960s and 1970s, they nonetheless confounded or subverted narrative expectations inherited from the commercial film industry and as such were experienced as assaults on conventional notions of what films should be. The obtuse "narratives" of Gregory Markopoulos, Willard Maas, or Maya Deren defied easy comprehension and forced viewers to use other arts—poetry, mythology, dance—as an aesthetic key for understanding. As Lauren Rabinowitz argues, "cinema was increasingly identified as an object divided on the basis of the intellectual discourse associated with different groups of media objects. By the end of the decade, 'highbrow,' 'lowbrow,' and 'middlebrow' had become the popular designations of hierarchical categories of aesthetic taste."[31] As before the war, the highbrow reception developed in tandem with avant-garde filmmaking, but the postwar counterparts pitted their film culture not only against a culturally reviled Hollywood but also against an emerging middlebrow culture.

That middlebrow film culture borrowed from the highbrow cineast the notion that cinema was an art and combined it with a nearly exclusive preference for commercial fiction features. In one sense, it continued a middlebrow impulse of Hollywood itself. Joan Shelley Rubin diagnoses a split tendency in middlebrow culture—on one hand democratic, on the other reverential to cultural authority—across early twentieth-century American culture, from the "great books" movement to book-of-the-month clubs and Alexander Woollcott's book-review radio broadcasts.[32] Similarly, the literary adaptations, biopics, and historical films of the 1930s promised for the masses the possibility of high culture experience. To studios, they were valuable not simply for preselling content but also for the association of cultural elevation they conferred, the sense that watching a film version of a canonical novel or play was a substitute for the aesthetic experience of the adapted work itself. *Dodsworth* is an ideal type in this use of literary source material: the film was based on the work of a novelist with high-culture credentials and secondarily on an acclaimed Broadway theatrical adaptation. Thematically, the film centers on "adult" material, the dissolution of a marriage because of a wife's infidelity; if anything, the film version emphasizes the bittersweet romance more than the source material does. Characteristically, the novel's keen class analysis in the myriad cultural references that European travel represents for its protagonist Sam Dodsworth is conspicuously missing in the adaptation. Prestige filmmakers were primarily interested in literary source material for romantic melodramas with a more complicated emotional tenor.

The postwar years continued this outward middlebrow citation of highbrow culture. Marianne Conroy has pointed to references rife in postwar Hollywood's narratives, from theatrical adaptations marketed as vehicles for method actors to the social problem films. In *Imitation of Life* (Douglas Sirk, 1959), she notes,

> The possibility that Lora might audition for a [Tennessee] Williams play is no sooner proffered than it is dropped. The play is "all cast" before she even appears in Loomis's office. . . . In fact, the specific play is largely beside the point of the reference; indeed, Williams himself matters only insofar as he is arguably the one American playwright a mass audience in 1959 would have recognized as a serious writer of "blockbuster plays."[33]

The postwar middlebrow film continued its goal to serve as an aesthetic substitute for high culture, but it also thematized legitimate culture as distinct from the Hollywood formula. Frank Sinatra unpacking his stack of Modern Library books in *Some Came Running* (Vincente Minnelli, 1959) or the montage of "classic" book covers in *I Remember Mama* (George Stevens, 1948) takes on, conspicuously, a high culture/cinema differentiation that the 1930s prestige film was all too eager to elide.

Postwar middlebrow film culture involved far more than explicit citation, however. Art films from Britain's Rank Studios or social problem films from Stanley Kramer and 20th Century–Fox did not so much offer anxious cultural references within their narratives as position themselves as the sort of cinema middlebrow consumers championed as "artistic." The distinction between "Hollywood" and "art" assumed a centrality in the classed reception of the postwar years. Aesthetic judgment came without any semiformalized basis of formal contemplation that marked highbrow discussions. In making claims of artistry for social problem

Table 1.1 Comparison of *New York Times* Critical Favorites and Top-Grossing Films

New York Times' Ten Best (1946)	Top-Grossing Films (1946)
Open City	*The Best Years of Our Lives*
Road to Utopia	*Duel in the Sun*
The Green Years	*The Jolson Story*
Henry V	*The Yearling*
Notorious	*Saratoga Trunk*
Brief Encounter	*The Razor's Edge*
The Well-Digger's Daughter	*Night and Day*
The Best Years of Our Lives	*Notorious*
My Darling Clementine	*Til the Clouds Roll By*
Stairway to Heaven	*Road to Utopia*
	Two Years Before the Mast
	The Green Years
	The Harvey Girls
	Margie
	Easy to Wed

Sources: Bosley Crowther, "The 'Ten Best,'" *New York Times*, December 1946, sec. II, 29; "60 Top Grossers of 1946," *Variety*, January 8, 1947, 8; Thomas Schatz, *Boom and Bust: The American Cinema in the 1940s*, vol. 6 of *History of the American Cinema*, ed. Charles Harpole (Berkeley: University of California Press, 1997), 467.

and other prestige pictures, these consumers were pursuing a parallel process of legitimization that the highbrows had effected in another context. Hollow citations and literary uplift continued, but increasingly, too, middlebrow taste valued in cinema a literary and theatrical "quality" and recognizable characteristics of "maturity": socially relevant content (the "race problem" cycle), theatrical scope in acting style (*Henry V* [Laurence Olivier, 1945]), pessimistic subject matter (*The Men* [Fred Zinnemann, 1950] and *The Snake Pit*), epic narrative scale applied to everyday subject matter (*The Best Years of Our Lives*), and eventually nontraditional sexual themes (*Bonjour Tristesse* [Otto Preminger, 1958]). This version of the middlebrow had less to do with the class references that could corroborate the audience member's status self-image than in positing one's preference for the "right" kind of film artistry as a conspicuous marker of one's social position. For quite a few people, cinema had become a realm of potential cultural legitimacy.

The rise and subsequent changes in middlebrow culture corresponded to the changing class structure of a rapidly expanding economy. Janice Radway traces the rise of the middlebrow in the first half of the twentieth century to the rise of the professional-managerial class, and Marianne Conroy similarly cites C. Wright Mills's notion of status panic and white-collar growth.[34] Both explanations are useful but insufficient: the "new middle classes" appeared a half-century before the period Conroy considers, and the mere existence of a professional-managerial class does not account for any change in middlebrow culture between the 1920s and the 1950s. Here, Bourdieu's sociology of taste can help. While older strains of middlebrow culture emerged from the class milieu of the old petite bourgeoisie (shop owners and small-scale proprietors), three new bourgeois class fractions favored newer strains of middlebrow culture, ones more inclined to the "virtuoso" gambits of cultural legitimization. The ascendant or "new bourgeoisie" represented the new business and management class sprung forth by the managerial revolution.[35] The new petite bourgeoisie includes "all the occupations involving presentation and representation (sales, marketing, advertising, public relations, fashion, decoration and so forth) and in all the institutions providing symbolic goods and services."[36] The class fraction is marked by the "well-armed pretension,"[37] a pretension to high culture based on a rejection of tastes typically associated with the petite bourgeoisie. Finally, the "executant" petite bourgeoisie includes junior executives and clerical workers, who fall in the middle between the newer and more classically middlebrow forms.[38] One likely engine for the change in middlebrow reception and the cultural legitimization of cinema is a changing balance between these "newer middle classes." While the managerial revolution of the late nineteenth and early twentieth centuries began to undermine the old petite bourgeoisie, the sustained economic prosperity of the 1940s swelled the ranks of the new and executant petite bourgeoisie while solidifying the stature and social hegemony of the new bourgeoisie. Class coalition is a useful notion in describing the social problem genre, which included the top box-office earners for their studios and straddled "mass" and "class" appeal.

Critical Distinction and Industrial Trend as Mutual Transformations

The journalistic film critic was both emblem and key catalyst of middlebrow reception. Already employed to make judgments on commercial narrative cinema, the film reviewer extended his or her charge to an aesthetic judgment that referenced cinema's existence as art. Robert Ray has pointed to a gap between popular and critical tastes in the 1950s, yet this dynamic was already emerging by the mid-1940s.[39] For instance, from 1946, the favorite films of *New York Times*' main film critic Bosley Crowther were not the year's box-office winners. A few, like *The Best Years of Our Lives* and *Notorious* (Alfred Hitchcock, 1946), appear on both lists, but more telling are films with strong box-office draw—*The Jolson Story* (Alfred E. Green, 1946) or *Saratoga Trunk* (Sam Wood, 1945)—that were even more generic and distant from the kind of prestige film Crowther preferred. In contrast to highbrow writers like Parker Tyler and Manny Farber, the mainstream critic did not see potential cultural worth in any film, high or low, but relied instead on the prestige drama, the art film, and the social problem film as the raison d'être of his or her criticism. A mutually influential process was thus in place by the late 1940s: Hollywood's prestige dramas began to incorporate more finely internalized modes of aesthetic judgment just as the popular press critics responsible for legitimization of Hollywood's product took the prestige drama as their main focus. Against a backdrop of the film industry's changing conception of the prestige drama, the postwar journalistic critics assessed the cinema's relation to other media and urged the production of films that could compete with higher arts.

Nowhere, at least in the latter 1940s, was the film critic's self-consciousness in discussing film as an artistic medium clearer than in reviews of problem films. The popular press's middlebrow tendency continually contrasted the prestige film and Hollywood's nonprestige product. Bourdieu, famously, has pinned this sort of differentiation as the basis of class judgment: "A difference . . . only becomes a visible . . . socially pertinent difference if it is perceived by someone who is capable of making the distinction [who] is endowed with the categories of perception."[40] Critical distinction was not new to the postwar years (the *Nation* in 1913 had classificatory schemata of its own), but postwar journalistic critics approached the social problem film through a series of distinctions that signaled the cinema's position in the sphere of the legitimizable: European or Hollywood, mature or immature, art or commerce, courage or cravenness, realism or artifice. Bourdieu's model not only draws attention to these binary contrasts but also reminds us that binary distinction need not serve a binary understanding of class. Even close historical studies like Lea Jacobs's reading of A/B film distinction in the 1930s often take the historical agents' class antinomies to imply class bifurcation.[41] Instead, aesthetic distinction just as often asserts a middlebrow taste. While highbrow taste differentiated Hollywood and the avant-garde, Hollywood and documentary film, or Hollywood and the European art film, the middlebrow critics contrasted different commercial narrative features to suggest that some were closer than others to more legitimate theatrical, literary, or visual arts.

The distinction between imported and domestic product was the most glaring. Films imported from Europe were instrumental in shifting the middle terrain in cinematic legitimization. Highbrow critics championed the Italian neorealist films and in so doing helped solder together cultural legitimacy and a self-consciously realist aesthetic. In Hollywood, neorealism inspired specific productions like *The Search* (Fred Zinnemann, 1948) and, arguably, a general narrative activation of location shooting. As Barbara Wilinsky has emphasized, the cosmopolitan values associated with watching foreign films were central to the discourses of reception during the emergence of the "art film" in the postwar years.[42] The films of Britain's Rank Studios—*Henry V*, *The Red Shoes* (Michael Powell and Emeric Pressberger, 1948), and *Brief Encounter* (David Lean, 1945)—implicitly challenged Hollywood's product by citing some higher art, such as theater, dance, or the psychological novel. European émigré directors had long had a role in the American film industry, and the postwar problem film cycle had directors, such as Anatole Litvak and Billy Wilder, who brought a sensibility of their European work to their American films. In the receptive context of 1940s cinema, though, critics treated films by émigré directors as "Hollywood," in distinction to imports that played in art houses.

Whether Italian or British, foreign films contrasted with Hollywood and guided middlebrow reception of the social problem film. One reviewer of *Crossfire*, for example, called the film "an example of what Hollywood can do . . . if it wants, or if it has the courage more than once in a blue moon. This RKO-Radio production is the sort of film that critics and a critical public have come to expect only from abroad."[43] A review of *The Snake Pit* contrasted European films ("purposeful, adventurous, courageous or merely grown up") with a Hollywood that "lacks the brains, artistry or daring to undertake such work locally."[44] Even a negative review of *The Boy with Green Hair* (Joseph Losey, 1949) criticized the film on the grounds that it was not enough like the neorealist films.[45] The industry reacted defensively: Warner Bros.' Jerry Wald countered, "Hollywood may be stumbling, but it's certainly more realistic than Broadway or the British."[46] Wald's statement reveals just how much had changed in the cultural terrain, so that one might expect Hollywood films to ape legitimate theater and foreign films more closely.

Meanwhile, critics contrasted maturity and immaturity as stand-ins for cinema's relation to other media. Sometimes "mature" applied to the implied audience of the film, since reviewers lamented a commercial cinema geared toward teenagers' tastes and sensibilities. One critic praised *All the King's Men* as "pleasantly free of the superfluous preachments that so often mar a Hollywood movie concerned with any topic more difficult than the mating customs of soda-fountain habitués."[47] At other times, maturity meant the sophistication of the medium relative to other, more institutionalized arts. Writes one reviewer of the films on anti-Semitism, "As great mass media, intimidated by the size of their audiences, [the cinema and radio] have lacked the courage familiar in fiction and on the stage. . . . But of recent months the movies have apparently decided to grow up."[48] Similarly, a review of *The Snake Pit* calls for an "adult medium" on equal footing with literature and capable of dealing "truthfully and unflinchingly with adult subjects."[49] The *New York Times* viewed the same film in an opposition to "Hollywood as usual," writing, "This latter fact, incidentally, is the only 'Hollywood' touch that Millen Brand and Frank Partos have permitted to show in their superior script. . . . *The Snake Pit*, while frankly quite disturbing, and not recommended for the weak, is a mature, emotional drama on a rare and pregnant theme."[50] In later contexts, "mature" and "adult" would connote material that pushed audience expectations of what was sexually permissible on the screen. Here, though, "adult" subjects are the high-minded ones—the superego to Hollywood's usual id.

Underlying the contrast between an adult and a juvenile medium was a parallel contrast between art and commerce, in which the middlebrow tendency castigated escapist cinema in favor of seriousness. In *Pinky*, *Time* was relieved to see the public "interested in movies that give serious treatment to a serious theme," and in *The Best Years of Our Lives* considered the problem genre's forthrightness a sign of its quality.[51] *Newsweek* praised the "intelligent and courageous handling" in *Best Years* and the "restrained and courageous treatment of a delicate theme" in *Lost Boundaries*; the magazine wrote of Stanley Kramer's *Home of the Brave*, "indisputably, it took courage for an independent producer to tackle this highly controversial theme."[52] The genre-wide equation of social relevance with courage and honesty was ultimately a restatement of a distinction between art and commerce. Studio films with "courage," after all, were putting their profits at risk and hence were received as serious rather than commercial in nature.

Finally, the popular press critics contrasted the realism of the social problem film with the artifice of Hollywood's usual product. Many of these reviews cited aspects of the filmmaking itself, including set design and cinematography, as lending an air of realism. "In spite of the fact that this cast has several top-ranking stars," wrote one review of *The Best Years of Our Lives*, "Wyler has succeeded in making these people as real as your neighbors. This natural tone is further heightened by the realistic sets."[53] *The Lawless* impressed a *Time* reviewer in part through its cinematography:

> Using unvarnished photography on the streets, interiors and people of real California towns, director Joseph Losey has given the picture a startling look of reality. For the setting of his manhunt climax, he takes imaginative advantage of the stony, rolling waste of a gold-dredging field. His mob scenes crackle with a spontaneous movement and raw vitality usually found only in bang-up newsreel footage.[54]

Bosley Crowther at the *New York Times* cited *The Lost Weekend*'s "case-history documentation in its narrative and photographic styles," and "a sharp tone of actuality in all of [Wilder's] studio work."[55]

Not all critics praised the social problem films. Some thought that individual films failed to live up to a quality genre, whereas others objected to the genre's didactic tone, whether from a highbrow disdain of middlebrow "uplift" or a lowbrow defense of mass entertainment. In general, the periodicals more aligned with highbrow taste were the most critical of the problem film. Reviewers like John McCarten in the *New Yorker* or Robert Hatch in the *New Republic*, both quoted above, took the mission of social relevance to heart yet often faulted problem films for aesthetic failings, insufficient realism, or lack of sociological analysis. Robert Warshow exemplified the highbrow suspicion of middlebrow taste: "As the mass audience escapes into easy sentiment, so the educated audience escapes into ideas, a tendency which does not necessarily reflect a real interest in ideas."[56]

Bosley Crowther straddled support and critique. In his tenure at the *New York Times* from 1940 to 1967, his support for the genre and the new "realistic" prestige films was tempered by criticisms of films that he felt did not do justice to social reality.[57] As Frank Eugene Beaver points out, Crowther argued that cinema uplift had a dual nature, aesthetic and social: "Crowther's demand for realism in pictures," he notes, "became synonymous with his demand for entertaining and significant stories."[58] As such, Crowther occupies a compromise ground between the highbrow sensibility of the *Nation*'s James Agee or the *New Yorker* and the middlebrow cultural reverence shown by the anonymous reviewers at *Time* or *Newsweek.* Significantly, the wider-circulating visual-digest magazines like *Life* and *Look* registered very little generic difference between the problem film and others. In passing along the publicity materials given by the studios, they sidestepped the issue of the films' prestige in favor of the sort of star coverage the middlebrows frowned upon.[59]

To a surprising extent, producers and makers of the problem films, too, shared many of the critics' distinctions. Writer Philip Dunne considered *Pinky*'s script "the most challenging and important subject for a picture that I have come across in years. . . . It can be an even more significant picture than *Gentleman's Agreement.*"[60] Darryl Zanuck warned the makers of *No Way Out* against "any element which even remotely has a feeling of 'movie' or 'Hollywood.' I do not say this disparagingly of the movies or Hollywood, but only as the term is applied by the critics."[61] He explicitly considered Academy Awards and critical reception in his deliberations on mid- and low-budget prestige films. As he noted on *The Snake Pit*, "It is neither courageous nor clever for us to try to present in this picture the intimate details of life in an insane asylum. We won't get either critical acclaim nor public praise for it if we do."[62] Hence, producers did not simply share the critics' perspective (Zanuck was too keen to foster "showmanship," that is, popular generic appeal), but instead sought the critics' approval, shifting their perspective to vicariously understand the critical mindset.

To gain critical and wider prestige, the studios appealed to the middlebrow taste formation in the marketing of the social problem dramas. The idea of "courage" became a recurring part of the self-congratulatory industrial discourse, including studio advertising and marketing. "*Gentleman's Agreement* calls a spade a spade," read the tagline in one newspaper ad. The rhetoric may have been inflated, but studios like 20th Century–Fox sought recognition from a broader slice of entrenched opinion brokers than had typically been engaged in discussion of cinema. Fox began to emphasize its problem films in the advertising budget. *Gentleman's Agreement* had cost a respectable $265,000 in publicity, below the big-budget prestige pictures *Forever Amber* and *Captain from Castile.* By 1949, the problem film *The Snake Pit* received $417,000 for advertising, over three times the amount of any other Fox feature and half of the studio's yearly trade press advertising budget.[63] The example of Stanley Kramer's *The Defiant Ones* shows that the split between an "exploitation ballyhoo campaign" and a "'prestige' campaign" was solidified and self-conscious by the 1950s.[64] The late 1950s career of Kramer embodied the contradiction of a producer-director for whom the earnest cinematic statement was impossible to tease out from commercial calculation. By that point, the prestige film's industrial transformation and the broader cultural elevation of the cinema had successfully converged.

Conclusion

Social theorists at times speak of "steering mechanisms," the underlying structural forces driving a historical phenomenon.[65] Two primary steering mechanisms—industrial reorganization and the middle class's reorientation in relation to the cinema—go a long way to explaining the relatively sudden popularity of Hollywood's social problem films. The larger historical context mattered too, as the following chapters show, but studio economics and cultural legitimation were proximate causes for Hollywood's turn to the social in its narratives. These smaller-scale factors were the conditions necessary for the larger-scale discourses to take hold in a culture industry removed from the intellectual and public policy fields. Rather than insincerity behind the studios' adoption of the mantle of "sociology," the Bourdieusian model suggests a more complex dynamic: studios had every financial and cultural incentive to adopt the critical dispositions of those reviewing their prestige films.

Just as important, the industrial and critical context of the prestige film shows how the social problem film was central to the trajectory of Hollywood in the middle of the twentieth century. Film histories tend to treat the problem films as a fad or brief experiment, but they were a catalyst for larger definitions of realism and ultimately influenced the move to postclassical cinema. In turn, earlier types of prestige cinema influenced the postwar problem films. A firm division between topical or politically committed Hollywood and more routine product is simply not tenable given the thematic and aesthetic connections. A fuller history must grapple both with the cultural distinction the problem films posed for contemporaries and the underlying continuity of industrial and historical trends that gradually pushed Hollywood in new directions.

2

Hollywood as Popular Sociology

Hollywood's postwar fascination with psychoanalysis might be more famous, but its embrace of the relatively new academic discipline of sociology was no less fervent. As with psychoanalysis, Hollywood filtered its narratives through a popular social science oriented toward public policy and translated for the general public by journalists. Additionally, the demands of entertainment narrative simplified the films' sociological implications. Nonetheless, from their earliest use of the "social problem" or "sociological" film label, a use that extends back to the 1910s, critics and contemporary observers tapped into a notion that social problem films were part of a larger policy discourse emanating from the field of sociology. Cynics might dismiss this connection as tenuous, but in their way these films did reflect changing models of sociology.

Something is unsatisfying about the label of "social problem film," however, in no small part because the word "social" is a vexing one. Like its conceptual cousin "cultural," "social" is a term with multiple meanings, each with a varying degree of specificity. By its nature, the social is an abstraction, and it can range in reference from face-to-face interaction to aggregate phenomena unseen by any one individual. The term "social" uncomfortably straddles academic and everyday usage, and the confusion only compounds in the popular press film reviews from the period that toss around the terms "social" and "sociological" in ways that, to a critical eye, seem fuzzy at best. For instance, a *Commonweal* reviewer in 1947 complained that given *Crossfire*'s Manichaean characterization of the villain and the multiple murders in the narrative, "it is hard to consider the first killing (committed only because the victim was a Jew) with the sociological import the film intends."[1] Reviews like these are largely responsible for the term film scholars most commonly use for these films, so a question of semantics lingers: if a set of social problems films is more or less identifiable, what exactly makes their problems social? Moreover, what does sociology have to do with the Hollywood feature film?

The matter is no easier when we turn to the films themselves. In *The Lost Weekend*, Ray Milland's character, Don Birnam, drinks too much and comes to understand that he is an alcoholic. Alcoholism could be understood in medical terms as a psychological and biochemical disease. It could also be understood in individualistic terms, as an emotional issue or moral failing. *The Lost Weekend* sees alcoholism as both but also offers a range of collective dimensions, including public health, law enforcement, and economic productivity. In effect, reviewers and other observers were capable of interpreting films like *The Lost Weekend* on multiple levels, so that the *social* is an analytical dimension partly asserted by the films, partly read onto them. A later generation of academic critics would critique the genre ideologically on the grounds that the films compromise a true, collective political analysis with individualized narrative. For many of the problem films, though, the social was less a collective opposed to individual experience than a way of making sense of individual experience. The politics of the problem film, in its historical context, boils down to a particular practice of textual reading.

The social problem film came to prominence at the same moment sociology was becoming a full-fledged discipline in the American academy. With the establishment in 1892 of a Ph.D. program at the University of Chicago and the emergence in the 1920s of a "Chicago school," the field gained more properly scientific aspirations with methodological reflection and empirical case studies. Institutionally, the founding of the *American Journal of Sociology* (1895), the American Sociological Society (1905), and increasing undergraduate and graduate programs in the field spoke to the discipline's birth.[2] By the end of World War II, one school of sociological thought, functionalism, established hegemony and in the process adapted the ideas of Emile Durkheim into a concept of society as a set of systems that are either functional or dysfunctional. This tendency to pathologize social relationships distinguished the postwar functionalist sociology from the formerly dominant Progressive and Chicago school sociologists. Rather than conceiving of problems *to* society, social science and public policy increasingly conceived of problems *of* society.

The functionalist approach to sociology permeated Hollywood's approach to topical subject matter. Just as "sociology" meant something different after the war than before, so, too, did the 1930s "social" or "sociological" film differ from the "social problem film" of the 1940s. From the Progressive era, through the Chicago school and the interwar pluralism, to postwar functionalism, the conception of the "sociological" and the "social" in Hollywood's social problem films frequently changed referent. Hollywood's topical dramas, too, increasingly portrayed social problems as problems *of* society. Examples from three cycles of problem films suggest the evolution of the social problem discourse popularized in Hollywood's features. First, the "slum" films *Dead End* (William Wyler, 1937) and *Mr. Soft Touch* (aka *Settlement House*, Gordon Douglas and Henry Levin, 1949) reveal the inheritance of Progressive-era sociology while pointing to a new Chicago school discourse. Second, *Knock on Any Door* (Nicholas Ray, 1949) and *The Sniper* (Edward Dmytryk, 1952) show the eventual triumph of functionalism in American criminology. Third, the "race problem" cycle of *Gentleman's Agreement*, *Pinky*, and *Intruder in the Dust* reflects the functionalist turn in race sociology. Each of these—urban sociology, criminology, and the sociology of race—reveals the limitations of postwar liberalism, but each also shows how popular sociology complicated Hollywood's discourses more than is typically acknowledged. Critics of the social problem film have a tendency to doubt, even dismiss, postwar social science as first and foremost ideological, yet to read through the sociology is to ignore the specificity of the intellectual formation of the period.

The Chicago School and Early Sociology: *Dead End* and *Mr. Soft Touch*

At the time of the postwar problem film cycle, American sociology still was relatively new. Its existence as a discipline was barely a half-century old, with initial academic programs started in the late nineteenth century. Still, even these early sociologists were not unified professionally. Many came from Christian-reformist backgrounds, while others were philosophers with pragmatist or Social Darwinist inspiration. The early sociologists shared a tendency toward evolutionary models (drawing analogy to the biological sciences) and a focus on the problems of modernity and industrial capitalism (and the politics of Progressivism). The Progressive conception of sociology was coterminous with reformism. Key works included reformist "surveys" like Jane Addams's work with Hull House (1895) or Jacob Riis's *How the Other Half Lives* (1901).[3] As Lee Grieveson has argued, this wave of Progressive social science was intimately connected with the political elite's anxiety about the power of the new medium of cinema. He notes, for instance, Jane Addams's advocacy for nickelodeons to serve as sites of educational uplift.[4]

The impact of Progressive sociology extended into 1940s cinema, and *Mr. Soft Touch*, an offbeat Columbia Pictures film, foregrounds several aspects of this version of the social problem discourse. The narrative follows the symbolically named Joe Miracle (Glenn Ford), a returning World War II veteran forced to turn to crime to steal back money stolen from him. As he tries to avoid a vindictive crime organization, Jenny Jones (Evelyn Keyes), a social worker and reformer, inadvertently gives Joe cover in the settlement house she runs. The film thereby interweaves three generic strains: a crime thriller, a social problem film, and a romance. At first the juxtaposition is comedic, drawing on a fish-out-of-water narrative, but *Mr. Soft Touch* gets more serious in tone after the first act. Ideologically, the film pivots from an initial satire of and skepticism about social work and aligns the spectator with the social work of the settlement house, particularly as Joe's internal conflict grows between aiding the settlement house and escaping with his money.

The film has much in common with 1930s problem films, particularly those that Warner Bros. produced, with their emphasis on the misunderstood criminal loner. But unlike the 1930s Warners' examples, *Mr. Soft Touch* more self-consciously foregrounds Progressivism. Jenny stands in for a broader vocation of social work and a social policy stance of helping the poor through state-aided charity. A courtroom scene establishes that Jenny has a close relationship with the judge, based on the activist leanings of his wife, whereas a fund-raising scene at the end shows the police as some of the settlement house's biggest supporters. However, the film also suggests the social work–oriented understanding of the social as an alternative to typical law enforcement. A police sergeant in one of the film's opening scenes quips sarcastically as Jenny tries to intervene in his arrest of Joe: "See . . . he's not to blame, he's just a victim of society." The film partakes of a 1940s social problem cycle, but ultimately reflects a prior reform-movement conception of the social—one of a crude environmental determinism.

The early Progressive era held an enduring role in defining the "sociological" in Hollywood's social problem films. *Mr. Soft Touch* came at the tail end of social problem films equating "sociological" with reformism. The first were a wide range of transitional-era and early classical Hollywood features and newsreels on a variety of issues. The film historian Kay Sloan has cited these as the first original cycle of the social problem film. "The social problem film," she writes, "originated in primitive melodramas made by filmmakers who actively sought social reforms during the Progressive Era . . . realistic melodramas made by groups like the National Association of Manufacturers, the National Child Labor Committee, the National American Woman Suffrage Association, the National Committee of Prison Labor, and even by a Progressive New York Governor, William Sulzer, who wrote and starred in his own melodrama."[5] As Sloan notes, the Progressivism of these films was as likely to be co-opted by business interests as not. By most indications (though film restoration continually changes the historical picture), the late 1920s saw a curtailment of these early activist melodramas, but a cycle of 1930s problem films would revive Progressivism, not only in tone but also in the type of issues they depicted, including prison reform, youth reform, and legal reform. The climax of *Wild Boys of the Road* (William Wellman, 1932), for instance, takes place in a courtroom, in front of a Progressive (and New Deal–identified) judge.

Despite their value as (refracted) illustrations of Progressivism, many of these 1930s films and especially a 1940s outlier like *Mr. Soft Touch* were in key respects out of sync with developments in sociology, whose academic center began to depart from Progressivism starting in the 1910s. The key development of the interwar years was an intellectual movement dubbed the Chicago school of sociology. Whereas late nineteenth-century scholars often contributed to a fledgling discipline in an uncoordinated fashion, the sociologists housed at the University of Chicago operated out of an established department with a Ph.D. program and a methodological self-consciousness.[6] They retained some ties to a Progressive reformist spirit: Harvey Zorbaugh's *The Gold Coast and the Slum* has similarities to the reformist "surveys."[7] At the same time, they resisted the moralism and impressionism of the Progressives, preferring instead a more scientific approach. In contrast to the evolutionary and Social Darwinist thinkers, the Chicago sociologists were resolutely empirical and worked largely with case studies of the city. Their "urban ecology" approach presented a model of observable social groups interlocked in conflict and competing interests.[8]

One of the clearest cinematic expressions of the Chicago school's work on urban sociology was William Wyler's 1937 *Dead End*, a drama set in a tenement district of New York City. Though based on a play rather than a nonfiction work, the drama holds striking similarity to both Progressive-era and Chicago school writing. The film opens and closes with crane shots of the New York City skyline (re-created with set work and special-effects miniatures), as well as a rolling title: "Every street in New York ends in a river. For many years the dirty banks of the East River were lined with the tenements of the poor. Then the rich, discovering that the river traffic was picturesque, moved their houses eastward. And now the terraces of these great apartment houses look down into the windows of the tenement poor." Muckraking works like *How the Other Half Lives* were a touchstone for the thematic contrast, echoed by the film's production design, but a comparison to Zorbaugh's *The Gold Coast and the Slum* is equally fruitful. Zorbaugh offers an extended contrast in social worlds in proximate location: "The Near North Side shades from light to shadow, and from shadow to dark. The Gold Coast gives way to the world of furnished rooms; and the rooming-house area, to the west again, imperceptibly becomes the slum."[9] Not only does the book's prose suggest a coexistence of social scientific inquiry and Progressive reform (this coexistence would mark the Chicago school before Robert Park's intervention on behalf of detached scientificity), it points directly to the central dramatic and thematic conceit of *Dead End*, where the East Side slums abut new high-rise apartment buildings for the wealthy. The contrast stressed the Progressive reformist elements of *Dead End*'s "social document," as contemporary critics would call it.

Dead End pushed toward an implicit urban ecology. Like the Chicago school case studies, the film's theme stressed the organic vitality of the city itself, and this sense of the city as an independent character comes through in Lillian Hellman's screenplay and in Wyler's execution, with its elaborate repurposing of theatrical sets as a determining but expressive space. At the same time, the film suggests that slums cause the dead end existence of the characters and that reform (Dave Connell's "tearing it down" to build new buildings) will rectify the problem. Richard Maltby reads the film as part of the 1930s gangster cycle's embrace of Chicago school sociology. "For the most part," he writes, "the Chicago sociologists were more concerned with the gang than with the gangster."[10] The Chicago school could not be reduced to the environmental determinism of *Dead End*, but Maltby demonstrates the influence of the Chicago school's model, in which the organic evolution nature of the city drove criminality and personal alienation.

Joseph Breen and those in the Motion Picture Producers and Distributors of America (MPPDA) picked up this reform mentality more than the Chicago school urban ecology. One letter from MPPDA's James Wingate to Breen detailed his response to a premiere of *Dead End*: "Last Tuesday after I viewed the picture, I had a long conference with Mr. Esmond stressing the fact that it was a social betterment theme and really a strong plea for slum elimination and better housing as a crime prevention. I told Mr. Esmond of the interest that the several social betterment groups had in the picture and of their enthusiastic approval of the same."[11] Later, Breen writes, via telegram: "The Film Dead End widely acclaimed in United States as important social document it has active support and endorsement of great number important sociological and social welfare groups church and women's club organizations stop. . . . Please ask Doctor Funder to view picture in Vienna he will readily recognize its importance and social message."[12] Ultimately, *Dead End* straddles Progressive-era reformism and a budding social scientific discourse. As a late 1930s entry into a largely Progressive cycle, it pointed to the new sociology sensibility of the postwar years, influenced by the social theory of Emile Durkheim.

Criminology and Functionalism: *Knock on Any Door* and *The Sniper*

Around the 1940s, four key historical changes coincided that marked a qualitative shift in the social problem discourse. First, American sociology itself grew as a discipline and finally gained solid footing in the academy. Second, sociology exerted a wider influence in American cultural life and public policy, in part because of a politics of liberal consensus. Third, social problem sociology emerged as a distinct subfield within the discipline.

Fourth, functionalism and its cousin, abstract empiricism, became the dominant school of thought in American sociology. These changes were related and mutually influencing. In themselves they do not explain why journalists, politicians, or filmmakers would take up the terms of sociology. Nonetheless, the changes in sociology explain the form and sensibility that wartime and especially postwar discussions of social problems would take. The differences between two films about criminal justice reform, *Knock on Any Door* and *The Sniper*, reveal the rapid change in popular sociology along the lines of this new functionalist social science.

After World War II, the discipline of sociology grew rapidly in size, contributing to a far-reaching influence in policy and journalistic fields. Craig Calhoun notes that the discipline's growth, increased prestige, and growing professionalization led to the postwar years' reputation as a "golden age" of sociology.[13] The discipline changed in tandem with the American university. The G.I. Bill did not merely expand the number of attendees; the land grant universities were some of the biggest benefactors, and the educational field shifted so that even private institutions oriented themselves (with the help of foundation funding) more toward the research functions they had previously avoided in favor of a focus on undergraduate education.[14] Whatever the source of the intellectual changes, sociology in the 1940s differed starkly from the discipline of the 1920s and 1930s.

By the 1930s, the Chicago school was no longer ascendant, and after World War II sociologists turned instead to a model in which small-scale social dysfunctions, not class conflict or individual morality, were on the research agenda. The historians of sociology Stephen Turner and Jonathan Turner speak of the "mismatch between the older idea of the history of social thought, with its critical tone, and the new statistical scientism, with its deep desire to make sociology like the natural sciences."[15] One dominant approach was the new type of social-psychological empiricism pioneered by Paul Lazarsfeld and others, which justified the increased funding by the government and business and filled the needs of opinion measurement and marketing and demographic research. (Sometimes this research had a direct relation to the social problem film, as in the media-effects research into the influence of the films on racist attitudes.)

Theoretically, meanwhile, functionalist sociology supplanted the Chicago school. Most readily embodied by the work of Talcott Parsons and Robert Merton, functionalism offered postwar social scientists, and sociologists in particular, a vision of society as a unified whole, in which the cultural relations between social agents (individuals) are responsible for social harmony or, alternatively, for social problems. From their reading of Emile Durkheim, the functionalists drew a number of related tenets. First, they understood social life as systematically structured, and the proper study of society as a focus on a macro- rather than microsociological view. In other words, they sought to be objectivist. The first third of Durkheim's *Suicide* in fact is a polemic against an individual or psychological explanation of the problem. As he writes on suicide: "But is the fact thus defined of interest to the sociologist? Since suicide is an individual action affecting the individual only, it must seemingly depend exclusively on individual factors, thus belonging to psychology alone. Is not the suicide's resolve usually explained by his temperament, character, antecedents and private history?"[16] No, argues Durkheim. "This total is not simply a sum of independent units, a collective total, but is itself a new fact *sui generis*, with its own nature—a nature, furthermore, dominantly social."[17] The social fact of suicide is not apparent at the level of individual observation but comes to the foreground only in analyzing statistical information of its victims' demographics. The functionalists followed his cue, Parsons with his emphasis on systematicity and Merton with his clear distinction between conscious motives and objective functions in social behavior.[18] As a result, the theoretical orientation of a good majority of postwar sociologists was neither toward the humanistic notion of the self-contained individual nor toward Marxian conceptions of political-economic structure.

Second, the functionalists argued that advanced societies function through the interdependence of their parts. Most of the time, they maintained, elements of the system function positively, that is, contribute to the overall continuation and furthering of the social system. Parsons's work theorized the tendency for stable social systems to structure social agents' behavior with norms and collective values.[19] As Merton notes, not all norms and systems function positively (one can conceive of both negative and neutral-vestigial functions), but despite their dysfunctions, societies do adhere as remarkably complex and stable systems of interdependence. Functionalists took this observation as the basis of a research agenda focused on positive and negative functions. On this matter, they took inspiration from Durkheim more than the other classical social theorists, since Durkheim's work posits an "organic solidarity" analogous to the function of cells in the human body, binding society on bases other than commonality among social agents (which he calls "mechanical solidarity").[20] In other words, Durkheim is trying to explain why the move toward social diversification that accompanies the division of labor (and from gemeinshaft to gesellschaft in Tönnies's famous typology) does not mean the breakdown of social cohesion.[21] Similarly, Parsons starts axiomatically from a stable society and explores which value systems keep this society functioning.[22] Arguably, the shifts in American demography and national culture gave fodder to functionalist conceptions of collectivity.[23]

Third, functionalism explained the negative functions of certain norms and behaviors as a pathology of social relations, anomie (normlessness or social alienation). Durkheim's explanation of suicide famously offers anomie as one of the key causes of melancholic suicide, a phenomenon he contends is nearly nonexistent in precapitalist societies.[24] He even ascribes much of class conflict to anomic lag in the changing division of labor.[25] The analytical emphasis on social ties and correspondingly on anomic conditions was taken up by Parsons and Merton and shared by the functionalist hegemony that marked theoretical sociology and more empirical "middle level" research in the 1940s and 1950s. The functionalists downplayed (though did not ignore) Marx's role as a social theorist and relegated social critique and a conflict approach to the margins.[26]

The spread of either functionalism or the aligned social problem sociology into more popular discourse was a complicated process. Hollywood films invoked Progressive, Chicago school, and functionalist ideas, but as popular sociology they were triply removed from academic sociology. First, even if writers, directors, and producers sometimes cited particular studies, they were more likely to be aware of public policy and journalistic versions of social science than to engage with the academic discipline as such. Second, cinematic references to sociology were often oblique and dependent on connotation. These films were entertainment fiction features first and foremost, and their thematic messages were often moral in nature. Third, the conceptions of the social were not always consistent. Some films invoked sociological ideas at variance with the main theme, whereas some films invoked multiple conceptions of the social simultaneously. As early as 1950 Howard Odum complained that sociologists used the term "social problem" with little consistency or clarity.[27] In popular usage, it was even less precise. By the time the discourse filtered into the realm of popular press and even trade press film criticism, its referent often seemed contradictory or confused.

An often-overlooked Nicholas Ray film, *Knock on Any Door*, exemplifies the diffuse and uneven process of popularization. Indeed, the film is a palimpsest for divergent schools of sociological thought, mixing Progressive, Chicago school, and functionalist discourses. *Knock*'s narrative is primarily about juvenile delinquency and secondarily about the problem of justice for young criminals. Nick Romano (John Derek) is a confused youth charged with murdering a police officer. A lawyer, Andrew Morton (Humphrey Bogart), at the urging of his social worker wife, Adele (Candy Toxton), reluctantly agrees to defend him against a murder charge. In making the case for the social determinism of crime, the film synthesizes several contemporary discourses of popularized social science. On the one hand, the reformist sentiment in the film shows the imprint of Progressive reform sentiment. The Skid Row scene in particular uses a washed-out style shot on fast film stock, its realism invoking an iconography of urban suffering inherited from Riis's *How the Other Half Lives*. The depiction of the reform school is a muckraking portrait of abuse. (Social problem films of the 1930s, like *Hell's House* [Howard Higgin, 1932], specialized in this issue.) More important, the dyad of Adele/reformer and Andy/lawyer is reminiscent of the close relation between social work, public policy, and sociology around the turn of the century.

On the other hand, the film's depiction of a city as a dynamic and determining social environment owes more to the Chicago school of sociology than to mere reformism. The Chicago sociologists made the social fabric of the American city their primary object of study and developed an "urban ecology" approach that examined simultaneously material determinants and primary and secondary group interaction. The Chicago school serves as the basis for the social-determinist theme of *Knock on Any Door*. Chicago school sociology coincided with the rise of criminology as a scientific subfield, and Edwin Sutherland's research set an agenda of differential association to explain the causes of crime—in Sutherland's words, "the causal or genetic process through which a particular person or series of persons, regarded individually, became criminals. This is a statement of lifetime processes, running through the entire career of the person, rather than an analysis of the attitudes of a person and the characteristics of his situation at the time of the crime."[28] The film's emphasis on turning points similarly abstracts Nick Romano's personal life to causal processes of character formation.

In addition to Progressive and Chicago schools, the depiction of Nick's descent into criminality shows the possible influence of nascent labeling theory, particularly the work of Frank Tannenbaum, who saw self-fulfilling prophecy in social and self-identity as a criminal.[29] This view echoes in Morton's monologue: "We the solid citizens of this community, we photographed and labeled this boy years ago." This version of labeling theory had neither the disciplinary self-critique nor the subjectivist focus on social interaction that labeling theory would represent in the 1960s. Here, it is merely one model of criminal causation among multiple ones.

The final soliloquy of Morton's closing arguments encapsulates the theme's intellectual pluralism. The lawyer invokes labeling theory: "We're scandalized by environment, and we call it crime." He indicts "society" for the production of criminal deviance. He critiques the press for sensationalism. He calls for tearing down the slums in order to get rid of poverty and crime. Here, the film's title is explained. "Knock on any door," Morton says, "and you may find Nick Romano." The phrase and the overdetermined cut to a medium shot of a teenager combing his hair are an extreme statement of social determinism.

What is missing is the functionalist approach that emerged in the 1940s and came to dominate postwar sociology of deviance. Criminology would adopt the postwar functionalist sociology, but little sense of anomie appears in *Knock on Any Door*, unlike other films in the postwar problem film cycle.[30] *Knock* therefore shows a notable historical lag between its criminological discourses and the postwar social science that was already gaining dominance in academic and public policy circles. The one exception is the confidence the film ascribes to scientific reform. For instance, after one flashback ends on Nick's arrest, Morton says, regarding reform schools, "The word reform means . . . to improve. It can also mean degrade, brutalize. There are reformatories with modern methods, where the delinquents are looked upon as individuals, with individual problems. And then, there are others, like the one where Nick was sent to." Charles Maland points to problem films' faith in the solution to problems, and confidence in "modern methods" was the hallmark particularly of postwar functionalism.[31]

Whereas the functionalism of *Knock on Any Door* was nascent, another criminology narrative made only three years later, *The Sniper*, had left behind Progressive and Chicago school sociology in favor of social psychology and functionalism. *The Sniper* is a police procedural about a serial killer whose psychopathic behavior is caused by his upbringing, and in addition to psychological causes, the film depicts criminality as a type of anomie in the functionalist sense. The film is a Stanley Kramer production for Columbia pictures, in a period between his early independent productions and his higher-profile prestige productions distributed via United Artists. Directed by Edward Dmytryk, the film also follows *Crossfire*'s template of procedural noir combined with social problem film content. From the opening, three intertitles announce the film's claim to a social problem discourse:

> A word about the picture which follows:
> High among police problems is that of the sex criminal, responsible last year alone for offenses which victimized 31,175 women.
> Adequate and understanding laws do not exist. Law enforcement is helpless.
> Here, in terms of one case, is the story of a man whose enemy was womankind.

The titles bear some resemblance to the exculpatory preface that Thomas Doherty notes as a hallmark of gangster and other 1930s films; such a preface provides the high-minded rationale for more exploitation genre material in the narrative.[32] Here, though, the tone is different, with simple, stark, sans-serif white lettering on a black screen and a low-volume moody scoring. The numbering of victims implies a quantitative study, not a qualitative social work orientation. Finally, in distinction to *Knock on Any Door*, which argues for reform of the legal system, *The Sniper* starts off with a dissociation of knowledge and the existing judicial system.

As with many problem films, one character bears the thematic weight for the narrative. In this case, the police psychiatrist, Dr. Kent, explains the genesis of the sniper's criminality, first to a skeptical but persuadable police lieutenant and later to a hostile group of well-connected citizens pressuring the police chief. In the former scene with the lieutenant, Kent traces the sniper's pathology both to deep-seeded psychological issues (in popular psychology typical of the period, his mother) and to a pattern of reinforced behavior. In the later scene, Kent appeals to legal reform for the psychological treatment of sex offenders. "If his first act had led to treatment instead of jail," he pleads, "three women wouldn't be lying dead today." As in similar scenes in *Crossfire*, the close framing of Kent, looking off forward frame left, as he talks to the citizen-activists puts additional emphasis on his account.

At face value, dialogue like the psychologist's would place the narrative as one of popular psychology, not popular sociology. However, the

FIGURE 4 *The Sniper*: framing as anomie.

film layers on top of the psychological narrative a depiction of the social alienation of the sniper, Eddie Miller (Arthur Franz). The procedural narrative frames the police's detective work with a subjective depiction of Eddie's increasing alienation from the primary groups among which he circulates in the city. As such, Eddie is the ultimate product of gesellschaft. For instance, a group of children rebuke Eddie as he approaches their baseball game. The scene starts and ends with Eddie isolated in the decoupage and the frame, the deep focus emphasizing his status as social outcast. Elsewhere, Eddie is on the margins of groups talking, whether passersby on the street, patrons at a restaurant, or workmates. The tight framing signals the psychologized dimension of Eddie's experience but also his atomization driven by social anomie. The narrative depicts Eddie's base pathology as psychological but the inability to thwart his base urges as a social failing.

That these two levels, social and psychological, overlapped so neatly in the film spoke to a broader dialogue between these two levels in the sociological literature of the day. Methodologically, the functionalist turn in sociology resulted in a move away from the group-and-conflict orientation of the Chicago school, toward studies that abstracted social dynamics. In surveying the changes in 1940s sociology, Andrew Abbott and James T. Sparrow refer to an "individual-collectivity" model that treated social life as two abstract levels, the individual and collective. They write:

> The relation between these two levels was theorized in various ways: as microcosm/macrocosm (the individual contains a picture of the "larger" society or its values); as normative (society provides "rules" that govern or "integrate" individuals); and as purely aggregative (society is merely the appearance of individual attitudes or behaviors taken as aggregates). But all three models shared the concept of sharply separated levels, related in ways that were timeless and abstract.[33]

Abbott and Sparrow see this model working across the major sociological works of the 1940s and early 1950s, including *An American Dilemma*, *The Authoritarian Personality*, and *The American Soldier*.[34] In other words, where functionalism might narrowly be construed as a theoretical school limited to certain thinkers, its individual-collectivity model was the operative *doxa* for parts of the discipline not considered strictly functionalist. Abbott and Sparrow in fact see it as responsible for the symbiotic relationship between theorists such as Parsons and Merton and empiricists like Paul Lazarsfeld and Samuel Stouffer. Sociological schools that would otherwise seem strange bedfellows found ground for dialogue in their scientism and their abstraction away from situated social conflict.

The role of the Frankfurt School in 1940s American sociology highlights the way that functionalism subsumed competing social models into a new synthesis. The Frankfurt School's home, the Institute for Social Research, had been in exile in the United States and housed as a semiautonomous unit at Columbia University. As its material support from the university waned, however, the Institute was forced to look for foundation funding willing to support largely empirically driven studies. The Radio Project, later the Center for Social Research, headed by Paul Lazarsfeld, employed Theodor Adorno and was broadly affiliated with those in the Institute. Later, the American Jewish Committee commissioned *Studies in Prejudice*, an examination of anti-Semitism in the United States.[35] As Martin Jay notes, these studies posed a dilemma for the Frankfurt School scholars: "From the first . . . the Frankfurt School was critical of the reductionist tendencies implicit in inductively oriented, empirical social science. In the exploration of social phenomena, it placed theory prior to the gathering of 'facts,' just as in politics it put theory before *praxis*. At the same time, of course, it was never satisfied with the cavalier dismissal of all empirical research."[36] Thus, although theoretically the Frankfurt School scholars opposed the empirically oriented work that edged toward positivism, during the 1940s their work often shared the methodological assumptions of the field. As Abbott and Sparrow demonstrate, *The Authoritarian Personality*, the Institute's large-scale study of fascist psychology, shared the individual-collectivity methodological synthesis of American sociology. Moreover, it did so by relying heavily on social-psychological opinion research in the Lazarsfeld vein, which Habermas, drawing largely on Frankfurt School antipositivism, would later critique as a deformed version of public opinion.[37] The theoretical occupations of the Frankfurt School certainly drove the study and made it distinctive from the mainstream of American sociology, but its reception in the United States came from its surprising legibility and its functionalist, relatively non-Marxist, methodology.

The crime-problem films varied in their thematic emphasis on psychological causes, but the postwar problem film cycles removed or downplayed individual moral culpability for socially deviant behavior and presented the primary and secondary social relations *as social relations*. In brief, they popularized the insights and arguments of a rapidly growing and entrenching academic discipline. The shift in popular sociology between *Knock on Any Door* and *The Sniper* in a span of just a few years shows how quickly the new functionalist *doxa* established itself in a wider public discourse.

Race Sociology: *Pinky* and *Intruder in the Dust*

The social problem films dealing with racial politics were among the most famous of the postwar cycle, and films like *Pinky* and *Intruder in the Dust* were important events that, however compromised by racist discourse, reflected a significant shift in both the U.S. government's civil rights policy and Hollywood's orientation as an industry toward racial representation. Ellen Scott has charted the political battles around censorship of racialized images in commercial cinema, giving a picture of a triangular relationship between governmental censorship (local, state, and federal), industry self-censorship, and a newly powerful civil rights representational activism.[38] The social problem discourse of race abetted but also complicated this relationship. Two films in particular, *Pinky* and *Intruder in the Dust*, repeated and reformulated the ideas circulating from public discussion of a specific sociological work, Myrdal's *An American Dilemma*. *An American Dilemma*'s readership exceeded a merely academic one, reaching into policy circles, the clergy, police forces, and newsrooms, and directly or indirectly the study popularized the functionalist and liberal understanding of race as a "social problem."[39] Beyond Myrdal, too, a broader functionalist turn was reflected in Hollywood's racial representations.

The sociology of race provides a useful microcosm for the changes that functionalism and the individual-collective model brought to sociology as a whole. Howard Winant suggests that American sociology's understanding of race comprised four distinct phases organized around central paradigms of race: a biologist paradigm, including Herbert Spencer–influenced work; a pragmatist paradigm, primarily the sociology of the Chicago school; a structural-functionalist paradigm that gained dominance in the postwar decades; and paradigms tied either to new social movements or the neoconservative movement.[40] An ambitious and voluminous sociological study of American race relations, *An American Dilemma* shifted the framework for understanding racial relations by ushering in a structural-functionalist paradigm tied to white liberalism and the instrumental needs of the U.S. government. In this paradigm, understanding race meant diagnosing a "social problem" whose dysfunctions threatened American society as a systemic whole. Winant writes, "The structural-functionalist view of race consistently stressed the integrative qualities of U.S. society; thus the overlap of the two uses of the term integration—one that summarized the key civil rights demands of the era, and one that frames sociological explanation in terms of social unity and commonality."[41]

This intellectual shift registered in the differing viewpoints of Gunnar Myrdal and Chicago school leader Robert E. Park. In the pages of *An American Dilemma*, Myrdal critiqued Park for a laissez-faire objectivity in face of race relations: "What we find is a systematic tendency to ignore practically all possibilities of modifying—by conscious effort—the social effects of the natural forces."[42] According to the historian Fred Matthews, Park responded to Myrdal and generally voiced suspicion that social harmony was a possible or desirable precondition for racial justice. "I think the liberals realize now," Park wrote in one letter to a colleague, "that the Negro's cause must in the long run win. The only thing is, they don't want it to win too soon and they don't want the change to be so rapid as to result in the disorders that we have had."[43] Although the Chicago school and the functionalists shared some common ground (both were highly critical of Jim Crow and both approached race as a systemic social artifact), the methodological emphasis colored the politics of their approach. In hindsight, Park's conflict approach may have been more prophetic than Myrdal's social-integration model; in the 1940s, Myrdal's approach carried the day. Even as late as 1967, Talcott Parsons, reflecting on the civil rights movement and the historical changes since *An American Dilemma* had been published, reasserted an essentially functionalist conception of social integration.[44]

At first glance *Pinky* would seem not to be invested in the sociological as a mode of understanding. The most overtly melodramatic of the postwar social problem cycle, the narrative follows the identity crisis that a passing light-skinned African American, Pinky Johnson, faces when she returns South to visit her aunt. As Scott notes, the source novel's author, Cid Ricketts Sumner, "a self-identified white Southerner, never advocated integration. But Zanuck employed liberal screenwriters Dudley Nichols and, later, Philip Dunne to adapt the novel, blending her gradualism with their liberalism."[45] *Pinky* screenwriter Philip Dunne's "behind the scenes" discussion for the *New York Times* suggests an explicit inspiration from Myrdal's work: "Every American citizen, white or Negro, has his own ideas on the subject of race in America. Few Americans have been able to approach it without passion or prejudice. (It is significant that the only truly dispassionate and unprejudiced appraisal of the problem is the work of a foreigner, Gunnar Myrdal, in his monumental *An American Dilemma*.)"[46] *An American Dilemma* gave *Pinky* a high-minded justification for its message about prejudice but also shaped the film's depictions of the black community and conception of the social problem. In story conference memos, one producer at Fox, Michael Abel, wrote of the script:

> Striking with the skill and daring of the surgeon's knife it lays open the foulest cancer in the American way of life, and by exposing, paves the way, let us hope, for its eventual eradication. The wretched condition of the Negroes in our southern states—the poverty, ignorance, fear and humiliation they suffer at the hands of the "superior" whites, are hammered here in powerful blows to the shame of the people in this country. It is high time the facts were faced openly and honestly; there has long been a crying need for a picture of this type.[47]

This tone is remarkably similar to the rhetorical approach, at once emotive and rationalist, of *An American Dilemma*. Throughout their deliberations the film's writers and producers acknowledged Jim Crow, discrimination, and segregation as the backdrop for the social message of the film, yet they emphasized the "conditions" of black life and so maximized the black southerner's status as object rather than subject.

An American Dilemma's project registers in the film's narrative. *Pinky* depicts the title character's transformation from passing as white and a life in the North to an acceptance of her race in defiance of Jim Crow conditions. Even in its passing melodrama, many of the incidents dramatize racial prejudice and show common ground with *An American Dilemma*. Myrdal writes, "If a Negro commits a crime against another Negro, and no white man is involved, and if the crime is not a serious one, white policemen will let the criminal off with a warning or a beating, and the court will let him off with a warning or a relatively light sentence."[48] Compare this observation with *Pinky*'s climactic courtroom scene. When the defense attorney asserts in cross-examination that the police officer let Pinky off without any charges, the policeman replies, "You generally always let 'em off with a good talking to, like you give her. You know how it is." Furthermore, the Manichaean characterization of the African Americans in the film sets up an objectified "Negro condition." Even though *An American Dilemma* explicitly warns against moralizing variants of prejudice, it does read "the Negro community as a pathological form of an American community." The function of subproletarian Jake is to stand in for this pathologized black experience, as in Darryl F. Zanuck's words that "[Jake] is supposed to be a shifty, dishonest, low-class Negro, a sort of agitator."[49]

Additionally, as much as *Pinky* owes its narrative of passing to literary and filmic precedents, it also moves passing from mere categorical ambivalence (the "caught between two worlds" trope of the tragic mulatto) to a stand-in for social and political conflict. "As a social phenomenon," *An American Dilemma* notes, "passing is so deeply connected with the psychological complexes—built around caste and sex—of both groups that it has come to be a certain theme of fiction and of popular imagination and storytelling."[50] By presenting the protagonist's dilemma as a choice between self-affirmation and freedom from economic oppression, *Pinky* combines the thematic preoccupations of fiction and cinematic storytelling with the social understanding of caste and sex.

FIGURE 5 *Intruder in the Dust*: "Our Conscience" of *The American Dilemma.*

Intruder in the Dust likewise adopts themes presented in Myrdal's publication. *An American Dilemma* organizes its quilt-work composite of qualitative and quantitative findings around a central conceit: that racial segregation and stratification affront core American ideals of freedom and equality and therefore pose a challenge to the American conscience.[51] In *Intruder in the Dust*, the protagonists' exchange at the end lays out a comparable message:

CHICK *(referring to Lucas Beauchamp)* They don't see him, as though it never happened.

JOHN STEVENS They see him.

CHICK No, they don't even know he's there.

STEVENS But they do. The same as I do. And they always will as long as he lives. Proud, stubborn, insufferable. But there he goes. Keeper of my conscience.

CHICK Our conscience, Uncle John.

Whereas Lucas Beauchamp's words close the source novel with an ironic ending (in which Lucas asks for his receipt), the exchange between John and Chick asserts the Myrdalian theme. One Faulkner critic has, convincingly, read the novel as an articulation of white moderate politics in the context of the 1948 presidential election.[52] In the process of adaptation, two versions of white liberalism are competing. It is not clear that Hollywood's adaptation is the more regressive of them, since, as Gordon Hutner has argued, *Intruder* was simply one of a series of novels by white authors to challenge prior cultures of racial prejudice.[53] In comparison to the novel, however, the film version of *Intruder in the Dust* does recuperate a straightforward Myrdalian view in distinction to the complicated ideology of the novel.

This social problem tendency clashed with the more conventional murder-mystery material of the narrative, as well as the film's circulation as a semifaithful adaptation of William Faulkner's novel. These contradictions inflected the marketing of the film across regional lines. *Intruder in the Dust* featured two trailers, one the studio designated for southern audiences, another for northern audiences:

SOUTHERN TRAILER

TITLE The faith of this BOY . . . The courage of this MAN . . . The heart of this Lady . . . Fighting against what unholy violence?

TITLE INTRUDER IN THE DUST [*over close-up of book*]

VOICEOVER Boiling like hot lava from the angry pen of one of the world's greatest storytellers, *Intruder in the Dust* brings to the screen the most striking characters you've ever met. Filmed on location to authenticate its raw, rugged, realistic background, *Intruder in the Dust* tells its story in tense terms of men of action and women of courage, of the furtive whine of a bullet fired from the shadows . . . the baying of hounds at the edge of a pool of quicksand . . . of the smoldering hate in a craven heart . . . of the silent terror of a man who waits alone in the night for he knows not what . . . of the sullen fury that grips a town and whips it to the brink of violence.

Intruder in the Dust, an outstanding American novel, is from the same studio which gave you *The Yearling*. And like that distinguished film, has been made with force, fire, and fidelity. MGM presents a faithful dramatization of one of the great novels of our time.

NORTHERN TRAILER

TITLE INTRUDER IN THE DUST [*close-up of book*]. [*Dissolve to*] You can't film *that* novel . . . but we did! Metro-Goldwyn-Mayer announces the savage story of one man . . . [*close-up of Lucas*] . . . this man . . . against the weight of the world!

DAVID CLARKE You crummy, bigoted, burr-headed [*attacks Lucas*] . . .

TITLE NO BEATING AROUND THE BUSH! NO SIDESTEPPING! NO DOUBLE-TALK!

DAVID CLARKE Nigger!

TITLE INTRUDER IN THE DUST [*over close-up of book*].

VOICEOVER The seething fury that grips a town and whips it to the brink of violence. . . . a mystery drama that quivers with suspense . . . the burning fever that spawns reckless, ruthless action—that's *Intruder in the Dust.* The strong force of pride and decency, which thrives even in the midst of terror. . . . The faith of this boy . . . the courage of this man . . . the heart of this lady. . . . That, too, is *Intruder in the Dust,* a faithful dramatization of the superb novel by William Faulkner, one of the world's greatest living authors.

[*Trailer excerpts four scenes of confrontation, emphasizing racial conflict.*]

TITLE INTRUDER IN THE DUST [*over close-up of book*][54]

The southern trailer de-emphasizes the racial conflict in the film, playing up the mystery genre, the character traits of the white protagonists, and the film's status as an adaptation. The national-release trailer, meanwhile, emphasizes the social problem content, lending sensationalism to depictions of southern racism. The combination of liberal didacticism and showmanship that producer Dore Schary had adopted in *Crossfire* takes on a specific regionalized appeal to a northern spectator.

Justifiably, critics have seen the layering of melodrama, exploitation, and social problem film as watering down the postwar race problem film cycle's civil rights liberalism.[55] From another perspective, however, the sociological discourse appeared in more melodramatic films as well as realist examples. Film scholars generally treat *Imitation of Life* as melodrama or as surreptitious auteur art cinema (or both), but there is also a social problem film strain within its narrative.[56] One key moment early in the film shows character Sarah Jane refusing the black doll and wanting Susie's white doll; a swift tilt shows the discarded doll on the floor. On one hand, this scene is the melodramatic moment par excellence, comprising sudden and dramatic musical scoring, the pathos encapsulated in overdetermined imagery, and the foreshadowing of an episodic narrative. (Sarah Jane will repeat her vain attempts at rebellion many times in the film.) On the other hand, this scene has a more specific referent and replicates the scenario of Kenneth Clark and Mamie Clark's famous study of African American children's impressions of dolls. This study tabulated children's responses to and perceptions of race in white and black dolls.[57] Kenneth Clark had contributed to Myrdal's *An American Dilemma*, and both Clarks were psychologists researching the social psychological foundations of broader social attitudes. The *Brown v. Board of Education* U.S. Supreme Court decision cited their study as evidence of the deleterious effect of educational segregation and in the process further publicized the study in the popular social science discourse surrounding the civil rights movement.[58] Although *Imitation of Life* was released a decade after the initial postwar race problem films, this intertextual citation reveals that popular sociology could appear in unexpected corners of Hollywood's output.

The Hermeneutics of Social Problem Cinema

Despite the at times palimpsestic nature of Hollywood's involvement in the social problem discourse, the decade and a half between the late 1930s, with *Dead End*, and the early 1950s saw an overall shift from the Progressive conception of the social to a Chicago school and ultimately a functionalist understanding. The reception of the social problem dramas of the late 1940s reveals one key tenet of the social problem discourse: a tendency to look beyond the individual for causes of phenomena. *Variety*, for instance, warned that *The Lost Weekend* "isn't a pretty story for more than one reason. Its moral, of course, crusades against alcoholism, but to casual readers of the book and patrons of the picture there may well be a wholesale condemnation of the suppliers of spirits."[59] Even when criticizing the films, journalistic critics often did so on the grounds that they did not illuminate better the deeper sociological causes of the problem. In a judgment mirrored by the *New Yorker*, Bosley Crowther's review of *Gentleman's Agreement* complained that protagonist Phil Green's "explorations are narrowly confined to the upper-class social and professional level to which he is immediately exposed. And his discoveries are chiefly in the nature of petty bourgeois rebuffs, with no inquiry into the devious cultural mores from which they spring."[60] Sociological analysis had diffused enough that some educated consumers of Hollywood's product wished for narratives that could suggest social causation.

The sociological ideas were not always front and center in the themes or narratives of these social problem films, but they were important as a signal that the conventional antimony between individual and structure is inadequate to make sense of these films. The stakes of this distinction are reflected in the writings of two prominent postwar critics of American cinema. Siegfried Kracauer wrote an article for *Harper's* on those "movies with a message" in which he compared *The Best Years of Our Lives* with *It's a Wonderful Life* (Frank Capra, 1946). "Wyler's characters are no less individuals than Capra's," he wrote, "but, unlike Capra's, they reflect the inner workings of the society to which they belong. The bankers in this film behave as typical bankers would—no better, no worse; and Fredric March as the ex-sergeant, himself no paragon of virtue, accuses them not so much of irregular villainy as of a stubborn insistence on regular practices that are apt to harm veterans."[61] The structural awareness Kracauer describes is synonymous with Marxist analysis, and he further argues that these problem films undercut their own liberalism by tacitly evincing doubt for the strength of social progress. In this regard, he would seem to agree with Robert Warshow, who, like other highbrow critics, critiqued the liberalism of the problem film. Warshow, however, saw *The Best Years of Our Lives* differently and criticized its narrative as a "falsehood":

> The falsehood has many aspects, but its chief and most general aspect is a denial of the reality of politics. If politics means the existence of real incompatibilities of interest and real *social* problems not susceptible of individual solution. The choice of subject is itself an evasion of politics, for the "veteran's problem" is not an issue, or at any rate it is false issue, since nobody is against the veterans and since they do not constitute a social group, except temporarily and very vaguely.[62]

Warshow's emphasis of the word "social" is telling. The social problem film, more than other classical Hollywood films, invited and continues to invite judgments that it either provides a thematic and analytical framework that exceeds the individualism that has defined Hollywood's ideology or misses the broader vision of social determination. The left critics of the genre tend to come down on Warshow's side of the argument.[63] The divergence between Kracauer's and Warshow's arguments suggests that the desire for a proper social analysis in cinema dates at least to the release of postwar problem films. The case that problem films reinforce individualism and therefore miss the social is just as tenable as the case that they figure social causation exceeding the individuals of their narratives.

The key to understanding the peculiar politics of the postwar liberal problem film cycle is the paradox of a worldview different from both Marxism and liberal humanism. As with the overwhelming majority of Hollywood films, the social problem dramas cast large-scale political problems as individual ones, and so prove the rule of a "Hollywood formula" and its ideological bent. All the same, the postwar problem films portrayed problems that elude both individual and diegetic solution. Phil Green faces a coordinated "gentleman's agreement" excluding Jews; Pinky faces a southern justice system that consistently rules in favor of whites over blacks; and in *The Snake Pit* protagonist Virginia Cunningham and her doctor face a chronic lack of funding for mental health treatment. Even when the pathologies and problems are personal (Susan Hayward's character's alcoholism in *Smash-Up*, for example), the very inclusion under the rubric of the social problem had the potential to elevate them to social issues proper. These narratives are more than failed leftism and failed social analysis: they represent a historically specific understanding of the "social problem" itself.

Postwar functionalism and social problem sociology distinguished themselves not merely from what preceded them but also from what was to follow. After the 1950s especially, a growing minority of conflict-approach sociologists, C. Wright Mills the most famous among them, established a counterbalance to the theoretical and statistical approaches dominant in the field.[64] By the 1960s, sociologists began to question the power dynamic behind social problem definition. Howard Becker's *Outsiders*, mentioned earlier, understood deviance as the product of social labeling, thereby reversing the functionalists' emphasis on social pathology. As both methodological reflection and New Left politics changed the direction of the field, social problem sociology no longer operated with the same unselfconsciousness that sustained its rise during a period of liberal consensus. The subtitle alone of Anthony Platt's study *The Child Savers: The Invention of Delinquency* rebuked the Merton-inspired studies of deviance (and departed from the attitude of films like *Rebel without a Cause* [Nicholas Ray, 1955]).[65] Factors internal and external to the field would bring about an end to the functionalists' Durkheimian view of the social problem, but for two solid decades that view held sway.

3

Hollywood and the Public Sphere

Sociological thinking may have come into vogue for Hollywood in the 1940s, but it was the journalist rather than the academic who was a common protagonist of the social problem film. A key example would be *Gentleman's Agreement*, made in 1947 by 20th Century–Fox. The film includes briefly the character of a scientist whose views are meant to stand in for contemporary anthropology's view of race as an artifice and social construction. However, the film's narrative centers overwhelmingly on journalist Phil Green (Gregory Peck), who is writing an exposé of anti-Semitism for a major news magazine, the fictional *Smith's Weekly*. The dialogue between Green; the publisher, Mr. Minify; board member Irving Weisman; and Ann Dettrey, fashion editor, in the *Smith's Weekly* board meeting scene is typical:

MR. MINIFY Mr. Green is going to do a series on anti-Semitism for us.
IRVING WEISMAN Really? Again?
MINIFY Not again. For the first time. We're going to split it wide open.
WEISMAN If you don't mind my saying as an old friend, I think it's a very bad idea—the worst, most harmful thing you can possibly do now.

MINIFY Not at all. Why is it a harmful idea?

WEISMAN Because it will only stir it up more. That's right. Let it alone. We'll handle it our own way.

MINIFY The hush-hush way?

WEISMAN I don't care what you call it. Let it alone. You can't write it out of existence. We've been fighting it for years, and we know from experience the less talk there is about it the better.

MINIFY Sure, pretend it doesn't exist and add to the conspiracy of silence. I should say not. Keep silent and let Bilbo and Gerald L. K. Smith do all the talking? No sir. Irving, you and your just-keep-silent-about-it committees have got just exactly no place. We're going to call a spade a dirty spade, and I think it's high time and a fine idea.

PHIL GREEN So do I. I couldn't agree with Mr. Minify more.

Gentleman's Agreement is about the press nearly as much as it is about the crusade against anti-Semitism. Some have seen in the problem films a reformist mentality, but it is worth noting that the social problem here does not require governmental action, which the dialogue does not even mention. Rather, the battle is over the very vehicle of mass persuasion at the protagonists' disposal, and Phil Green seeks to act upon the sphere of public debate. The film takes pains to point out that this debate extends beyond the realm of the diegesis, even into legislative bodies and radio, hence the references to Mississippi senator Theodore G. Bilbo and America First Party organizer Gerald L. K. Smith. Contrary to what Weisman says, the film implies, you can write (and film) anti-Semitism out of existence.

Even when social problem films did not revolve around the journalist figure, they adapted news articles, as in *The Best Years of Our Lives* and *Lost Boundaries*, or otherwise invoked the aesthetics of the investigative exposé, as in *The Snake Pit.* Implicitly or explicitly, social problem dramas seek to act on an audience as a citizenry and to serve as part of a fourth estate. In theoretical terms, they activate a notion of the public sphere, that is, an abstract collectivity tied to the process of public deliberation. The cinema had since its inception provoked a sense of its power as a mass medium, but the cultural expectations of its participation in a mass public sphere fluctuated throughout the twentieth century. The social problem film, with its unique mix of entertainment fiction and nonfiction social analysis, brought the issues of the public sphere to the fore.

The social problem film by its nature invokes a public sphere, since problem films are narratives whose topicality implies social relations as part of the problem and a public audience capable of acting on the problem in some abstracted capacity as the public. To this extent, the problem film merely makes explicit the potential persuasiveness of cinema as a mass medium—a potential to which contemporary observers in the 1940s were especially attuned. As much as propaganda fostered an anxiety about cinema's role in the public sphere, the liberal consensus also broadly welcomed the use of cinema for persuasive ends. In the middle of the twentieth century, journalism was the dominant expression of the mainstream, official public sphere, whereas documentary cinema offered a new and developing model for a specifically cinematic public sphere. Discursively and textually, Hollywood's social problem film formed an analogy with both of these public sphere institutions. Journalism and documentary film were cultural products that participated in public debate, and any attempt to understand Hollywood's disposition to speak to "social issues" must grapple with the relation of the social problem film to each.

The Mass Public Sphere and Its Critics: *Meet John Doe* and the Social Comedies

While the postwar social problem film would often depict the mass public in distinct ways, it owed a considerable debt to earlier films to highlight the masses as an entity. By the 1930s, especially, films drew upon populist and New Deal iconography of masses of workers, but they increasingly invoked the sense of the masses as citizens. The credit sequence of Frank Capra's *Meet John Doe* (1940), for instance, begins with a montage of shots of workers and city dwellers. Immediately after the credits, construction workers change the sign of the venerable newspaper *The Bulletin* (motto: "a free press for a free people") to *The New Bulletin* ("a streamlined paper for a streamlined era"). Thus the film sets up a thematic connection between the economic problems of the "common man" during the Great Depression and his representation through the press. Charles Maland points out Capra's role (with screenwriter Robert Riskin) in synthesizing screwball comedy and the social problem film.[1] More than those of any other Hollywood director, furthermore, Capra's films establish the mass public sphere as a political problem.

A number of political thinkers have sought to explain the nature of a realm of public debate central to democracy. Perhaps most notably, Jürgen Habermas theorized the concept of the public sphere via the term "*öffentlichkeit*," which also translates variously as publicity, publicness, and the public.[2] However, the public sphere does not simply mean the public realm in the everyday sense of the term, as distinct from the realm of private or domestic life. Rather, the public sphere is the instrument of debate in democratic theory. Its realm is separate from the state but is vital to the state's functioning; it rises above private business interests yet consists of individuals acting privately. Some have questioned whether the public sphere actually ever rose above the private interests of a bourgeois male elite.[3] Habermas admits the exclusivity of the bourgeois governments, but claims that the liberal public sphere of the eighteenth and nineteenth centuries was ideology but not merely ideology, because it defined the liberal bourgeois state against previous governmental forms and because the ideal has since continued to inform models of democracy.

The main complication to the ideal of the liberal public sphere was one that earlier critics, notably Walter Lippmann, writing in the 1920s, and C. Wright Mills, writing in the 1950s, have also noted: the public sphere tends toward systematic corruption in modern, industrial democracies.[4] The critique of the public sphere's corruption has taken several forms, but it centers on a few claims. Legitimation is stripped of its deliberative nature and turned into mere acclamation for the real operation of power, which takes place increasingly in extraparliamentary sites. Private interests encroach upon public ones, especially in new practices like public relations and political marketing. The shift from the press to mass media further reduces the possibility for deliberative debate, either because of the media's restriction of senders relative to receivers or because of the news industry's political economy. Finally, through the institution of public opinion polling, a social scientific (abstract empiricist) understanding of the public as a statistical aggregate comes to replace genuine, debating publics.[5] Each signals a transition from the liberal public sphere of democratic theory to the mass public sphere of actually existing democracy in advanced (and postindustrial) capitalist societies.[6]

This corruption of the public sphere played out with multiple important developments, as new public sphere institutions arose to meet the demands of and even constitute the new mass public. Public relations had its beginning in the interwar years with trailblazers like Ivy Lee and

Edward Bernays first attempting damage control for high-profile and image-battered monopoly firms (including, respectively, Standard Oil and General Electric) and later trying to formulate general principles of the profession.[7] Not until after 1945, however, did public relations cohere as an industry and widespread practice, with a professional organization and a proliferation of university-level education.[8] Meanwhile, scientific opinion measurement professionalized with new survey and statistical tools and expanded in scope during World War II.[9] Some mass-public forms, like political marketing, would flourish only in the televisual age, but by the 1940s many of the recognizable public sphere practices had been set.

These institutional developments accompanied a broader cultural constitution of a mass public. The historian Sarah Igo has argued that social science and polling practices fostered a culture in which citizens began to imagine themselves as part of an abstracted collectivity. Igo points to key sociological studies like *Middletown*, the Gallup surveys, and the Kinsey reports as catalysts for a new understanding of the "average American" as a statistical and cultural construct. "Many contemporary observers," Igo notes, "viewed surveyors' aggregating techniques as the inevitable product of a 'mass society.' But national polls and surveys . . . were as much responsible for creating a mass public as they were reacting to its arrival."[10] Igo's account provides a useful periodization, whereby a culture of an abstracted mass public developed in the interwar years, only to strengthen by the postwar period.

In the realm of entertainment cinema, certain Hollywood comedies and social problem dramas, Capra's most of all, adopted Lippmann's critique of the mass public. *Meet John Doe* is the apotheosis, in which newspapers and broadcast media are both the vehicle for comic development and the object of institutional critique. Newspaper reporter Ann Mitchell (Barbara Stanwyck) invents a story about a chronically unemployed man, "John Doe," who plans to jump off the city hall building in protest of government corruption. Through complications, John Willoughby (Gary Cooper) becomes John Doe only because of the distorting power of the press and of broadcast media. Over the course of the film he comes to believe in the role he has been chosen to play. As Charles Wolfe notes, "The very premise of the film calls into question the possibility of an authentic relationship between 'hero' and the 'people' by transposing the former into a performer and the latter into an audience."[11] The film's theme is contradictory in that the debased mass public sphere is both the problem (it fools the citizenry into acclamation for business interests) and the solution. An abstracted public sphere is a structural narrative agent: newspapers and broadcasts present information to a consuming public, which acts accordingly. Especially in the climactic John Doe convention scene in which the montage alternates between John's attempted speech, the socially typed convention goers, and the representatives of the press, crowds come to figure the debating citizenry as a public entity.[12]

What had in the 1930s been a signature Frank Capra critique of the mass media became in the 1940s and 1950s a regular trope. The most striking example is *Magic Town* (William Wellman, 1947), in which Jimmy Stewart plays a pollster, Rip Smith, who discovers and ultimately corrupts a town that is a perfect statistical bellwether. The dramatic turning point comes when the citizens of Grandview gain awareness of the town's role and begin to asset their free will against a presumed demographic destiny. Up to this point the town of Grandview perfectly predicts the public opinion of the entire nation, and the actions of Rip Smith as pollster are premised on the townspeople's conformity to their true social selves. Ultimately, narrative complications thwart the social science researchers and public opinion pollsters, but whether as an active, insightful critic or as a historical index (in fact, the film is both), *Magic Town* diagnosed a problem that seemed new and vital in midcentury America: the power of a mass public sphere conceived in social scientific terms and given power by mass mediation.

Many postwar films, too, continued in the vein of public sphere critique. *A Face in the Crowd* (Elia Kazan, 1957) presents a dystopian view of television as an enabler of political demagoguery. *Scandal Sheet* (Phil Karlson, 1952) used the B-film thriller format to lament the erosion of journalistic integrity. Even setting aside films about the press, media critique was far more pervasive than generally acknowledged. The political advertising scene in *The Last Hurrah* (John Ford, 1958) is one good example: its internal framing and shot distance present the on-air televisual performance as an unnatural imitation of true, filmic performance. Subtextually, such critiques distanced cinema from the competing medium of television, whose rise was challenging the film industry. The depictions were more than competition between media, however, since postwar narratives repeatedly featured protagonists from the new professions of the mass public sphere. This includes not only the pollster in *Magic Town* but also the advertising executives of *Mr. Blandings Builds His Dream House* (H. C. Potter,

1948) and *The Hucksters* (Jack Conway, 1947), the political marketer of *The Senator Was Indiscreet* (George S. Kaufman, 1947), and the publicist of *The Fearmakers* (Jacques Tourneur, 1958). Comedies like *It Had to Be You* (Don Hartman and Rudolph Maté, 1947), *A Letter to Three Wives* (Joseph Mankiewicz, 1949), and *It Should Happen to You* (George Cukor, 1954) commented wryly on the impact of advertising. The social problem film was therefore just one of many genres to depict and comment on the public sphere professions.

The Journalism Analogy: *Hell's House*, *The Life of Emile Zola*, and *Gentleman's Agreement*

Despite the Lippmannesque strain of mass public critique in Hollywood films, postwar social problem films invoked journalism as a profession not to critique it but instead to privilege the journalist's professional ethos as model citizenry. There are some exceptions, but a general pattern holds: whereas social comedies in the Capra vein satirized and critiqued the mass public and public sphere institutions, prominent social problem films of the 1930s and 1940s were fully sympathetic with the journalist and implicitly aligned the film's thematic point of view with his or her crusade. As such, these films posed an analogy between cinema and journalism. They often did so through a journalist character that allegorically stands in for the studio, the filmmakers, or the film's circulation in public debate. At other times, the intimations of the journalistic dimensions of the social problem narrative were subtler. Either way, the analogy strengthened from the 1930s into the 1940s and changed in nature. Hollywood's invocations of the public sphere became less pro forma and more integral to the narrative. Unlike the ironic use of the journalist-protagonist in *Citizen Kane* (Orson Welles, 1941), the figure in the problem films collapsed the public sphere aspirations of journalism with the films' themes.

For the 1930s cycle of social problem films from Warner Bros., the press played an important if supporting role to the narrative. The Warner Bros.' producers, Darryl Zanuck especially, conceived of these as "ripped from the headlines" films, and Penelope Pelizzon and Nancy West have argued that the films drew upon the aesthetics of tabloid journalism of the 1920s and 1930s. They chart how Warner Bros. adapted to the temporality of cinema by staging tabloid news as cinematic allegories.[13] Narratively, the films included journalists as characters but also journalism as a more diffuse narrative entity. For instance, *I Am a Fugitive from a Chain Gang* (Mervyn LeRoy, 1932) follows the struggles of a convict, James Allen (Paul Muni), dealing with a flawed justice system and inhumane incarceration. Newspaper headlines provide crucial exposition in montage sequences, but the journalists are a palpable, though invisible, agent to bring about the reform the film supports.[14] At the same time, the public sphere is an exterior force in the narrative, and Allen is an object of journalism rather than its subject.

Hell's House, on the other hand, depicts a journalist who is also a main character but limits his importance as an agent of the public sphere. In the film, a young boy, Jimmy, is wrongly sent to a children's reformatory prison on account of his bootlegger friend. The journalist Frank Gebhardt gets involved in a crusade to free Jimmy; he thereby represents the protagonist within the film's Manichaean worldview but one whose main narrative function is to be a typical representative of institutions of authority and a foil for the "outlaw" or real protagonist, here the bootlegger played by Pat O'Brien (who corresponds to similar everyman characters in the Warner Bros. cycle played by Humphrey Bogart or Paul Muni). Gebhardt talks about reform and a muckraking journalism that will achieve a desired effect in the political sphere. Surprisingly, though, for all of Gebhardt's call for reform in *Hell's House*, it is striking that the journalist's individual actions and not his published articles further the narrative's advancement. Gebhardt functions here as other figures of authority do in the Warner Bros. cycle, from judges to congressmen. Although *Hell's House* represents a step toward an articulation of the public sphere, the film's allegorical resonance links Warner Bros. as a studio with Pat O'Brien's character, not the reform-minded Gebhardt.

One film of the 1930s cycle to draw an analogy between journalists and the Hollywood studio was *The Life of Emile Zola* (William Dieterle, 1937). Warner Bros. used the life of the literary figure to follow up the earlier biopic success of *The Story of Louis Pasteur* (William Dieterle, 1936) and to congratulate itself for the (in its mind) Zola-inspired type of social consciousness films it made in the 1930s. In one representative scene, the young Zola (Paul Muni) discovers his social consciousness by stumbling on vagrants sleeping underneath a bridge. Most of the stylistic tropes familiar to Warner Bros.' social consciousness films are present: the extreme low-key, low-lighting cinematography that puts Muni in the shadows; the panning shot of the urban poor, who stand in as mere objects of Zola's gaze;

even the punctuating dissolve. Muni's role as a writer exposing the conditions of miners in his novel *Germinal* has a clear parallel to Muni's role as a miner himself in *Black Fury* (Michael Curtiz, 1935). Accordingly, *The Life of Emile Zola* allegorizes Warner Bros. as a protest voice. At the same time, the journalist Zola gets recuperated by the writer and Great Man Zola; the conventions of the biopic mean that Zola does not represent journalism as a field or institution so much as a distinctive voice of individual courage.

To the extent the 1930s Warner Bros. films depicted journalism as a field, they invoked a Progressive-era practice of muckraking journalism. The postwar problem film cycle, by contrast, could present a professionalized journalist. In the diegesis of *Gentleman's Agreement*, Phil Green is an excellent journalist, but there is no implication that his ability or work ethic is singular. This paradoxical combination of ordinary and powerful registers in the mise-en-scène of *Smith's Weekly* office space, for which the studio sets adopt an International Style minimalism much more pared down from the generic Deco style of corporate offices in 1930s Hollywood (figure 6). Rather than a luxurious, vaguely "rich" setting, *Gentleman's Agreement* cites a distinctly bourgeois and professional referent. The professionalized depiction of journalism changes the effect of the journalist character in the social problem narrative. The editorial meeting scene of the film mirrors the film's own aspirations to act upon the public sphere, and the boardroom conversation restages Hollywood's decision to make problem films as a fictional choice in the publishing industry, with Mr. Minify standing in for Darryl Zanuck and Irving Weisman for the Jewish studio moguls. Thus the film's narrative not only invokes the journalistic field, it also allegorizes the film industry's realignment to public debate. If, as Pelizzon and West have argued, allegory is a central strategy for the early 1930s headliner cycle, allegory in the 1940s prestige films moves away from an external commentary on political machines of American cities and toward a broader idealization of Hollywood cinema as a journalistic institution.

One striking element of *Gentleman's Agreement*'s implicit analogy between journalism and cinema is its exaggerated emphasis on journalism as exposé. In writing on anti-Semitism, Phil Green is going to "split it wide open" and do so through one convention of investigative journalism, social passing. As historians of journalism and cultural historians have noted, the exposé as a journalistic form emerged in the Progressive era out of the political economy of national magazines aimed at the middle classes.[15] Muckraking journalism had circulated discursively in Hollywood

FIGURE 6 Mise-en-scène of the professionalized journalist in *Gentleman's Agreement*.

films, but the postwar cycle of problem films amplified the equation of cinema and exposé. Another key film in the cycle, *The Lost Weekend*, differs in that its writer-protagonist is a participant in his subject matter. The exposé narrative poses as a kind of journalistic investigation and contrasts the "normal" life of middle-class America with the sordid realm of the social problem. The 1930s cycle partook of the exposé rhetoric, as in *Hell's House*, but in the 1940s the investigative journalist becomes less an inert narrative agent and more the subject of the narrative.

Notably, even if these social problem films of the 1930s and 1940s depicted journalists, writers, and other mass public sphere agents, they differed from two cycles about newspapers. First, Pelizzon and West identify a tabloid-racketeer cycle of the early 1930s that "portray[ed] their protagonists as racketeer types, ready to extort, bribe, or obstruct justice." The cycle shared with the social comedy a critical stance but, instead of the Lippman critique, assumed the class vantage of broadsheet journalism against tabloids.[16] Second, a genre of the "journalism film," which builds the central theme and conflict around some procedural and ethical dimensions of journalism, has spanned the decades from the 1930s to contemporary Hollywood.[17] The social problem films, in contrast, whether containing a journalist as the central character (*Gentleman's Agreement*) or an incidental character (*Hell's House*), focus on the more diffuse public sphere rather than the practice of journalism per se. In *Gentleman's Agreement*, Phil Green's success in finishing his article matters for the narrative only to the extent that Phil has an epiphany about the extent of anti-Semitism and presumably will have an impact on a reading public to fight it. In *The Lawless*, the struggles of newspaper owner Larry Wilder (Carey Macdonald) to keep the press open and running is a manifestation of his fight against anti-immigrant bigotry in a California town. For *The Lost Weekend*, Don Birnam's exposé novel is self-therapy for overcoming the need to drink and ultimately a public airing of the alcoholic's mindset. Like many comparisons, this analogy between cinema and journalism was not perfect, but by invoking it, social problem films created an ideological position poised between a literal invocation of journalism as a profession common to the journalism films and the Lippmannesque critique of the mass public sphere common to social comedies.

The Griersonian Text: *The Lost Weekend* and *Gentleman's Agreement*

The idea that cinema could be an instrument of the public sphere emerged during the transitional-era cinema of the 1910s and continued throughout the 1930s problem film cycles. However, nonfiction rather than fiction cinema would forge a closer relationship to journalism and a broader acceptance as a public sphere instrument. Newsreels explicitly took on the journalistic role of reportage and in the talking-picture era overlapped with radio news in style and journalistic ethos. Newsreels would form the basis for 20th Century–Fox's pseudodocumentary cycle, which had close ties to social relevance. At the same time, Griersonian documentary posed a specifically cinematic public sphere form. As John Grierson himself noted,

> It is worth recalling that the British documentary group began not so much in affection for film per se as in affection for national education. . . . We noted the conclusion of such men as Walter Lippmann, that because the citizen, under

> modern conditions, could not know everything about everything all the time, democratic citizenship was therefore impossible. . . . We turned to the new wide-reaching instruments of radio and cinema as necessary instruments in both the practice of government and the enjoyment of citizenship.[18]

Thereby drawing from Lippmann's notion of intelligence work, Grierson imagined a distinct social function for documentary as an enabler of public debate and an educated citizenry. Thus, when Grierson complains that the city symphony films fail to show workers in their economic specificity, his critique is both formal and social.[19] Griersonian documentary as a concept refers both to the Lippmann-inspired public sphere aspirations and the aesthetic forms of expository documentary.

Theorists have critiqued both aspects of Griersonianism as either benignly or malignantly ideological, and recent scholarship has begun to integrate newsreels, essay films, and other nonfiction cinema into a documentary historiography that has heretofore excluded them.[20] Furthermore, documentary as a cinematic field was still in a developing phase, often without autonomy from the state. Nonetheless, in its context, the wedding of a public sphere project to an aesthetic template was highly influential, including in Hollywood. Aesthetically, Grierson differentiated documentary from the journalistic other of the newsreel and gave a formal and definitional impetus to documentary by arguing for a structured use of actuality footage into a transparent and expository argument. In practice, documentarists in the 1930s formulated a nonfiction cinematic language that built the aspirations of the public sphere into documentary form itself, with abstracted voiceover, intellectual montage editing, and extreme long shots and aerial establishing shots. *The City* (Ralph Steiner and Willard van Dyke, 1939) is a good example from the U.S. variant of the documentary movement, with its expository argument about the impact of capitalism on the life of the workers proceeding through oratory voiceover narration and Soviet-influenced montage.

In the 1930s and the 1940s, Griersonian documentary gained influence in the United States and entered into the film industry's consciousness. Institutionally, documentary photo leagues and a short-lived government-sponsored documentary unit comprised a distinct American documentary movement. Documentary histories often stress the shift of politics of documentary more aligned with left populism in the United States, but in other dimensions 1930s American cinema developed along Griersonian lines.[21]

Both avowedly left documentarians and more institutional filmmakers adapted Griersonianism to their own ends. American documentaries developed their own nationally inflected voice, yet they combined actuality footage, intellectual montage, and voiceover narration much like British documentaries. Newsreels and the semidocumentary *March of Time* series in turn selectively adapted this documentary language and played a role in popularizing it for audiences.[22] Grierson played the role of active evangelist for the public sphere mission of documentary by publishing in popular and trade periodicals in the United States.[23] Similarly, trade publications like *American Cinematographer* showed a strong interest in documentary, especially during World War II.[24] The rise of the nonfiction propaganda film during World War II expanded the familiarity with documentary as an idea and aesthetic form.[25]

The documentary movement impacted Hollywood films institutionally and stylistically. Hollywood studios produced documentaries, both as shorts and as wartime propaganda films.[26] At the same time, Hollywood fiction films borrowed certain stylistic features of documentary films. Montage sequences, faster film stocks, handheld and aerial cinematography, and location shooting are all techniques that had uses outside of a documentary mode; nonetheless, documentaries influenced Hollywood's use of each in the 1940s. The stylistic aping could at times be written off as mere faddishness. For instance, the postwar cycle of pseudodocumentaries like Henry Hathaway's *The House on 92nd Street* (1945), *13 Rue Madeleine* (1947), and *Call Northside 777* (1948) combined location shooting; a high-contrast, harshly lit shooting style; subject matter "based on a true story"; and voice-of-God narration. The cycle proved to be short-lived, arguably representing a new narrational gimmick that Hollywood would exploit, then discard. Jesse Lerner remarks that "the so-called 'semi-documentary' saved studios money by beefing up low-cost narratives shot on a studio sound stage (most typically noirs or tabloid crime dramas) with stock B-roll filmed on location and an authoritative documentary-style voice-over."[27] These films are in fact more complicated, since some of the Hathaway features had a solid A-picture budget and since all of them have formal innovations. Nonetheless, this cycle was so finite and so fixated on its hyperrealism that scholars have read in it historical discourses specific to the United States in the postwar years.[28]

However, the problem films suggest something more complex and more lasting in the importation of documentary style. Rather than mere gimmick or surface style, the documentary qualities of the postwar films create a socially objectifying stance on their subject matter. Hollywood films invoked documentary's aspirations through narrational means, and this formal configuration could be called a Griersonian text, since its stance speaks to the twin heritage of Griersonian documentary. Social problem films and other postwar dramas clearly are not documentaries or even likely to be misapprehended for having documentary form, yet they adopt both formal and social elements of Griersonianism. A few key formal strategies recur—intellectual montage, documentary camerawork, location shooting, and objectifying narration. These devices work in three ways. They stress social typification over conventional characterization. They give cues for reading individual problems as collective or public ones. Finally, they place characters in some form of sociological specificity.

The Lost Weekend and *Gentleman's Agreement* demonstrate how these strategies encode socially objectivizing knowledge in a given narrative. One succinct indication of the documentary impulse would be the opening sequence, which frequently adopts the extreme long shot of the city or town before entering the diegesis. A remarkable number of postwar films begin this way, even to the point that the documentary-style opening appears in surprising genre material, such as the historical drama (*The Unforgiven* [Cecil B. DeMille, 1947]) or the film noir (*The Long Night* [Anatole Litvak, 1947]). The documentary-like impulse was particularly strong in the social problem dramas, however. *The Lost Weekend*, for instance, begins with an establishing shot of the Manhattan skyline, then pans and cranes to the apartment building of the main action: Don Birnam (Ray Milland) packing for a weekend in the country while a liquor bottle hangs hidden outside his window. The film's conclusion repeats the opening shot, only reversing its track and pan to end on an extreme long shot of the city skyline. In general, the film adopts a fast-film documentary look for many scenes.

Social typification is generally a dividing line between the way documentaries treat persons and the way narrative films construct them. Griersonian documentary understands its social actors as reflecting larger ideas, and its intellectual montage edits scenes according to the logic of the social actors' abstract categories. For instance, in *The City*, a series of shots of children in the street depicts the subjects not in their individuality but as indices of "city children." Hollywood montage sequences were often the first place to adopt a comparably expository role. Many montage sequences from the

1940s are particularly striking in their invocation of social analysis, from the documentary style of *All the King's Men* to the direct quotation of *The City* within *Humoresque* (Jean Negulesco, 1946). In *The Lost Weekend*, one montage sequence depicts Don Birnam wandering block after block of shuttered pawnshops on Third Avenue. Dissolves alternate tracking shots of the pawnshops with Don's weary expression and location markers such as street signs and elevated train tracks. The montage reveals an iterative narrative event (Don walking aimlessly) but also the situated actuality of lower-rent Manhattan, shot on location. Don's travel through the actual geography of the city figures his class descent throughout the lost weekend.

Openings or endings are also privileged moments of typification. André Gaudreault and Tom Gunning have argued that early cinema was marked by monstration as opposed to narration—showing rather than telling.[29] The pan shot of *The Lost Weekend*'s opening signals a return to the elements of monstration within the feature film. The track in, then later out, implies that Don's story is a historically real and socially situated one. The dialogue reinforces this suggestion, as Don says, "And out there in that concrete jungle, I wonder how many others there are like me." One pseudodocumentary, *The Naked City*, would develop this one-of-many conceit even further, with its opening and closing documentary montages. Another, *Boomerang!* (Elia Kazan, 1947), would take the pan shot to its formal extreme of a 360-degree circular pan around Bridgeport, Connecticut (not named as such), to establish an everytown setting.

With far less flourish, *Gentleman's Agreement* shows the sublation of the pseudodocumentary into neutral, "realist" narration. The opening as well is an extreme long shot of the Manhattan skyline; it pans left and tracks down. The next shot is a location shot of Phil Green and his son, Tommy, in the park. These shots highlight contemporary Midtown as the social milieu of the story. The next transition scene in the Midtown office building uses location shooting and further blocks its action in a style departing from the transparent, perfect observer of the classical style, instead placing office workers coming between the camera and the action (a practice reestablished at other points in the film, as in the lunch with Phil and Ann Dettrey). Though understated, the effect is the same as in *The Lost Weekend* and the pseudodocumentaries. Phil Green's story is in some ways atypical (he is a transplant to New York, in a creative profession, and upper middle class), but his experience is shown to be part of the social dynamism of postwar Manhattan. Rather than thematizing class as a political problem, the film implies a Durkheimian typification of division of labor and organic solidarity.

Meanwhile, problem films use location shooting to signal social information. *The Lost Weekend*'s location shooting recurs at key points in the narrative. First, during Don Birnam's visit to Bellevue Hospital, the lighting and setting shift from an expressionist approach to two documentary-style shots—one a pan of Don sneaking out of the hospital lobby, the second an exterior pan of the hospital entrance. The shift to location shooting underscores the implied critique of medical treatment of alcoholism and thus is thematically significant. *Gentleman's Agreement* punctuates a largely studio-shot film with transitions filmed on location. For instance, near the end of the first act of the narrative, one shot shows Phil Green walking across the Brooklyn Bridge en route to the *Smith's Weekly* office; it tracks into Phil, holds static in medium shot to show his pensive expression against the backdrop of the East River and the bustling drive, and then pans right to follow his journey back into the Midtown street life. At first glance, the inclusion of the location shooting would seem perfunctory. However, in the context of the narrative, the literal and figurative pause in the action signifies an internal conflict, since Phil is deciding to take the story assignment. Perhaps unusual for classical Hollywood, the film invokes a psychological revelation by presenting a transition with no dialogue. The revelation of the next scene is that this unspoken internal conflict is Phil's desire to take on a broader conflict. Since the external conflict also cannot be visualized, the cityscape comes to stand in for it.

Finally, the problem films comment on characters through narration that asserts an agency beyond the action. David Bordwell has suggested that certain classical Hollywood films assert an authorial voice by foregrounding self-conscious narration.[30] The moments of self-consciousness, he argues, tend either to emerge from generic or storytelling convention or to suggest an auteur hand. *Gentleman's Agreement* provides a good example: as Tommy and Phil prepare to enter Rockefeller Plaza, they pause in front of a statue of Atlas. A high-angle shot looks down on them: Phil, the shot implies, will assume an Atlas role or, alternately, that the role of "carrying the weight on his shoulders" will be assumed by a greater, more abstract power (society in aggregate? the state?). The ambiguity is at the heart of the film's relationship to the social problem, since the story is both Phil's individual story and also a social conflict that exceeds the narrative. Unlike

FIGURES 7 AND 8 *The Lost Weekend*'s opening shot: documentary monstration as narrative exposition.

1940s examples from other genres (including those directed by Otto Preminger or Jean Negulesco), the implied author narration is not mere stylistic flourish but objectifies its subject matter much like a documentary film.

The narration of *The Lost Weekend* lies somewhere in between classical suppression and assertive authorial voice. The opening and closing both evince a narrational distance to Don Birnam in a film that mostly lacks such distance. The track into the bottle and then into the window to frame Don looking out immediately suggests an omniscient knowledge: the spectator has key narrative information and anticipates Don's look out the window to establish his knowledge of this information. Such "private" character revelations are not alone to the problem film, certainly, but here the narration takes on a diagnostic characteristic: the spectator knows the full extent of Don's alcoholism, more than the other characters (to whom Don constantly dissembles) and more than Don himself (who does not see his pathology for what it is). The reprise of the shot at the end re-creates this knowledge gap with a difference, as Don now has the knowledge the

spectator has held the entire time: "My mind was outside that window," he recognizes in his voiceover. The combination of Griersonian documentary style and assertive narrational voice presents a psychic split (the narrative's "two Don Birnams") and a social split (the gap between spectator and Don Birnam) that the narrative must overcome.

Gentleman's Agreement and *The Lost Weekend* may be unusual to the extent they contain and even foreground all of these devices, but the majority of the social problem films use at least some of them. The resulting Griersonian gaze functions within the parameters of classical continuity and establishing shot patterns, yet intellectual logic in addition to narrative logic drives its editing relations. It reveals the social space of diegetic action and combines presentational and observational modes of cinema. It yokes abstraction (social typification and claims of social causation) to the robust storytelling expected of prestige films. Without venturing fully into the pseudodocumentary terrain of Fox features like *The House on 92nd Street*, problem films like *The Lost Weekend* and *Gentleman's Agreement* nonetheless adapt certain strands of documentary narration to fiction films. In doing so, they suggest the potential of entertainment cinema to speak to a critical mass public.

FIGURE 9 Objectivist narration in *Gentleman's Agreement*.

The Film Audience as Public Sphere

Journalism and documentary contributed to the problem film's construction of the social as an abstract entity. In addition to a textual invocation of a public sphere, though, a discursive tendency to equate entertainment cinema with the public sphere flourished in the 1940s. During the postwar years, especially, the audience and the debating public became aligned concepts in the film industry and the field of film criticism alike. The postwar years in fact brought more points of contact between Hollywood and social science than the Chicago school or functionalist sociology alone would suggest. Rather, the abstract empiricism of media research abstracted the film audience as a deliberative one. Built into the production and reception of the genre was an internalization of the public sphere as its hypothetical point of address, an amorphous entity of public opinion that could act upon problems as public problems. The flipside of Hollywood's depiction of public sphere institutions was a broad-based conception of the mass film audience as a public sphere.

The most concise way to understand the shift is to contrast Progressive-era reformist anxiety of cinema's influence with the postwar understanding of the film audience. From the Progressive era through the 1920s and 1930s, the emergence of the cinema as a mass medium had frequently provoked both concern of its influence on the public and a desire to use its persuasive powers. However, much as Progressive and even early Chicago school sociology conceived of problems to society rather than problems of society, the Progressive discourse about the film audience frequently conceived it as an inert public capable of being manipulated, stirred, or corrupted—not an active, debating public. Lee Grieveson, for instance, connects transitional cinema's censorship battles to a conception of the "vulnerable" audience fostered by the emerging fields of psychology and sociology and by Progressive activist movements.[31] The extant social problem films from this period adopted this reformist vantage and middle-class values in protecting the innocent from moral and financial danger.

The 1940s brought a scientized media-effects research agenda, which sought to quantify the social-psychological attitudes that resulted from watching movies. This research emerged from the empirical work that Paul Lazarsfeld and Columbia University's sociology department were doing on the effect of entertainment media on public opinion and consumer attitudes. Hence dubbed "media-effects research"—or in C. Wright Mills's critique, "abstract empiricism"—this approach was a crucial part of what Habermas considered the "social-psychologization" of public opinion. For Habermas, scientific "public opinion" research abstracted public legitimation away from actually defined groups in a liberal democracy, and the methodological danger of positivism overlapped with the debasement of the public sphere into a mass public.[32] All the same, in Lazarsfeld's diagnosis, the basic transformations of the public sphere in the twentieth century provided the impetus for a research agenda measuring the effect of mass media on public opinion: namely, the rise of cinema and radio, the spread of advertising, and the example of totalitarian propaganda.[33]

Media-effects scholars, in fact, privileged the topic of racial prejudice and the race problem cycle as objects of study for empirical media-effects audience research. The social science literature included a number of such studies, usually measuring the effect of *Crossfire* and *Gentleman's Agreement* on audience attitudes.[34] These studies often made explicit the connection between audience research and public opinion measurement. One 1949 study by J. E. Hulett Jr. even noted how the problem of public opinion pointed out methodological limitations of media-effects research: "There is no way of directly making estimates or predictions from such studies which will answer the question about motion pictures which is the primary concern of the sociologist and the student of public opinion: granted these effects of motion pictures upon individual spectators, how can we discover the net effect of the motion picture upon the public opinion process and upon collective action in the whole community?"[35] Both proponents and skeptics of the view of the feature film's persuasiveness thus shared a conceptual equation of audience and public.

In this light, the slippage between the audience and the public takes on deeper significance in the popular press reviews of the problem film. The journalistic critics, of course, were a distinct group from the media-effects social scientists, but they shared with the social scientists the conception of the social problem film audience as an object of persuasion. Even the most typical of popular press reviews referenced the public sphere as the genre's addressee: "*Pinky* is the most ambitious and costly of this season's crop of Negro problem films—including *Home of the Brave* and *Lost Boundaries*. *Pinky* was finished after its B-budgeted rivals had proved at the box-office that the public is interested in movies that give serious treatment to a serious theme, e.g. the sorry plight of the U.S. Negro."[36] No other genre prompted critics to muse about the ability of an audience to become an active public sphere and to eschew "escapism" in favor of "seriousness." *Newsweek*'s judgment that "it took a lot of courage for Paramount to bring Charles Jackson's terrifying case study of an alcoholic to an escapist-minded audience" was typical, as were praises for "adult material" that edified the audience.[37] Although reviewers occasionally faulted the films for their lack of dramatic values, most praised the films for their quality and their "courage," which meant less the courage to tackle issues than the courage to risk unprofitability for the sake of social relevance. "The screen and the radio," wrote one reviewer, "as great mass media intimidated by the size of their audiences . . . have lacked the courage familiar in fiction and on the stage." The problem films, particularly *Gentleman's Agreement* and *Crossfire*, convinced him or her the movies had "grown up."[38] The following *Life* magazine review of *The Snake Pit*, furthermore, makes explicit an analogy between cinema and exposé journalism: "*The Snake Pit* is partly an introductory lecture on psychiatry, partly an exposé of overcrowding and neglect in state hospitals for mental diseases, partly a good old-fashioned freak show; but partly and most importantly, it is Hollywood's first honest and unflinching look into the minds of the insane, with all their terror and bewilderment and frustration."[39]

It was not only critics but also the industry itself that held these views. Compare the *Life* review to the edifying language from the director himself:

> *The Snake Pit* was not conceived with the intention of pandering to morbid curiosity in dramatizing mental illness and the various scientific processes used to effect rehabilitation, Mr. Litvak asserted. His purpose in making the picture, aside from his fascination with the subject's inherent drama, was to "awaken public interest in this vital matter, to reassure people that mental disorder is an illness which can be cured and to direct attention to the facilities now available in our institutions."[40]

Here, too, Litvak presents fictional filmmaking in journalistic terms and invokes a crucial public interest. Screenwriter Philip Dunne made similar claims for *Pinky*, writing of the divergent view on race in America, "We are aware of our problem: lacking agreement even among ourselves how could we hope to reach 140,000,000 Americans, representing nearly 140,000,000 differing points of view?"[41] Dunne equates the film-watching experience to an active public sphere balancing 140 million opinions, and in the process he equates the film audience with the citizenry proper.

The rhetoric of this sort may have been inflated—James Agee would quip that "Hollywood's heroism is calculated to land buttered side up"—but producers and studios were sincere.[42] Much like the wider interpretive community, the makers of the 1940s and 1950s cycle increasingly considered the social problem amenable to change through their capacity as "public opinion" to bring about governmental action or even a change in public debate itself. In remarks on *Pinky* discussed earlier, Fox producer Michael Abel's corporate memo reveals the sincerity in which the studio saw its role as something comparable to the journalist's role in the public sphere: "Striking with the skill and daring of the surgeon's knife it lays open the foulest cancer in the American way of life, and by exposing, paves the way, let us hope for its eventual eradication. . . . It is high time the facts were faced openly and honestly."[43] The rhetoric is remarkably similar to the character Wiseman's boardroom speech in *Gentleman's Agreement.*

Darryl Zanuck and 20th Century–Fox considered entrenched opinion brokers to be privileged spectators for their message pictures. This vision guided their marketing strategy, and *Gentleman's Agreement* provides a useful example of the reorientation of prestige film exploitation to the public sphere. Fox advertising executive Charles Schlaifer wrote a report detailing the film's exploitation campaign, seeking to gain insight for the promotion of other mid-A budget prestige films, especially those in the problem film cycle. The new idea that Schlaifer and Zanuck devised was a series of advance screenings for opinion-makers, industry competitors, and political leaders—these would take the place of a premiere.[44] "The primary purpose of these screenings is to influence New York newspaper reviewers," Schlaifer wrote, but he added, "The secondary purpose of these screenings is to influence nationally syndicated opinion-makers who write either columns, features, or editorials."[45] Exploitation as an industrial practice frequently sought to appeal to community voices, but here the selection of opinion and community leaders dovetailed with sociologists' contemporary understanding of the opinion leader as a central figure in the mobilization of mass opinion.[46] Furthermore, Darryl Zanuck and Charles Schlaifer understood that the exploitation potential of their problem films lay in an invigorated and widespread tendency among observers to treat topical cinema as a matter of public debate. Their success in marketing *Gentleman's Agreement* bore their ideas out.

Official and Unofficial Public Spheres

The public sphere dimensions of the genre contributed to what contemporaries meant by a "social problem film" as much as the assumptions of popular sociology. As chapter 2 outlined, sociology's changes as a discipline in the first half of the twentieth century from Progressive and Chicago school sociology to Durkheimian functionalism helped shape the particular version of popular sociology that Hollywood adopted by the 1940s. It posed an abstracted two-level relationship between the individual and collectivity and emphasized anomie or social dysfunction over crude environmental determinism. Hollywood features never approached their subject matter with a sociological rigor, but the intellectual discourse did shape the narratives and the critical discussion around them. However, the popularization of sociology by and large came from academic sociology's indirect influence rather than a direct engagement with the intellectual field. Social problem sociology, a burgeoning field, was itself an applied field rather than pure sociology, and secondary sources filtered Hollywood's interest in social problem sociology: journalism, public debate, and the occasional best-selling study. (Even here journalistic coverage and reviews of these studies were probably more influential than the books themselves.) The filmmaking professions were culturally distant from the academy proper, but the industry did reflect developments in the literary, journalistic, and political fields.

The postwar years were a period in which filmmakers and critics reconceptualized the public dimension of entertainment cinema, and the problem film was a privileged genre in a new, mature Hollywood that many observers considered to be aesthetically and thematically serious. The postwar social problem film built an appeal to a debating public into the template of entertainment, narrative cinema. While it is tempting to see the equation of audience and public as a natural expectation of a popular culture medium, in fact Hollywood's attempt to engage its audience as a virtual public was a historically specific development. Over time, the industry shifted from conceiving of this audience as an inert body to control to conceiving the audience in social scientific terms of public opinion formation. As the industry and observers in America's cultural elites came to worry about unconscious media effects, they also came to militate for Hollywood's active role shepherding a critical mass audience.

Habermas's structural transformation thesis therefore suggests one reason why Hollywood began sending "messages" in the way it did, when it did. It helps reframe the film historians' typical understanding of the problem film as a series of cultural representations and images: of Jewish Americans, of African Americans, of mental illness, of juvenile delinquency, of veterans, and so forth. Whatever the utility of methodologies geared toward understanding the specific messages of Hollywood's problem films, they leave untouched the very historical development of message cinema to begin with. A fuller historical account must look at the public Hollywood imagined as the recipient of its messages, since this public was as important to the politics of the genre as the messages themselves. If functionalist sociology explains the move away from crude social determinism, the institutions of the public sphere help explain, on a macro level, why Hollywood would invoke sociology to begin with. The move from Progressive sociology and the Chicago school to functionalist sociology matched the consolidation of the public sphere in the United States, particularly by the 1940s.

The public sphere institutions overlap, but each has its own historical trajectory and its own impact on the problem film. The official public sphere centered on the journalistic field and included at its margins journalism's primary cinematic correlative, documentary film. Documentary in particular influenced the social problem film in its public debate aims as well as its narrational forms. Journalism and documentary film were both cultural products that participated in public debate, and any attempt to understand Hollywood's disposition to speak to "social issues" must grapple with the various analogies that the industry imagined for itself: between cinema and journalism and between Hollywood and documentary film. In the 1940s, Hollywood increasingly measured itself against these public sphere realms.

However, the problem film had such a dynamic relationship to the public sphere in part because cinema not only borrowed from and referenced the official public sphere but also brought with it a dimension of an unofficial public sphere. At a closer view, Hollywood combined elements of both the official public sphere and the vernacular modernism that Miriam Hansen has argued as constitutive of classical Hollywood. By the late 1940s, Hollywood increasingly depicted a sense of the social that was diffuse, abstract, and functionalist in its purview. Paradoxically, however, this depiction was not always through movies steeped in a social science discourse but also through narratives that figured, more evocatively, the contours of an abstracted sociality.

4

A Genre Out of Cycles

Under the influence of functionalist sociology, Hollywood's social problem films by the 1940s started to invoke a more abstract sense of social causation. However, this historical narrative presents some challenges. By most historical accounts, social problem films predated the 1940s. Peter Roffman and Jim Purdy's genre study, for instance, focuses on the 1930s as the heyday of the problem film, comprising multiple cycles and an extended bibliography of films.[1] Kay Sloan traces the genre back even farther, to the first two decades of the twentieth century.[2] These earlier examples were precursors to the postwar problem films and are by now an important part of the genre's history. However, the postwar problem films were distinctive from earlier problem films, both in their nature and their level of prominence. Only in the postwar years did the social problem film become a full-fledged genre. As Sarah Kozloff succinctly puts the issue, "The name 'social problem' originally referred to a cycle of films made right after World War II that focus on anti-Semitism, racism, war trauma, and other social ills. Subsequently, film scholars applied the label to earlier and later films so that the contours of a genre emerged over time."[3] This historical disjunction is just one barrier to defining the problem film as a genre.

Genre study can at times be a debate about labels, and in the case of the problem film, the labels have an important story to tell. Before World War II, the term "sociological film" was used occasionally and sparingly, whereas in the postwar years, the term "social problem film" became widespread as a standard genre label. As the previous chapter demonstrates, sociology changed in this period, becoming a professionalized discipline, so the referent for the "social" changed in meaning. Much as Chicago school sociology (dominant in the 1920s and 1930s) and functionalism (dominant in the 1940s and 1950s) offered competing intellectual frameworks based on divergent conceptions of the social, the "sociological" label that spans the 1930s and 1940s cycles meant different things in each context. The industrial and critical recognition of a genre grew at the same time that the films themselves adopted more forthrightly the social problem discourse associated with postwar functionalism. For this reason, two vectors of genre formation, common to much genre theory, define the problem film. Rick Altman distinguishes between "a self-conscious critical vocabulary" and a "user vocabulary" of film genre.[4] Similarly, Steve Neale notes, "A distinction needs to be made, then, between those studies of genres conceived as institutionalized classes of texts and systems of expectation and those studies that use critically or theoretically constructed terms as the basis for discussing classes of films."[5] One can therefore distinguish between a critical-textual genre and a historical genre. Whereas a textual genre delineates the narrative and formal expectations emerging from repetitions across films, a historical genre posits generic expectations and groupings dependent on context. On both counts the social problem film changed in the postwar years.

Beyond the issue of definition, examining the social problem film as both a historical and textual genre gives an insight into the evolution in Hollywood's and critics' understanding of the term. The conditions were favorable for the change of the prestige film and the adoption of a new type of middlebrow film. The impact of sociology in the public sphere gave an impetus toward adopting popular sociology as one avenue for the prestige film. However, the translation of these macrolevel roots of the problem film to Hollywood's implementation and the critics' reception was not an automatic process. An account for how film cycles coalesced into a genre gives an indication of the mutual influence of Hollywood and contemporary film critics. Taken as a whole, the emergence of a social problem film out of distinct cycles speaks to the broader transformation of the prestige film.

A Theory of Film Cycles

The irregularity of the social problem genre stems foremost from the fact that it comprises several, often distinct, cycles. Unlike genres, which generally develop conventions and audience expectations with historical longevity, cycles are short-term imitations, usually based on the success of an initial film.[6] Amanda Ann Klein has challenged the lack of attention that genre theory pays to cycles, noting that "cycles are generally understood as messy structures in flux, poised either to become stable genres or to disappear quickly. . . . Film cycles are fascinating precisely because they resist neat categorizations and have the potential to disrupt or complicate the discrete categories frequently generated by genre studies."[7] For Klein, examining cycles gives a fuller view of a genre by showing the cultural and aesthetic contradictions glossed over by more broad-scale approaches. Despite her focus on cycles as a low-status cultural product, her methodological intervention holds true for Hollywood's prestige product as well, since dramas, melodramas, and class-A pictures were as cycle oriented as more identifiable genre films. Her call for critical attention to cycles is a reminder that cycles comprise genres but have their own life and trajectory. In the case of the problem film, the postwar prestige cycle overwhelmingly drove the process of genre formation, but other cycles demonstrated distinct conventions and differing levels of genre coherence that both supported the overall process of genre formation and operated as countercurrents to this process.

During the first cycle of the Progressive era (roughly from 1900 through the silent period), commercially exhibited films adopted an explicitly didactic approach and encompassed a broad spectrum of themes ranging from outright Progressive activism to Victorian moralism.[8] There is little historical indication that this cycle had a significant direct impact on future cycles. It receded into the background as Hollywood in its classical form emerged as a dominant entertainment mass medium. For this reason, the transitional cinema problem cycle functions as a precursor rather than a direct historical influence for studio-era problem film cycles. Nonetheless, as Lee Grieveson has demonstrated, the Progressive cycle saw the first convergence of cinema and social science discourse. As he argues, the discourses seeking to contain social ills fed attempts at censorship in the transitional years.[9]

During the studio era, there were at least five industrial cycles of what scholars now call social problem films. Each had its own industrial cause, underlying ideology, generic label, and aesthetic features. Warner Bros.' *headliner cycle* (1932–1939) comprises much of what gets labeled the social problem genre of the 1930s, and its run as a cycle is perhaps the most cohesive, since it is identified with one studio, one narrative formula, and a finite historical duration. Warners conceived these low-budget films as "ripped from the headlines" and hence called them "headliners." *I Am a Fugitive from a Chain Gang* is sometimes credited as the first in the cycle, although the release of RKO's *Hell's Highway* (Rowland Brown, 1932) and Warners' own *Hell's House* preceded it. Left-oriented film historians have championed the Warners' cycle for presenting Great Depression problems and Rooseveltian political solutions more directly than the norm in 1930s Hollywood, but some take exception to recuperation of political protest within tidy individual narratives. Roffman and Purdy, for instance, argue that "through repetition of the same [Hollywood] Formula, the genre as a whole served as a formulized ritual to assuage extreme political dissatisfaction . . . and to reinforce the establishmentarian values encapsulated in the Formula."[10] Tino Balio notes that *Variety* even gave a name to the film's personalization of politics: "Burbanking."[11] Protagonists in the cycle are frequently dupes getting caught up in nefarious radicalism/reaction (Paul Muni in *Black Fury* or Humphrey Bogart in *Black Legion* [Archie Mayo, 1937]) or else unfairly punished for criminal activity because of mistaken identity or coincidence (*Wild Boys of the Road* or *Hell's House*). Aesthetically, films like *Wild Boys* could gesture toward a realist sensibility, with location shooting and unconventional blocking, but generally the films were defined by an action-oriented narrative and stripped-down aesthetic. The cycle would die out by 1938's *Blockade* (William Dieterle), but the romanticized misunderstood criminal character would recur in Warners' output, even getting a distinctly postwar treatment of familiar themes in 1947's *Deep Valley*.

Alongside Warner Bros.' low-budget films, other studios and producers released a *populist A-film cycle* (1932–1947) that expressed Popular Front and New Deal politics from a distinctly less proletarian vantage. These productions were marked by higher production values that matched their higher budgets, and the realist aesthetic they adopted could foreground intricate sets and a fluid camera style that were out of reach for the headliners. Three prestige directors—Frank Capra (most of his 1930s work, including *It Happened One Night* [1932] and *Mr. Deeds Goes to Town* [1936]), King Vidor (*Our Daily Bread* [1934]), and William Wyler (*Dead End*)—account for the mainstays of this cycle, and their example would influence the template taken up in the postwar prestige cycle. The populist drama and literary adaptation *The Grapes of Wrath* would be the most famous and canonical drama of the group. The politics in these films differed from the individualizing narratives and praise for benevolent authority of the "headliners." In contrast to Warner Bros.' "Burbanking" approach, the A-film cycle figured economic problems and social conflict as more properly historical matters. Capra's work, for instance, invoked the abstract relations of modern capitalism and made the anonymous crowd his second protagonist (as in the John Doe convention scene in *Meet John Doe* or the bank run in *American Madness* [1932]). In the process, his and other films of the cycle thematically commented on the power and problems of a mass public sphere. Capra's work led to a significant offshoot in the early 1940s, the social comedy, which in films like George Stevens's *Talk of the Town* (1942) or *The More the Merrier* (1943) amplified the Capra-esque side of the screwball comedy. This tendency would culminate in some of the social comedies of the late 1940s, like *The Farmer's Daughter*, a satire on political machinery, and *Magic Town*, a comedy about opinion polling.

Two films released at the end of World War II set in motion a *postwar prestige cycle* (1945–1950) of problem films. First, in 1945 Paramount produced *The Lost Weekend*, a cautionary tale about a writer trying to recover from alcoholism. Second, Samuel Goldwyn released William Wyler's *The Best Years of Our Lives*, a three-hour prestige film about the difficulties of three veterans returning to small-town life after the war. The former inspired a Susan Hayward–helmed imitation from Universal, *Smash-Up: The Story of a Woman*, as well as the broader cycle of films dealing with alcoholism, drug abuse, and mental institutionalization. *Best Years*, meanwhile, set a new tenor for the postwar prestige film: serious and "realistic" in its cinematic mode and historical reference. A cycle of short-term imitation spread across the major studios' A-film product and proliferating prestige-oriented independents. These films even set the tone for studio films not strictly associated with the social problem genre.

No one mimicked them as keenly as Darryl Zanuck, whose previous social problem film productions at Warner Bros. (most famously *I Am a*

Fugitive from a Chain Gang) and in the early 1940s at Fox (*The Grapes of Wrath* and *The Ox-Bow Incident* [William Wellman, 1943]) and desire to elevate the studio's cultural prestige positioned him ideally to take advantage of a new social problem prestige cycle. A year after *Best Years of Our Lives*, 20th Century–Fox made *Gentleman's Agreement*, an attack on "gentleman's" anti-Semitism. It was not the first film on the subject, since RKO's *Crossfire* preceded into release by a few months, but it was the first decently budgeted A production of the antiracist cycle, and it became Fox's top-grossing film of 1948. Similarly, the next two films in the studio's problem film cycle were among Fox's biggest hits: *The Snake Pit* starred Olivia de Havilland as a misunderstood woman committed to a mental health asylum, and *Pinky* concerned the difficulties of a black woman who passes as white and is thrust back into a Jim Crow South when she returns home. Other studios produced additions to the cycle, such as MGM's *Intruder in the Dust*, which turned William Faulkner's novel into a race problem film.

Films gris and ambitious B films (1947–1955) emerged from the postwar prestige cycle and ran parallel to it. Alongside 20th Century–Fox's prestige productions, independent producers and B units of the major studios took up the problem film as a means of upgrading low-budget productions. One formula that worked, at least in getting the productions approved and financed, was *film gris*'s combination of relevance with the stylistic and thematic qualities of film noir. RKO's *Crossfire*, for instance, combined a treatise against anti-Semitism with multiple flashbacks and stark cinematography. In between hearings of the House Un-American Activities Committee (HUAC), Edward Dmytryk followed up with Eagle-Lion–produced *Give Us This Day* (1949), a trenchantly socialist adaptation of the 1939 proletarian novel *Christ in Concrete* by Pietro di Donato. The narrative of a bricklayer's attempt to make a living and support a family during the Depression aims toward neorealism but is framed with a noir flashback structure. Joseph Losey's *The Lawless* did not use a mystery narrative like *Crossfire*, but it told the story of the hostility toward Mexican American workers with expressionistic camerawork common to noir. Finally, *Body and Soul* and *Force of Evil* (Abraham Polonsky, 1948), the anticapitalist allegories written by Abraham Polonsky, took proletarian or underworld characters as emblems caught up in larger forces of greed and generated by the capitalist system. These films' economical filmmaking signified "hard-hitting" realism, suitable for contemporary subject matter and psychological conflict. For producers who worried about the widespread appeal of the problem film (as many still were in the 1940s), the action orientation, convoluted narrative structure, and exaggerated style of noir provided showmanship to interest audiences in them.

Throughout the 1950s and 1960s, the social problem film entered a *self-conscious cycle* (1950–1967). The key examples were self-conscious because they drew upon not merely narrative ideas and general sensibility but upon narrative tropes and established genre conventions. 20th Century–Fox began a new race problem cycle—one centered around psychological conflict rather than passing—with *No Way Out*, a narrative about a rabidly racist criminal (Richard Widmark) who battles his African American doctor (Sidney Poitier). The films of Sidney Poitier, in fact, were mainstays of the social problem genre in the 1950s and 1960s: *Blackboard Jungle*, *The Defiant Ones*, *Pressure Point* (Hubert Cornfield, 1962), and *Guess Who's Coming to Dinner*. Jackie Byars identifies how social problem melodrama of the 1950s matched prestige melodrama production values to problem film topics, like drug and alcohol abuse in *The Man with the Golden Arm* (Otto Preminger, 1955) and *Come Back, Little Sheba* (Daniel Mann, 1952).[12] One parallel B-film cycle explored similar problem film territory as the A films. Sam Fuller's work (*The Crimson Kimono* [1962]) and the Dore Schary–produced MGM Bs (including *Go for Broke!* and *Bad Day at Black Rock*) tackled prejudice against Asian Americans, while a number of cheaper juvenile delinquency films emerged after the success of *Rebel without a Cause.* The B films of the period undoubtedly took social problem content and pushed it over into the realm of exploitation (as Fuller's *Shock Corridor* [1960] did with the mental illness narratives of *The Snake Pit* and *Possessed* [Curtis Bernhardt, 1947]), but this, too, was a sign that the cycle had become entrenched enough to play with a formula. It was also a sign of the affective quality of the prestige films themselves. Increasingly, in their focus on psychological conflict, the films used expressionistic technique as a marker of their realism. The ideal type would likely be Stanley Kramer's *The Defiant Ones*, which blended realist and expressionist aesthetics to signal social relevance and to carry an extended literary conceit. Despite the distinctiveness of Kramer's producer-auteur image, the film also reflected the style and thematic seriousness of prestige independent production in the 1950s: Hollywood films defined against the "Hollywood film."

Guess Who's Coming to Dinner was the last prestige film of the postwar self-conscious cycle. By the cycle's end, the genre had reached a rococo phase, built around exaggeration of the affective elements of the postwar problem films. Exploitation films adopted the generic formula of the problem picture as narrative kitsch, as in the B-film variation of *High School Confidential!* (Jack Arnold, 1958) or the A-film example of *Valley of the Dolls* (Mark Robson, 1967). Even a more straightforward independent social problem film like *I Want to Live!*, produced by veteran producer Walter Wanger, alternated an exploitation narrative of a tough-talking prostitute caught up in an underworld lifestyle (shot in a kinetic, low-key style) with a meticulously paced, "realistic" portrayal of Barbara Graham's final time on death row. Susan Hayward's performance itself alternates between camp and restraint.[13] Producers had difficulty continuing to copy even successes like *Guess Who's Coming to Dinner* in a climate of uncertainty about audience preferences and industry viability, not to mention the radically shifting racial politics of the late 1960s and early 1970s. Hollywood studios tended toward either spectacle genre films or else the smaller-scale features of the Hollywood Renaissance, a newer generation of filmmakers influenced by the international art cinema and an auteurist conception of Hollywood's past. Those wanting to make, or watch, serious midbudget films now had an alternative to the social problem film.

The Social Problem Film as a Historical Genre

The "social problem film" was a term used by producers and viewers in the 1940s and 1950s and in a more embryonic form in the 1930s. To them, related cycles of films were coherent and recognizable. In fact, the postwar coherence of the genre has bequeathed the label to subsequent historians and critics of the genre and has encouraged historians to read generic coherence back into the prewar and even silent-era "problem films." An account of the social problem film as a historical genre, therefore, starts with a reconstitution of the contemporary and subjective understanding of what a problem film was. This reconstitution looks first to the production cycles as understood by the industry rather than simply applying the broad label of a "social problem" genre. Secondarily, it assesses the use of "social problem film" as label and concept. Three key parties in Hollywood—the producers of problem films, the Motion Picture Association of America, and the trade press—shifted in their recognition of social problem films going into the late 1940s. In the postwar years, the functionalist discourse of the social was the basis for a process of genrification, as disparate cycles cohered into a full-fledged genre. How the film industry categorized films with socially relevant content thus serves as a vital counterpart to the textual contours of a genre that seems otherwise irregular.

The Producers

At first glance, the trajectory of socially relevant cycles would seem to fit into an evolutionary model of genre, popularized by Thomas Schatz's work on genre, with an early cycle, recombination, a classic phase, and finally maturity and self-reflexivity. Theoretically, though, the evolutionary model has problems, least of which is reifying what is essentially an analytical concept.[14] Beyond the larger problems of genre theory, the social problem film does not fit an evolutionary model for specific reasons. Evidence suggests that key parties in the film industry converged in their understanding of problem films as problem films only in the postwar years. Whereas a textual genre may extend back to the Progressive era, the historical genre of social problem film shifted over time, consolidating as it moved from a prototypical 1930s cycle toward a full-fledged 1940s genre.

Hollywood producers were an important constituency in the formation and propagation of the social problem film as historical genre. The case study of Darryl F. Zanuck in particular reveals how larger generic changes impacted even the thinking of the producer responsible for a number of problem films that were to be influential within the film industry.[15] Remarkably, Zanuck was associated with two of the major cycles of the genre, the headliner films in the 1930s and postwar prestige films in the 1940s. In neither did he produce the initial film of the genre, but he holds some key responsibility for each cycle.[16] For some, this responsibility suggests that the entire cycles sprung from the agency of producers. Russell Campbell argues that *The Grapes of Wrath*, *Gentleman's Agreement*, and *Pinky* all emerged from the same personal agency, "a man of liberal instinct, more than intellect."[17]

Despite Zanuck's influence over the direction of the problem film cycles, the 1940s cycle differed from that of the 1930s. Warner Bros. did not consider its films social problem films, but 20th Century–Fox did.

Zanuck in the early 1930s also differed in his conception of the genre from Zanuck in the late 1940s. Oddly enough, Zanuck's own words suggest a shift from the "headliner" to the "message picture." His own grouping of films would overlap with a problem film genre only in the 1940s. As the "headliner" label would suggest, topicality (reflecting current events) more than relevance (commenting thematically on current events) drove the 1930s Warners' cycle and provided the formula for further production. Zanuck's overview of the company's products for the *Hollywood Reporter* in 1932 shows how central the "headliner" idea was across a wide range of Warners' output:

> It is my sincere belief that the moving picture public will continue to respond to the "headline" type of screen story that it has been the policy of Warner Brothers–First National Pictures to produce during the past two years.
>
> A headline type of story must not be confused with the gangster or underworld cycle of productions that have flooded theatres in the past. Somewhere in its makeup it must have the punch and smash that would enable it to be a headline on the front page of any successful metropolitan daily.
>
> Sometimes the story is a biography or an autobiography, like *I Am a Fugitive from a Chain Gang.* Sometimes the story is that of a fictitious character, based on headline incidents from the life of a real character, such as *The Match King.* In the latter case, the story is deliberately veiled, such as changing the character's name and altering some of the unimportant details, yet retaining enough of the original story matter so that the average picture-goer easily grasps the identity of the notorious personality being exploited.
>
> Sometimes the story is of an exposé nature, like *Grand Slam*, which endeavors to tear the lid off the contract bridge racket. In this case we use a formula that calls for a mixture of drama and comedy, bordering slightly on satire. . . .
>
> . . .
>
> The first of these productions was *Doorway to Hell.* Then came *Little Caesar, Public Enemy, Smart Money, Five Star Final*, etc. We have touched on a great variety of subjects . . . a maternity ward in *Life Begins*, labor problems of the new South in *Cabin in the Cotton*, etc.
>
> . . .
>
> We have just completed a musical exposé, *Forty-second Street* . . . *Frisco Jenny*, featuring Ruth Chatterton, is based on the life of a very notorious San Francisco Barbary Coast hostess. . . .

> It is my belief that the producer of pictures today, in search for entertainment, finds himself in a position very similar to that of the editor of a metropolitan newspaper. By this I don't mean that romance and romantic stories are not "headline material." Love stories and sex stories make very good headlines, and sometimes very good pictures. *Baby Face* with Barbara Stanwyck, and *Ex-Lady*, with Bette Davis, are two of these particular types we are now producing.[18]

Rick Altman sets forth the difference between Zanuck's conception of the "headliner" films and later problem films: "While during Prohibition it is hard to imagine a gangster film that would not in some way be a contemporary and thus headline-type film (whence the origin of both the gangster genre and the would-be headline genre in the same list of films: *Doorway to Hell* [Archie Mayo, 1930], *Little Caesar* [Mervyn LeRoy, 1931], *Public Enemy* [William A. Wellman, 1931], *Smart Money* [Alfred E. Green, 1931]), the other films mentioned by Zanuck were eventually assimilated by Hollywood at large to the biopic, the musical, and the social problem film."[19] For Altman, the "headliner" is a prime example of the production-based genre that fails to catch. The implications are broader, too, since Zanuck could not "create" a social problem genre on his own. That creation required generic imitation across the industry and the application of modes of generic perception to Warners' or 20th Century–Fox's releases.

Moreover, the headliner was not limited to the Zanuck's idiosyncratic view. One *Variety* article explained that Jack Warner was irate at other studios that copied the headline cycle. "'Blessed Event' and 'I am a Fugitive from the Chain Gang' were Warner's particular peeves," the article said. "Didn't mention any by name, but meant Universal and Radio, which made 'Okay America' and 'Is My Face Red?' in the columnist trend. 'Destination Unknown' is about to start at U., and Radio has released 'Hell's Highway,' chain gang stories."[20] The article suggests that topicality was the rubric under which both Warner and *Variety* put Warner Bros.' output. Moreover, other studios participated in cycle building immediately after Warners' initial films. In Altman's scenario, Warners put forth a "headliner" cycle that later got copied for its social relevance: "It's not that other studios failed to imitate Warners' successes; other studios just read those successes differently from Zanuck and thus imitated other parts of them."[21] True as this was over the long run, the *Variety* piece suggests the converse—namely, that Warners' headline material got copied for even more specific narrative content, like the narrative formulas comprising the prison film.

In contrast, the memos and story conferences of Zanuck at 20th Century–Fox in the 1940s and 1950s show a growing self-consciousness of producing message films. Although he did not use the term directly, Zanuck's statements continually lumped the prestige "message" films together. Note the following:

> This story, of course, suggests immediate comparison with *Gentleman's Agreement.*[22]
>
> I visualize this picture [*No Way Out*] in the same category as *Boomerang, Street with No Name*, and *Call Northside 777*, and while it is in the same milieu as *Gentleman's Agreement* and *The Snake Pit*, it does not, of course, demand such an expensive overall production.[23]
>
> Throughout the years I have learned, in making pictures like *Grapes, Pinky*, and *Gentleman's Agreement* that it is foolish to get into a so-called controversial story and then try to white-wash it or avoid the controversy. I think that in *Island* we would be foolish to go into a black-versus-white story and then avoid the situations which are controversial.[24]

His comments on *No Way Out* indicate that at least some of the films were seen in the trajectory of the pseudodocumentary films like those of producer Louis de Rochemont,[25] yet Zanuck places each film into a trajectory of making more and more "controversial" or "frank" portraits of their subject matter.

The producer links this subject matter to the features' increased relevance to the public sphere. For *No Way Out*, he writes, "In other words, I visualize an exciting, violent story dealing with a very profound American problem."[26] Accordingly, although the exact term "social problem film" may not have appeared, Zanuck and his writers mention directly the "Negro" or "race problem" with the racial-message cycle:

> I think it has a good chance because it avoids the extremes of opinion in dealing with its problem.[27]

> I see *No Way Out* as a very original and exciting melodrama, dealing in tense, suspenseful terms with a phase of the Negro problem and race prejudice.[28]

> I believe it has the makings of an unusual and stirring picture which should have marked popular appeal, unless the appetite of the public will have been sated before it can reach the screen by several films already in release or production dealing with the Negro problem.[29]

When Zanuck does bring up the specter of the message film, it is often in the negative, a denial that the film in question is merely a didactic feature:

> But *Pinky* is not merely a social message. If it were, it would be only a futile, expensive gesture accomplishing nothing.[30]

> *This [*Pinky*] is not a story about how to solve the Negro problem in the South or anywhere else. This is not a story particularly about race problems, segregation or discrimination. This is the story about one particular Negro girl who could easily pass as a white and who did pass for a while. This is the story of how and why she, as an individual, finally decided to be herself—a Negress.*[31]

In their denial, these quotations suggest the opposite—namely, that social messages are initially what these films are. The last comments particularly indicate that the fear was not so much that these films depict social problems, but that such a depiction gets in the way of the humanistic drama required to sell movies. At stake is not simply profitability, already impaired by limited access to domestic theaters of the South, but also the image and ideology of Hollywood as a politically neutral institution.

Zanuck evolved in his approach to producing racial problem stories. Whereas in *Pinky* the humanistic emphasis of Pinky's personal story takes precedence over her social conditions, in *No Way Out* the two are more at tension with one another.

> Prejudice should be, in my opinion, the background and the foundation upon which we tell the main story. Always in the foreground should remain the personal story. In other words, I visualize an exciting, violent story dealing with a very profound American problem. However, never at any time do I want the problem to become bigger than the story. The personal story must at all

> times be superimposed in the foreground over the problem story. This does not mean that they cannot be completely intertwined, which is the result we must reach for.[32]

By the time of *Island in the Sun* (Robert Rossen, 1957), Zanuck manages to combine this humanistic stance with a call to more social analysis of race and an incitement to activist filmmaking (however moderate that activism).

> What has been done with the personal relationships is, in most cases, wonderful. But I think we have lost size and scope. We tell a nice love story between two young people—Euan and Jocelyn—but that's all it is, just a nice love story. It has no size. As an illustration of what I mean by this: In *The Grapes of Wrath* we told the story of *one* Okie family, but you had the feeling that this was a picture about *all* Okie families. In *Pinkie* [*sic*], we told the story of one girl and one man, but you felt that there was really more to it than just this love story.[33]

Whereas earlier Zanuck argued consistently for the personal story over the political or problem story, or, with *No Way Out*, argued for their synthesis, here he recognizes that presenting just a personal story evaded the larger social and political implications and that representing black characters *as three-dimensional characters* at that point in film history was a politically meaningful move. Furthermore, he rewrites the history of his own productions, to act as if what he agitated for all along was the tempering of humanist narratives with social implications. His words can be read as symptomatic of historical and social trends, and the shift from considering the problem to be Jim Crow economic and social oppression facing southern blacks (in *Pinky*) to "personal prejudice" (in *No Way Out*) echoes broader changes in civil rights rhetoric.

Overall, the example of 20th Century–Fox, which did, after all, produce about half of the 1940s prestige problem pictures, suggests that problem films were seen by at least one prominent maker as a coherent exploitation of a new market for "gritty," "realistic," or "controversial" subject matter, particularly racism, but elastic enough to encompass mental illness treatment or economic hardship. The terms "social problem," "message," and "social consciousness" film rarely if ever come up as category labels for this type of film, yet these features—*Pinky*, *The Snake Pit*, *No Way Out*, and *Island in the Sun*—were conceived and grouped as a type of film along lines of a social problem film genre and not according to characteristics of a more meaningful textual genre, such as the melodrama, historical drama, or thriller. Finally, Zanuck's denials of formulaic generic status of individual films suggest that he recognized the likelihood these films would be seen as message or social problem films. His denial that *Pinky* is about a social problem suggests that other films of similar subject matter are. The 20th Century–Fox producer had a disproportionate influence on the industrial success and narrative form of the social problem film, but his attitudes reflected a broader shift in the conception of the genre.

The Trade Press

The trade press, more in reviews than in trade news coverage, was far more ready to use a number of terms designating the social problem film as a recognizable category than Zanuck was. In *Variety*'s reviews of the pre–World War II cycles, the term "social problem" appears only once (for *The Grapes of Wrath*), but a whole host of other related and similar terms appear: "great contemporary social conflict" (*Cabin in the Cotton* [Michael Curtiz, 1932]), "social document" (*Wild Boys of the Road*), "treating an economic problem" (*Our Daily Bread*), "sociological cinematic exposition" (*Black Fury*), "social denunciation" (*Legion of Terror* [Charles C. Coleman, 1936]), "sociological meller" (*They Won't Forget* [Mervyn LeRoy, 1937]), and "social responsibility" (*Dead End*).[34] This tendency alone attests that some conception of the problem film did exist in the 1930s, especially among the trade press critics.

A number of factors, though, complicate the trade press's use of the term "problem film." First of all, the magazines' news coverage sometimes directly contradicted the reviews. *Cabin in the Cotton*, for instance, is mentioned in the Picture Grosses as a "straight filmer"[35]—"straight" referring to traditional showmanship, as in *Variety*'s film review of *Black Fury*: "Enough basic melodramatics for straight theatre values are there." Second, even the reviews that mentioned sociological significance sometimes foregrounded the "headliner" aspect:

> Warners has taken yesterday's headlines and fashioned a melodrama which gives the emotions a rough going over [for *Black Legion*].[36]

> "Black Fury" falls in the same category with Warners' previously fortunate topical releases—the same up-to-the-minute celluloid interpretation of what are almost current events.[37]

> Almost as timely as today's newspaper, [*Fury* is] an indictment against Judge Lynch.[38]

The headliner rubric therefore held sway, even for the critics remarking on social relevance.

Third, and most significant, melodrama remained a key generic lens through which almost all the reviews were understood, especially those in the Warners' cycle. As Steve Neale has pointed out, melodrama for the trade periodicals at the time referred to narratives of action and accelerated plot development, not to the stylistic or emotional excess of the weepies emphasized by later scholarship.[39] The above quotes for *Black Fury* and *Black Legion* demonstrate that the films were thought as much as "melodramatic" as "social." So, too, does the review of *Legion of Terror* point to a hybrid of genre categories: "In 62 minutes a place has to be made for romance and meller as well as horror and social denunciation."[40] Whereas *Variety* reviewed *Dead End* and *Our Daily Bread* in language decidedly removed from implication of an action orientation, for Warners' less-expensive topicals, it tempered any citation of the "sociological" with an emphasis on melodrama, action, and generic combination.

By the postwar years, the specter of "melodrama" had slipped into the background, in no small part because the postwar prestige films played down action and adventure in favor of a more "dramatic" tone, that is, a tone more consonant with the later scholarship on melodrama as emotional excess. *Variety* did not at first use problem film terminology to describe the earlier films in the cycle like *The Lost Weekend* and *The Best Years of Our Lives.* By mid-1948, however, the publication used the terms "problem pic" and "message pic" both in headlines and body of the articles:

> Howard Hughes . . . is understood to have ordered that the entire tolerance message be chopped from the film [*The Boy with Green Hair*]. . . . All "message" pix have been killed or are being edited, as is "Boy," to take out the moral angles.[41]

> Territory [the South] has comparatively few Jews and has been notoriously weak for social problem or "message" pix. . . . Fox execs are hoping for similar success on another social problem picture, "The Snake Pit."[42]

> Execs at 20th-Fox, who had been anxiously awaiting returns from a group of post-Christmas openings of "Snake Pit," were breathing easier this week. Problem pic, which previously had highly successful engagements in New York and Chicago, proved almost as strong in smaller towns. . . . [Box office] equaled or bettered those of another problem pic which 20th is using for comparison purposes, "Gentleman's Agreement."[43]

> "Snake Pit," 20th-Fox's chief problem picture for 1949, may emerge as its top grosser of the year.[44]

> Darryl Zanuck's personal production for 1949 will be "Pinky," a film with a message, depicting social conditions in the South.[45]

> 1949 is definitely living up as the year of the Negro problem pic.[46]

> The public will buy "message" pix but they gotta be good.[47]

The trade reviews followed suit, with references to *Pinky* tackling the "problem" of anti-black discrimination head-on and the "racial and lynch problems of the south" exposed in *Intruder in the Dust.*[48] By 1950, the usage is conventionalized, so that the review of *Right Cross* refers to a "shift of the social problem in Charles Schnee's script," and that of *Blackboard Jungle* mentions the "other social problems" besides juvenile delinquency covered. The late 1940s prestige cycle served as a demonstrable tipping point in the trade press consideration of a genre.

The Motion Picture Association of America

The Motion Picture Producers and Distributors of America (MPPDA) and its successor, the Motion Picture Association of America (MPAA), were less important in this context for their active role in production, confined mostly to censorship and legal and public relations stewardship, than as an extant trace of how films were categorized according to their subject matter. The trade association's generic classification took two forms. First, the MPPDA/MPAA released information on film subject matter in their annual reports in the 1930s and 1940s. Second, the association's production-oriented branch, the Production Code Administration (PCA), gave each production submitted from 1934 onward a classification according to type of film (a blank to be filled in) and any

Table 4.1 Motion Picture Producers and Distributors of America's Summary of Member Productions, by Genre Category, 1939–1940

Genre	1939	1940
Social category	54	35
Crime and horror	139	108
Musical	19	27
Western and action	160	115
Miscellaneous	212	238
Total	584	523
Social category (% of total)	9.2%	6.7%

Source: Annual Report to the Motion Picture Producers and Distributors of America, by Will H. Hays, president (New York: privately printed, 1941), 17. Percentages added.

relevant "angle" (a box to be checked alongside the possible contents: military, political, foreign, racial, religious, family life, juvenile, medical, or psychological). As an industry body devoted to anticipating potential difficulties with film-going publics and public institutions, these trade associations provide a useful historical indicator of the mediation between production and reception.

In the 1930s, the MPPDA and the PCA both recognized the social problem genre. The MPPDA's annual reports mention "pictures featuring various current social problems and contemporary political events" and "films with dramatic and problem themes."[49] Later in the decade, they listed the industry's entire product by subject matter.

The statistics in the annual reports from the 1940s are far less general. They break down subject matter/genre into six main categories—Melodrama, Western, Drama, Crime, Comedy, and Miscellaneous—and divide these into subcategories, in which musical or social problem films fall. These tabulations would seem to corroborate the view that the problem film was transhistorical, or at least made a strong showing in both the 1930s and 1940s.

So, too, does the PCA's classification of subject matter. If the films from Roffman and Purdy's filmography are typical, the PCA either did not prepare a certificate for the title (especially in the early 1930s) or used "social problem drama" as a classification.

Table 4.2 Motion Picture Producers and Distributors of America's Summary of Member Productions, by Genre Category, 1940–1944

Genre	1940	1941	1942	1943	1944
Melodrama					
Action	39	65	75	18	26
Adventure	12	9	12	2	3
Comedy	43	59	56	9	21
Juvenile	13	16	14	8	6
Detective-Mystery	10	6	7	7	7
Murder-Mystery	40	45	41	22	33
Musical		1		3	1
Social problem	48	16	6	18	7
Romantic	7	6	2	1	
War					4
Psychological-Mystery					1
	212	*223*	*213*	*88*	*109*
Western					
Action	99	110	108	78	71
Mystery	1	4	2	1	10
Musical	5	5	2	4	4
	105	*119*	*112*	*83*	*85*
Drama					
Action	4	8	11	12	5
Adventure		1		8	
Biographical-Historical	14	6	10		5
Musical	5	6	4	4	8
Romantic	3	9	6	2	6
Social problem	25	32	48	63	39
Comedy			1	1	9
Psychological					4
War					4
	51	*62*	*80*	*90*	*80*
Crime					
Action	20	24	14	2	5
Social problem	7	1	1	5	
Prison	4		2		
	31	*25*	*17*	*7*	*5*

(continued)

(continued)

Genre	1940	1941	1942	1943	1944
Comedy					
Romantic	36	42	29	29	42
Musical	39	35	30	67	56
Juvenile	8	6	6	13	6
Human interest	10				
Farce	21	44	27	9	20
	114	*127*	*92*	*118*	*124*
Miscellaneous					
Cartoon feature		3	2	1	1
Fantasy		3	6	3	1
Documentary		2	4	5	4
Horror		7	14	16	16
Religious		1		1	3
Allegorical		1			
Travelogue		2	3		1
Historical			1	1	1
Sport			2	2	
Farce–Murder Mystery				1	11
	17	*19*	*32*	*30*	*38*
Total	530	575	546	416	441
Social problem total	80	49	55	86	46
Social problem percentage	15.1%	8.5%	10.1%	20.7%	10.4%

Source: Annual Report to the Motion Picture Producers and Distributors of America, by Will H. Hays, president (New York: privately printed, 1945), 17. Social problem film totals and percentages added. "Miscellaneous" category not broken down for 1940.

By the late 1940s, and into the 1960s, the PCA had become more systematic in its records, as the certificates are standardized for every film. There, too, the classification the films considered to be part of the postwar problem cycle are usually marked as social problem films or social problem melodramas. The "angle" even suggests what the "problem" might be.

The exceptions themselves are instructive. Only some of the films dealing with mental illness, alcoholism, or drug addiction (*The Snake Pit*, *The Lost Weekend*, and *The Man with the Golden Arm*) were deemed problem films, whereas others (*Possessed*, *Shock Corridor*, and *Come Back, Little Sheba*) were domestic or psychological dramas. For *Rebel without a Cause*,

Table 4.3 Production Code Administration Records, 1930s Problem Films

Film	PCA certificate	Classification	"Angle"
Imitation of Life (1934)	No cert.		
Black Fury	No cert.		
One More Spring	2/4/35 memo	Drama–Social Problem	
Fury	No cert.		
Black Legion	No cert.		
Dead End	4/30/37 memo	Crime	
They Won't Forget	2/28/37 memo	Drama–Social Problem	
Blockade	4216	War	Military, political, foreign
Dust Be My Destiny	5407	Drama–Social Problem	
One Third a Nation	2340	Drama–Social Problem (slum, clearance of housing, etc.)	Political

Source: The Production Code Administration Archives, Margaret Herrick Library, Beverly Hills, CA.

the PCA lists juvenile delinquency films in their own category. Finally, *Boomerang!* and *Force of Evil* suggest that pseudodocumentary style or noir aesthetics could code the film as a genre other than a problem film.

So far this evidence might support a transhistorical social problem genre. Memos of the PCA, however, clearly show that in the 1930s, the term "social problem" applied to a far greater range of films. In them, an astounding variety of films fit the label of "social problem dramas." The inclusiveness of their "social problem" rubric explains the high tallies of social category films in the MPPDA reports. The question remains why clearly generic material—say, *Cleopatra* (Cecil B. DeMille, 1934) or *The Gay Divorcee* (Mark Sandrich, 1934)—qualified as problem films.

The more detailed synopses in the memos provide some answer. In one memo the PCA flags potential story problems:

Table 4.4 Production Code Administration Records, Postwar Problem Films

Film	Certificate	Classification	"Angle"
All the King's Men	13747	Drama–Social Problem	Political
Best Years of Our Lives	11972	Drama–Social Problem	
Boomerang	11999	Drama–Murder Mystery	
Crossfire	12325	Drama–Social Problem	Racial
Defiant Ones	18985	Drama–Social Problem	Racial
East of Eden	17086	Drama–Social Problem	Military, family life
Force of Evil	13413	Melodrama-Crime	
Gentleman's Agreement	12488	Drama–Social Problem	Religious
The Grapes of Wrath	5789	Drama–Social Problem	Political
Home of the Brave	13715	Melodrama–Social Problem	Racial, military
Imitation of Life	19184	Melodrama–Social Problem	Racial
Intruder in the Dust	13920	Drama–Social Problem	Racial (Negro)
Island in the Sun	18381	Drama–Social Problem	Racial, political, foreign
It's a Wonderful Life	11656	Drama–Social Problem	Religious
The Lawless	14310	Drama–Social Problem	Minority group
Lost Boundaries	13889	Drama–Social Problem	Racial, documentary
The Lost Weekend	10517	Drama–Social Problem	
Man with the Golden Arm	20011	Drama–Social Problem	
The Men	14228	Drama–Social Problem	Medical, psychological
No Way Out	14257	Melodrama–Social Problem	Medical, racial (Negro)
On the Waterfront	16916	Drama–Social Problem	
Pinky	13731	Drama–Social Problem	Racial
Possessed	11828	Drama-Psychological	
Rebel without a Cause	17504	Drama-Juvenile	Juvenile, psychological
Shock Corridor	20495	Melodrama-Psychological	Psychological
Snake Pit	12490	Drama–Social Problem	
The Southerner	10664	Drama–Social Problem	
The Well	15138	Melodrama–Social Problem	Psychological, racial
Wild One	16106	Melodrama–Social Problem	Psychological

Source: The Production Code Administration Archives, Margaret Herrick Library, Beverly Hills, CA.

Table 4.5 Films Listed as "Drama–Social Problem" in Selected Production Code Administration Memos, 1934–1937

Memo Date	Films listed as drama–social problem		
3/22/34	*Among the Missing*	*Imitation of Life*	*Sisters Under the Skin*
	Catherine II	*The Key*	*Uncertain Lady*
	Finishing School	*Laughing Boy*	*Where Are Our Children*
	Firebrand	*Professional Correspondent*	*Without Honor*
	The Green Hat		
5/21/34	*British Agent*	*Honor Bright*	*Of Human Bondage*
	Cleopatra	*I Love an Actress*	*100% Pure*
	Du Barry	*It Ain't No Sin*	*One More Rive*
	Fanny	*Kansas City Princess*	*Pursuit of Happiness*
	Grand Canary	*Kiss and Make Up*	*Sour Grapes*
	Here Comes the Groom	*Life of Virgie Winters*	*Stamboul Quest*
	Here Is My Heart	*Little Man What Now*	*Walking on Air*
		The Man Who Reclaimed His Head	*A Woman of Affairs*
9/1/34	*Firebird*	*La Tendresse*	*We Live Again*
	The Good Fairy	*The Mighty Barnum*	*A Wicked Woman*
	Lady Beware	*Outcast Lady*	*Within This Present*
10/15/34	*Biography*	*Frankie*	*Painted Veil*
	Bordertown	*Gay Divorce* [*sic*]	*Party Wire*
	By Your Leave	*Lottery Lover*	*Right to live*
	Enter Madame	*Marie Antoinette*	*Vanessa*
	Evelyn Prentice	*Night Life of the Gods*	
1/31/36	*Anthony Adverse*	*Hell Ship Morgan*	*Small Town Girl*
	Awakening of Helena Ritchie	*Lady Consents*	*Suzy*
	Fury	*My Brother's Wife*	*These Three*
		The Old Maid	
10/31/36	*Another Dawn*	*Depths Below*	*Parnell*
	Banjo on My Knee	*Go West Young Man*	*Reunion*
	Camille	*Jungle Princess*	*Theodora Goes Wild*
	College Holiday	*L'Equipage*	
2/28/37	*Angel*	*Call It a Day*	*Mazurka*
	As Good as Unmarried	*Marie Walenska*	*Steel Highway*

Source: Internal Production Code Administration memos, March 22, 1934; May 21, 1934; September 14, 1934; October 15, 1934; January 31, 1936; October 31, 1936; and February 28, 1937, The Production Code Administration Archives, Margaret Herrick Library, Beverly Hills, CA.

> *Gay Divorce[e]* (RKO): We are happy to report that this originally questionable story has been handled with great care and the resulting picture is a first-class musical, with the emphasis thrown to the dancing and singing of Fred Astaire and Ginger Rogers, instead of the questionable elements of the divorce-by-collusion racket.
>
> *Party Wire* (Columbia): This story deals with the evil results of gossip in a small town, focusing on the mistaken report that the unmarried heroine is pregnant.[50]

In each, violation of sexual morality is the "social problem" or, more properly, the problem *to* society. This conception of the social problem film makes sense of the industry's inclusion of the marked woman film in the category, but it also challenges a generic definition based primarily (as the postwar examples are based) in the social, not individual, nature of society.

Meanwhile, certain of the 1930s problem films were not considered so by the PCA. The PCA includes one type of film central to Roffman and Purdy's study, the labor relations film, in the category of "Crime": "We will also include in this category from now on stories dealing with industrial unrest, strikes, etc., a matter in which the studios are showing increasing interest as a subject for pictures. At the moment there are three pictures of this type in production, as follows: *Black Hell* (WB) . . . *Mills of the Gods* (Columbia) . . . *Call to Arms* (Columbia)."[51] Later, too, the PCA would classify *Dead End* as a crime film, while calling *Bluebeard's Eighth Wife* (Ernst Lubitsch, 1938) a problem film.[52] As with Steve Neale's case that the trade press rarely, if ever, used the term "melodrama" in the way scholars have, the PCA files from the 1930s demonstrate that although the concept of the social problem film has been used by some branch of the industry from at least the mid-1930s to at least the early 1960s, its meaning changed considerably between prewar and postwar years.[53]

Since the industry's appellation of a social problem genre varied historically, the genre-as-label approach allows a fuller understanding of the changes in the social problem film's coherence. An important shift occurred in the generic constitution of the problem film between the 1930s and the postwar years. The postwar problem film shows an instance in which producers, industrial associations, and the trade press converged in their generic definitions. The 1930s did produce some problem film

FIGURE 10 Frontal address and affect in *Gentleman's Agreement*.

cycles that now are considered foundational to the genre—cycles recognized by industry labels and trade press reviews. Still, generic labels were applied differently and inconsistently before the war. Notable semantic differences of the term "social problem film" separated prewar and postwar periods.

Affect and the Postwar Problem Discourse

Much as a film cycle exhibits conventions that have yet to gain a stable syntax that comes with consistent audience expectations, the process of genre formation consists of the establishment of stable conventions and expectations widespread enough to lead to a recognizable genre. In the postwar years, the success of the social problem cycles brought a prominence to the films, both because of their popularity (*The Best Years of Our Lives*' theatrical run in New York City lasted well over a year) and because critics and journalists talked about them as a category. Genrification had a self-fulfilling element, then, with the circulation of the label reinforcing

FIGURES 11 AND 12 Competing registers in *The Snake Pit*: emphatic narration (left) and banal realism (right).

the genre. As chapter 2 suggests, the different referent for the "social" and "sociological" helps explain some of the difference between the postwar problem film and earlier cycles.

However, genrification involved more than the genre labels. With the postwar cycles, previously unstable conventions gained stability. Social problem films never developed the kind of narrative formula that a B Western, screwball comedy, or MGM musical did. That is, their narrative events do not proceed according to a regular syntax or structure. Furthermore, since social problem films depict different topical subjects, they do not share a common iconography.[54] Social problem films do share some formal and thematic traits, though, even if the commonalities are not immediately apparent. One answer lies in Sarah Kozloff's observation that social problem films "blend two narrative modes: 1) realism, to prove that the story and problem are authentic, and 2) melodrama, to move the viewer to pity, outrage, and (perhaps) action."[55] The prestige problem films in the postwar years do not function fully as what critics

and scholars tend to deem melodramas. They are tonally restrained and avoid stylistic excess, and while all Hollywood films have elements historically borrowed from popular melodrama, the prestige problem films are not much more inclined toward these elements than any other. In their largely realist narratives, though, are moments of melodramatic style, which might be labeled moments of affect, and the wedding of affect to an otherwise objective narration is a defining trait of the social problem film. These moments pause the narrative chain, and their visual and aural registers signal an emotional gap between what should be and what is. These moments of affect could arise from characters' subjective awareness, or they could expose the difference between the spectator's awareness of the problem and the characters'. Frequently, they oscillated between both.

Films across the genre differ in how they use affective moments, but they do tend to have them. *The Lost Weekend* contains many moments of intensified narration, often centered on protagonist Don Birnam's mental torment. His evening in Bellevue Hospital, punctuated by other patients' screams, is a pivotal moment in which he not only realizes his descent but also begins to understand his problems as a type of mental illness. In *The Best Years of Our Lives*, Al Stephenson's (Fredric March) banquet creates pathos in the gap between the role proscribed for the banker and the person he has become (and wants to be). In *Gentleman's Agreement*, Phil Green (Gregory Peck) is refused a reservation at an upscale hotel because the owners think him Jewish. As the manager walks away from Phil, a frontal shot frames the protagonist gazing straight at the camera. The shot is complex, since it is not a literal point of view of the hotel manager (who in any case has turned away), but it figuratively places the spectator in the position of the hotel managment rather than Phil. A direct address shot in the context of classical Hollywood, rare in itself, would only be used for an objective vantage (as opposed to the 180-degree reverse shots that Jonathan Demme would use in the postclassical *Silence of the Lambs* [1991]). The narration therefore positions the spectator as a putative discriminator, while able to see the effect on Phil.

These moments of affect could be surprising because they appear in films with an ordinarily restrained style. *The Snake Pit* is almost extreme in the contrast. The most notable (and famous shot) captures Virginia's (Olivia de Havilland) shock at finding herself in the mental health asylum's "snake pit." In a stylistic flourish, the scene moves from her personal story to the objective view with a sweeping high-angle crane shot to capture the totality of the institution (figure 11). A fade-out not so much offers narrative closure as it emphasizes the social conflict that has no resolution in the narrative. The shot is a typically expressive shot for director Anatole Litvak, who uses emotive camera movement frequently in the noir film *The Long Night*. However, much of the film is particularly restrained in its cinematography and camerawork, with a minimal mise-en-scène and a medium gray tonal palette (figure 12).

Any of these moments could qualify as melodramatic tropes, and in fact they do function much like affective moments in other dramas. What distinguishes the social problem films is, first, that the affect comes in films produced, circulated, and received as realist dramas and, second, that they yoke affect to narrative moments in which the discourse of the social most readily appears. In this project, the 1940s problem films represent the synthesis of elements of the two 1930s cycles. Similar to the headliner cycle, the social problem genre approaches topical material through a melodramatic style. Similar to the 1930s populist cycle, the genre takes an objectifying view of the "problem." These two strains combined as the films came to depict the social in abstract terms. By locating historical agency in neither the individual nor an embodied collectivity of the masses, the problem films forged a genre language that would remain in place for future decades.

The Prestige Problem Film in Context

The postwar problem film cycle was coherent enough to resonate outside of the films specifically created and marketed as part of that cycle. A selection of films across studio and genre—all produced in 1947, the year of key problem films *Gentleman's Agreement* and *Crossfire*—indicates that a problem film sensibility extended well beyond the highly visible prestige cycle:

1. *Daisy Kenyon* (Otto Preminger, Fox) touches on two major problems—the internment of Japanese Americans during World War II and child abuse—in the framework of a women's picture melodrama structured around Joan Crawford's star image. Unusually, the social problem subplots are secondary to the central melodramatic tension of the narrative, namely whether Daisy (Crawford) will choose the dependable Peter (Henry Fonda) or the philandering, charming Dan (Dana Andrews).
2. Columbia's *Son of Rusty* (Lew Landers) gives a socially relevant twist on the boy-and-his-dog adventure B-film. A returning vet, Jed Barlow, picks a small town in which to settle down, only to find that his psychological troubles have led to social stigma and eventually to a trumped-up misdemeanor charge and a trial. Only the eponymous dog can get the boy to overcome his fear of the man, just in time to come to Jed Barlow's defense. During the court scene, Barlow's defense attorney articulates the theme of the film: "We are not assembled here today to try any case against Jed Barlow. . . . The whole town of Lawtonville is on trial . . . for their unbearable attitude of intolerance to a fellow man."
3. *The Romance of Rosy Ridge* (Roy Rowland) is a typical MGM period-piece sentimental drama, but beneath the surface is a latent problem film about racial tolerance. Henry Carson (Van Johnson) is an affable wanderer who comes to a frontier town and ends up caught in the middle of both a romance and a town feud fed by

simmering resentment from the Civil War. Despite the film's lack of African American characters, a terror organization in the narrative shows clear intimations of the Ku Klux Klan and shifts the theme to a plea for tolerance.

4. *Deep Valley* (Jean Negulesco) continues Warner Bros.' fondness for the misunderstood criminal character. However, the criminal here is a shell-shocked veteran, psychologically wounded and in need of understanding—a theme shared by films like *The High Wall* (Curtis Bernhardt, MGM) and *The Long Night* (Anatole Litvak, RKO).
5. *Living in a Big Way* (Gregory LaCava, MGM) criticizes war profiteering and promotes cooperative housing development—all in the context of a musical romantic comedy.
6. *The Unfaithful* (Vincent Sherman) is on the surface a Warner Bros.–formula noir in the vein of *Mildred Pierce* (Michael Curtiz, 1945). But allegorically it presents the trail of its crime as a reflection on the legacy of home-front sacrifice. "Have we forgotten the war so quickly?" the defense attorney asks.

On top of these, numerous films invoked topical content in a more superficial or lighthearted way: *Suddenly It's Spring* (Mitchell Leisen, 1947) with the topic of postwar divorce rates; *Road to Rio* (Norman Z. McLeod, 1947) with a gag about Jim Crow; and *A Likely Story* (H. C. Potter, 1947) about the housing shortage. All of these examples show a grappling with the changes wrought by World War II and suggest that topical material and liberal themes were less exceptional than film histories often make them out to be. All the same, the identification of short-term imitations as the film industry approached them does help our historical understanding of even the films, like *The Romance of Rosy Ridge* or *The Unfaithful*, that fall outside a narrow cycle definition.

There are good reasons why critics do not consider the films outside of the prestige cycle or the noirish *films gris* to be social problem films. Either the social problem elements are muted or there is another genre that takes primacy (musical, adventure, and so forth). Just as important, the genre categories of the canon prevent historians for looking for the connections, since many of the B films and middlebrow films are now largely forgotten and do not conform to the topical idea of the canonical social problem films. However, these marginal examples show how widespread both the social problem discourse and the aesthetics of social problem affect were across genres. Some problem films overlap with noir or action films, but others overlap with melodramas, historical films, sentimental dramas, or musicals.

A tension therefore exists between inclusive and exclusive definitions of the problem film. Most narrowly, a closer industrial history can start from the historically finite cycles, both to reconstitute the problem film as a historical genre category and to chart the cycles' evolution. However, beyond the exclusive categories, the social problem film spanned from prestige cinema to elements of genre cinema, often genre films with prestige film elements. The process of genre formation, as the industry encouraged and responded to audience expectations, should not obscure the fact that the social problem film was not a self-contained entity but rather a sensibility that differentiated itself culturally from a wide range of other Hollywood films. As the next chapter explores, the generic context of the 1940s prestige films was just as important as the preceding 1930s cycles in fostering a new social problem film genre.

5

Realist Melodrama

Hollywood in the 1940s took a decided turn toward a realist aesthetic, and the postwar social problem films were a privileged genre in this trend. As Hollywood aspired to participate in the public sphere, it turned increasingly to realism as a suitable style to match topical subject matter. From subject matter to visual treatment, the problem films adopted a self-consciously contemporary realism that distinguished the films from earlier romanticized styles and genre treatments. Throughout Hollywood's studio era, realism was operative as an aesthetic or ideal, but starting around 1940 and decidedly more after World War II, the visual language of Hollywood changed. Moreover, contemporary observers had the sense of a drastic change, as the reception of social problem films suggested. *Newsweek* praised *The Lost Weekend* for its location shooting and its set design, writing, "Paramount should be credited for making one of the best movies of this or any other year. . . . Not the least of the film's assets are its realistic sets. The Birnam apartment actually looks like a New York apartment; and the street scenes, which were photographed in New York, are the real thing."[1] Realism poses thorny theoretical problems as both a critical category and cultural construct. Nonetheless, both in their aesthetics and their reception, Hollywood moved toward the "realist" side of expressive possibilities.

Nothing would seem more straightforward than the causes of postwar realism in Hollywood's films. Film historians have identified three major sources. Documentary film influenced Hollywood's cinematic language, in famous examples like Gregg Toland's cinematography for *The Grapes of Wrath* or James Wong Howe's for *Air Force* (Howard Hawks, 1943)—but also in smaller, less grand ways.[2] This influence reached its apex in the pseudodocumentary or "semidocumentary" cycle of postwar films that sometimes overlapped with the problem film, as films like *House on 92nd Street* or *Boomerang!* explicitly borrowed documentary language and aped documentary style in the context of a feature film. As Lisa Dombrowski argues, these genres were complex blends of classical cinematography and documentary-influenced rule bending but ultimately spearheaded a broader turn toward realist cinematography in postwar Hollywood.[3] Similarly, historians point to the effect of World War II, in what Robert Ray identifies as a new willingness on Americans' part to engage with world events and contemporary events.[4] Finally, some scholars highlight the impact of the Great Depression and the proliferation in the 1930s of realist literature, painting, and photography. Peter Roffman and Jim Purdy in particular argue for the influence of New Deal movements on Hollywood's realism and social problem films:

> That John L [Sullivan of *Sullivan's Travels*] should express such socially conscious sentiments ("How can I do a musical at a time like this?") was natural to the period. From the advent of the Depression to the rise of McCarthyism, a strong sensibility of social concern was given play in America. In politics, FDR and the New Deal functioned as the focal point of this sensibility, and in the arts, agitprop drama, proletarian literature, and documentary photography represented a major strain of cultural expression. The economic breakdown of the Depression, the rise of fascism and the war against it, and the idealistic vigor of the postwar years all fostered a concern with social conditions, an impulse toward political change.[5]

In this account, New Deal politics, interrupted by wartime unity, brought New Deal aesthetics to an otherwise resistant Hollywood.

This account seemingly dovetails with the analysis of chapter 3, which argues that the social problem film encoded a "Griersonian text"—a documentary-like sensibility implicating the viewpoint of the mass public sphere. New Deal art movements, leftist cinema of the 1930s, and wartime journalism each had an undeniable impact on the postwar cinema. However, in stressing them as causal factors, the canonical account has overlooked the widespread realist style of prestige films that do not conform to the New Deal cultural canon. This style differed from the proletarian novel, the Works Progress Association (WPA) photo essay, or the newsreel. Even though films like *Gentleman's Agreement* and *The Snake Pit* invoked documentary in parts, they ultimately resembled the other quality dramas that Hollywood was releasing. The social problem films were just one part of a broad turn to a particular kind of realist cinema in the 1940s, and the aesthetic language of earlier dramas formed much of the basis for the postwar problem film.

The surprising missing link was therefore the paradoxical realist melodrama that was popular in the early to late 1940s. Often adapting best-selling literary work, this cycle included both canonical works like *How Green Was My Valley* (John Ford, 1941) and less-remembered dramas like *The Human Comedy* (Clarence Brown, 1943). Some of these films invoked topical concerns, but mostly they were removed from the New Deal lineage. Other realist films were more explicit in their New Deal politics (as *The Grapes of Wrath*, for instance) or in their documentary influence (*Air Force*), but the literary adaptations walked a middle ground aesthetically by appropriating realism and topicality within the strictures of the novelistic drama. Critics did not praise each of them, but collectively the films comprised a category of prestige dramas that the industry and critics alike considered among the best quality films Hollywood produced. Richard Maltby remarked of the state of film history in the late 1990s, "What is certainly true of the history of classical Hollywood as presently written is that the industry's prestige product has been excluded from the critical canon as criticism seeks to construct a Hollywood cinema worthy—thematically, aesthetically, ideologically—of study."[6] His observations still hold, since the prestige drama remains underexamined. Understanding the social problem film therefore requires reconstituting this prestige style. Scholars have elided prestige film aesthetics either by emphasizing canonical realism (or modernism) or by treating melodrama as merely a genre of excess. The 1940s adaptations were neither, exactly, and as such informed the aesthetics of many of the postwar social problem films.

Many films would fit into this category of the prestige realist melodrama in the 1940s. Five examples show the development and form of the genre. *Kings Row* (Sam Wood, 1942) adapted Henry Bellaman's 1940 novel of the same title about the dark underside of a small American town. A more upbeat portrait of small-town life, MGM's film *The Human Comedy*, has a William Saroyan script about home-front adjustment during World War II. (Unusually, Saroyan novelized the script and published it before the film's release.) *A Tree Grows in Brooklyn* (Elia Kazan, 1945), based on Betty Smith's 1943 eponymous best-selling novel, is a coming-of-age story set around the turn of the century in a poor immigrant neighborhood in Brooklyn, New York. *A Bell for Adano* (Henry King, 1945) is the film version of John Hersey's 1944 Pulitzer Prize–winning novel about an American army major negotiating the culture clash of U.S. occupation of Italy in World War II. Finally, whereas Sinclair Lewis's 1945 novel *Cass Timberlane* was written during the war, the film version (George Sidney, 1947) invokes the changes of immediate postwar American life. All five source novels were on *Publishers Weekly*'s Top 10 best-selling list of their publication year, yet by most measures none qualify as genre fiction. Significantly, the sources of all these films were novels marketed and discussed in the popular press in advance of the films.

Together, these adaptations show a multifaceted but unified trend of novelistic realism that lay behind the 1940s prestige film. Chapter 1 outlined how middlebrow culture was not a single entity but, in the case of Hollywood, comprised at least two dispositions to legitimizable popular culture. The taste changes within the cultural field of cinema paralleled a flourishing of a broader middlebrow literary culture.[7] Particularly important were what the literary historian Gordon Hutner calls middle-class novels (a term he uses for its specificity and nonpejorative quality): fiction books published in hardback and aimed for a wide middle-class readership.[8] Film studies as a field has generally overlooked such literary sources, but middle-class novels served as source material for the major problem films in the melodrama and social problem cycle alike, and the middlebrow literary readership overlapped with the audience Hollywood envisioned for its dramatic films. The half-forgotten source novels were central to Hollywood's sense of both "literary" and "realist" material. As Phil Green, the main character in Laura Hobson's source novel *Gentleman's Agreement*, notes, Somerset Maugham and Sinclair Lewis were his literary heroes.[9] Middlebrow liteature served as an aesthetic model for Hollywood's newer realist prestige style that would assume dominance in the 1940s, as popular literary realism drove the unusual synthesis of narratonal detachment and sentimentality in the 1940s Hollywood drama. Although film historians see *The Grapes of Wrath* as a key film in the social problem cycle, films like *A Tree Grows in Brooklyn* hold a greater claim on influence for *The Lost Weekend* or *Gentleman's Agreement*.

The film industry had the particular challenge of translating this literary style to the screen. Cinematographers in particular fashioned a realist style amenable to the storytelling demands of the melodramatic source material. Moreover, their trade discourse suggests that "realism" as a category was elastic enough to include attributes not commonly associated with realism. Studio house styles helped generate stylistic change in favor of the newer prestige style. Realism was as much a subjective category of aesthetic distinction as an objective formal quality, and house styles emerged from intra-industry differences in conceptions of realism, even as trade discourse of realism developed industry-wide. Because of a broader shift in discourses of cinematic realism, literary adaptation came to embody what Bill Nichols calls the "discourse of sobriety" of social problem diagnosis.[10]

Most of all, the synthesis of literary source and cinematographic approach makes sense of the curious juxtaposition of realist discourse with more sentimental material. Hollywood drew direct inspiration from the public sphere realms of documentary film and the middle-class novel, yet in putting these two realms in dialogue, within the context of commercial cinematic conventions, filmmakers created a distinct version of the vernacular modernism that Miriam Hansen argues was always present in classical Hollywood cinema. That is, social problem films participated in a discourse of sobriety but also contained elements of emotional pathos more familiar to melodrama. Previous accounts could reconcile these with a sell-out narrative in which serious leftist artists were compromised in their dealings with the culture industry. Realist melodrama, however, was not a bug but a feature of 1940s Hollywood—an approach that corresponded to the literary and public sphere cultures of the day.

The Middle-Class Novel

Histories of the social problem film tend to ignore or downplay the fact that many of the major examples were adaptations of novels. Both *The Lost Weekend* and *Gentleman's Agreement* were best-selling novels before they were films. Film historians have pointed to Hollywood's ongoing fondness for presold properties. Studios looked to novels, short stories, and plays (including those based on novels) as the source of narratives. Moreover, adaptations had a built-in marketing hook, and the studio practice of seeking out best-selling literary properties was commonplace. Jeanne Allen, for instance, notes that Warner Bros. swiftly bought the option on Olivia Higgins Prouty's *Now, Voyager* (Irving Rapper, 1942), based on the popularity of Prouty's previous novels.[11] Not every film adaptation signaled its status as such, but for many films, marketing or reception, or both, situated the film intermedially, in relation to older and more prestigious media.

Hollywood adapted widely, from pulp novels to magazine stories, but one of its mainstays was the serious, dramatic novel. Gordon Hutner refers to a middle-class novel "better than formula fiction but not as good as high art."[12] This class of fiction was "middle class" on a few grounds. It was the mainstay of hardcover publishing and geared toward a bourgeoisie and petite bourgeoisie with the income, leisure time, and cultural disposition to buy, read, and discuss such books. The works in turn found their champions in the mass-market weekly magazines geared toward the middle class. Hutner argues that canonical approaches blind scholars to the literature that broad swaths of the American public read in the twentieth century. American realism as a literary subfield continues to focus on canonical authors and to bypass realist novels from the 1920s to the 1950s.[13] However, these decades contain many novels that updated realist aesthetics to address their contemporary situation.

The novels constructed a middle-class implied reader who sought to make sense of the relationship between the public sphere and intimate life. In this regard, the middle-class novel continued a bourgeois literary tradition from the eighteenth and nineteenth centuries. In Jürgen Habermas's account of the public sphere, the literary public served as a correlative to the political public sphere. Not only did the social spaces of coffeehouses and salons serve expressly political functions at various points, but also literature, with the rise of the novel and the psychological theatrical drama in particular, fashioned an internalized sensibility that translated between public and private realms. Habermas writes of the audience-oriented subjectivity that connected the bourgeois family's identity with its public presence: "The relations between author, work, and public changed. They became mutual relationships between privatized individuals who were psychologically interested in what was 'human,' in self-knowledge, and in empathy."[14]

Hutner argues that a similar readership address characterized the middle-class novel. Middle-class novels, he maintains, "were not the ones that everyone was talking about, but in the world before television, they were a valuable means of circulating not only cultural capital, but also social awareness, if only by providing a few evenings' interesting instruction about the life of the middle class and the state of society."[15] Their centrality to a national literary culture gave these novels a role in the middle-class's self-imagining. The middle-class readership from the 1920s through the 1950s saw in the novel a negotiation over the tensions and relationship between public identity and private life. Sinclair Lewis's books—*Arrowsmith* or *Dodsworth*, for instance—are frequently about the interplay between the heterosexual couple and their social position within a bourgeois (or petit bourgeois) community. Similarly, John P. Marquand's novel *H. M. Pulham, Esq.* gently satirizes the Harvard-educated Bostonian as he reflects back on missed career opportunities (advertising instead of stock brokering) and missed loves. Works in this vein were not social problem novels, but they did comprise a literary tradition against which books like *Gentleman's Agreement* and *The Lost Weekend* were measured.

Two adaptations show how the prestige adaptation and the social problem film sprang from a common sensibility. The novel *A Bell for Adano*, winner of the 1945 Pulitzer Prize, follows the account of an Italian American army officer as he navigates the cultural conflicts involved with the American occupation of Italy in World War II. Thematically, both novel and film argue for a culturally sensitive engagement with the Italian people. As author John Hersey writes in his foreword to the book, "The theories about administering occupied territories all turned out to be just theories, and in fact the thing which determined whether we Americans would be successful in that toughest of all jobs was nothing more or less than the quality of men who did the job."[16] Recently, some scholars have argued that postwar cinema created a global humanist spectatorship allied with U.S. foreign policy, and nowhere is the relation between the intimate sphere and the public sphere more evident than in Hersey's novel and Fox's Henry King–directed prestige adaptation.[17] In a similar vein, Sinclair Lewis published *Cass Timberlane* at the war's end, in 1945, and the narrative (film and novel) surveys the moral dilemmas of a middle-class judge in a medium-size midwestern town; his midlife crisis doubles the crisis in public culture of a middle-class society eroded by industrialization and urbanization, the crisis that C. Wright Mills would document in his 1951 study, *White Collar*.[18]

The middle-class novel falls outside the three mainstays of adaptation studies of cinema: canonical modernist fiction, genre fiction, and committed fiction of the Left. The last category, in particular, has preoccupied historians and critics of the social problem film, who read the genre against the postwar struggles of Hollywood's Left. Films in the postwar cycle of *films gris*, for instance, often had their basis in the proletarian novel or drama. *Christ in Concrete*, for example, adapted Pietro di Donato's 1939 novel about Italian American construction workers. Similarly, some of the writers and directors facing the blacklist in the late 1940s had a background in proletarian theater and literary projects of the WPA.[19] For instance, Abraham Polonsky, Elia Kazan, Joseph Losey, and Nicholas Ray all worked in 1930s left theater, and each eventually was involved in social problem film or *film gris* productions.

Understandably, canonical histories have discounted the middle-class novel adaptations as insufficiently politicized or insufficiently formalist. However, the genre included stylistic innovation as well as significant cultural negotiation over American politics. The literary historian Michael Szalay, for instance, traces Betty Smith's background in the Federal Theater Project and reads *A Tree Grows in Brooklyn*'s thematic emphasis on insurance and catastrophe against the New Deal's tenet of social insurance. Furthermore, he links Smith to the modernist literary discourse around the New Deal.[20] Aesthetically, *A Tree Grows in Brooklyn* is decidedly neither committed nor modernist fiction, but it shows how the often-recuperative themes of middle-class realist literature still managed a critical exploration of ideas similar to more canonical fiction.

Lists of best-selling novels suggest the importance of the middle-class novel in 1940s popular culture. As Hutner notes, not all best sellers would fall into the category of the middle-class novel, and not all middle-class novels sold well. Nonetheless, certain serious, realist novels had a disproportionate visibility and impact. To take just one year, 1944, *Publishers Weekly*'s top best sellers have a number of prominent examples:

1. *Strange Fruit* (Lillian Smith)
2. *The Robe* (Lloyd C. Douglas)
3. *A Tree Grows in Brooklyn* (Betty Smith)
4. *Forever Amber* (Kathleen Winsor)
5. *The Razor's Edge* (Somerset Maugham)
6. *The Green Years* (A. J. Cronin)

7. *Leave Her to Heaven* (Ben Ames Williams)
8. *Green Dolphin Street* (Elizabeth Goudge)
9. *A Bell for Adano* (John Hersey)
10. *The Apostle* (Sholem Asch)

Of these, Hollywood adapted seven in the mid-1940s, at least four of which were exemplary prestige realist melodramas: *A Tree Grows in Brooklyn*, *The Razor's Edge*, *The Green Years*, and *A Bell for Adano*. Similarly, while top-grossing films for the middle of the decade included genre films and star vehicles like the Bing Crosby–Bob Hope road pictures or RKO's light comedies, many middle-class novel adaptations were some of the top-grossing films of their release year: *Cass Timberlane* ($4.05 million), *The Green Years* (Victor Saville, 1946) ($4.65 million), *The Razor's Edge* ($5 million), and *Gentleman's Agreement* ($3.9 million).[21] The best-selling novel was tangential to the literary canon, but literary histories have pointed to the naturalist impulse strong in 1940s fiction, and more recent revisionism in the field has questioned the historiographical distinction between best-selling fiction and high literature.[22]

In one sense these adaptations comprise Hollywood's middlebrow, yet middlebrow as a concept does not adequately describe the middle-class novel adaptation. Some elements of the middlebrow do apply: key among them is deference to more established art forms, especially literature, or to written history. The most common means is through the genre iconography of the credit sequence, which frequently features books but also uses typography and graphics to connote seriousness. Ideologically, these films positioned themselves in the middle, figuring a conflict with both poor or working-class roots and upper-class snobbery. *A Tree Grows in Brooklyn* and *I Remember Mama* (George Stevens, 1948) are archetypal in this sense. In each, a coming-of-age story chronicles class mobility and creation of a middle-class subject that stands in for a collective middle-class national identity (and a "realist" take on the Horatio Alger mythology). Similarly, *A Bell for Adano*, novel and film, presents the immigrant American as capable of resisting both the brutality of war occupation and the deadly indifference of military bureaucracy. The prevalence of art and artists in their narratives made these dramas not too different from classically middlebrow genres like the biopic (*Song of Love* [Clarence Brown, 1947]) or the Anglophile film (*The Green Years*). The prestige films, therefore, were part of a wide range of dramatic films exhibiting a middlebrow veneration of serious culture.

At the same time, Hollywood films produced a discourse on their own taste formation that was hardly naive and at times was actually sophisticated. *Cass Timberlane* is one example of a film actively critiquing bourgeois and petit bourgeois values. The narrative follows the eponymous midwestern judge (Spencer Tracy) who falls for a younger woman, Ginnie (Lana Turner), who lives on the other side of the tracks. Cass has an existence somewhat independent from the town's bourgeoisie. He reads, in one character's words, "journals that no one has heard of, except the FBI." His romance with Ginnie and willingness to break social convention is evidence of this insider-outsider status he has with the town's society, but it also makes him question his own idealism and independence. Thematically, the film explores the *Babbitt* theme (which criticizes the conformity and small-mindedness of the American middle class) but seeks to unearth the collusion between the Babbitts and those in the middle class dependent on the Babbitts' influence and money. As *Cass Timberlane* shows, these films could involve their spectator in the class critique.

Realism and the Middle-Class Novel

The middle-class novels' brand of realism, in the lineage of late nineteenth-century American realism, gives historical specificity and critical precision to their place in larger taste formation. Canonical literary accounts treat the era of American realism as long passed by the 1940s, but its impact remained strong.[23] The realist novel had French roots rather than American, but William Dean Howells's writing and criticism formulated an American school of literary realism—and, accordingly, a project of literary realism that American literary historians have recognized.[24] Literary scholars have debated the exact nature of Howellsian realism, but basically the style involves objectivist narration, social satire or critique, and subject matter turning its gaze back on its mostly middle-class readership. As Hutner notes, Howellsian realism served as the defining aesthetic of the middle-class novel from the 1920s through the 1950s, helped in large part by other major authors working in the realist vein, notably Edith Wharton and Sinclair Lewis.[25] Whereas modernist authors like John Dos Passos combined narrative experiments with an exploration of ideological contradictions, the realist novels presented a unified and coherent story world around the subjectivity of their (often middle-class) characters.

The middle-class novel was a largely objectivist narrational form. Howells drew explicit reference to historical writing as a model for the novel and, as literary scholars have noted, created narration that provided omniscience while minimizing the obtrusiveness of the omniscient narrator.[26] *A Bell for Adano* is a good example of this approach. In one chapter, the ongoing dynamic between navy lieutenant Livingston and army major Jappolo involves the major's subtle ability to convince the lieutenant to help him out:

> "Well anyhow, thanks a million. . . . Oh, say, before I hang up, I just happened to think. I heard the other day of another way you could use your initiative and earn yourself some more friends, and do a hell of a lot of good in the bargain."
>
> "How's that?" said Lieutenant Livingston, rising like a famished trout to a well-cast fish fry. . . .
>
> When he had hung up, the Lieutenant thought to himself, what a good guy, you never can tell about a meatball until you get to know him.[27]

In this passage, the narration steps in to editorialize about Livingston ("rising like a famished trout"), but the intrusion is minimal and secondary to the ironic presentation of Livingston's subjectivity. Because of the narration, the implied reader knows things that the lieutenant does not: that the major gets what he wants by flattering the naval officer and that the traditional white Anglo-Saxon Protestant (WASP) view of immigrant Americans is a foible for Livingston and, by extension, the group he represents. This system became part of literary theories of the "classic realist text," and Colin MacCabe, for instance, uses *Middlemarch* as an instance of classic-realist metalanguage—that is, the bracketing of character subjectivity within the objective worldview of the novel.[28]

Sinclair Lewis represented the satirical variant of realism that would gain influence in American middle-class literature. One critic of the late 1940s, John Flanagan, remarks of *Main Street* that "the novel appeared at the precise hour when readers suddenly freed from the tensions of a world war and conscious of the need for self-examination were willing and almost avid to learn the truth about themselves."[29] The following passage in *Cass Timberlane* manages to be both a satire of the middle class and a reflection of the role satire had taken in the literary public:

> Some of these smart-aleck critics claim that Middlewestern businessmen haven't changed much since that book—what's its name—by this Communist writer, Upton Sinclair—"Babbitt," is it?—not changed much since that belly-ache appeared, some twenty years ago. Well, we'd like to tell those fellows that in these twenty-odd years, the American businessman has changed completely. He has traveled to Costa Rica and Cuba and Guatemala, as well as Paris, and in the *Reader's Digest* he has learned all about psychology and modern education. He's been to a symphony concert, and by listening to the commentators on the radio, he has now become intimate with every branch of Foreign Affairs.[30]

Not every realist novel adopted Lewis's satirical style, but some, such as the comedic realist novels of John P. Marquand, excelled in it. Satire generally became one mode of a larger realist style, and *A Tree Grows in Brooklyn* and *The Human Comedy*, for instance, both weave satirical passages into otherwise somber or sentimental material.

The middle-class novel's satirical vein created the sense that middle-class novels were opposed to Victorian sensibility. Lea Jacobs has argued that American cinema in the 1920s responded to a shift in literary and taste cultures, from refined and "old-fashioned" to antisentimental and "modern."[31] Middle-class novels like *Kings Row* and *A Bell for Adano* could be forthright about nontraditional and even antinormative sexuality. This battle between Victorian morality and modernity raged in the middle-class novels themselves, as in *A Tree Grows in Brooklyn*'s conflict between Francie's traditionalist mother and her aunt Sissy, who has unmarried attachments with a string of men and refuses traditional patriarchal roles. The attempt, even eagerness, of respectable middle-class literature to embrace elements of modernity that went against bourgeois strictures of the Victorian era complicates Miriam Hansen's model of vernacular modernism, which pits both high-modernist and (some) popular culture against the bourgeoisie's traditionalism.[32]

Despite the social critique and anti-Victorian sensibility, however, the middle-class novels generally recuperated social contradictions in a humanistic theme. *The Human Comedy* is the most glaring example in its recasting a wartime home-front story as an allegory with connections to Homer's *Odyssey.* It follows a young boy, Ulysses, who works after school as a telegram delivery boy. Given the ongoing war, his job consists mostly of delivering death notices to families of servicemen. Its narration takes a poetic turn in many places, and chapter titles make semiaphoristic statements about moral truths, such as "There Will Always Be Pain in Things" and "Love Is Immortal, Hate Dies Every Minute." Other middle-class novels are more straightforward in their realist style, but they, too, invoke interpersonal connection and emotional resolution in the face of intractable historical and social conflict. In the case of *A Bell for Adano*, the individual efforts of Jappolo to understand the Italian people and serve as a cultural ambassador suggest Hersey's utopian hope that a Pax Americana could overcome the war's conflicts and the challenges of postwar reconstruction.

A Tree Grows in Brooklyn is striking in its combination of realism and sentimentality. Francie's story is a view onto a broad sweep of historical challenges for poor Irish Americans at the start of the twentieth century, but told from the child's point of view. The novel treats the hardship as fodder for sentimental nostalgia. "She'll never have the hard times we had, will she?" Francie's brother, Neeley, asks about their newborn sister. Francie replies, "No. And she'll never had the fun we had, either."[33] Ideologically, this nostalgia captures a broader historical nostalgia for Americans reflecting back on the opening decades of the century. The realist tone helps establish the nostalgia, as in this passage from the opening of one of the chapters: "For the little while of the Christmas holidays, it had been almost like the old times in the Nolan family. But after New Year's things reverted to the new routine which had grown on them since Johnny's death" (368). The split between the two stylistically straightforward sentences sets up an affective pattern of longing and loss that is a microcosm of the book's larger bildungsroman structure. Like Francie and Neeley's dialogue above, past and present, nostalgia and progress, are separated out into contrasting positions not easily reconciled. The novel's central conceit of the tree also becomes a source of sentimental affect. In the book's final chapter, Francie notices the tree in the backyard:

> The tree whose leaf umbrellas had curled around, under and over her fire escape had been cut down because the housewives complained that wash on the lines got entangled in its branches. The landlord had sent two men and they had chopped it down.
>
> But the tree hadn't died . . . it hadn't died. (442)

Here, the objectivist narration of the novel appropriates Francie's emotional investment in the longevity of the tree. The pathos emerges in the gap between the forward-moving historical time of the novel's narration and the endurance of its key symbol.

The middle-class novel was hardly monolithic. It encompassed a range of approaches, including *Kings Row*'s appropriation of Sherwood Anderson's modernism and *The Human Comedy*'s neo-Victorian sentimentality. Betty Smith emerged from the activist theater milieu of the New Deal, whereas John Hersey wrote *A Bell for Adano* out of his experience as a war journalist. Nonetheless, these works served as a category of novels with an underlying literary project. Upon closer examination they were hybrid cultural forms, grafting affective qualities sometimes associated with romanticist or sentimental fiction onto nonsentimental forms. Hollywood adaptations inherited this hybridity of affect and realism and adapted it, sometimes in surprising ways. In doing so, they kept a number of traits from the underlying literary source, beyond the subject matter: objectivist tone, sentimental affect, humanist thematics, and social critique, including critique of the readership's middle-class identity and milieu. From a critical perspective, at least, these could be contradictory traits, but in the context of 1940s culture they were experienced as a strong, stable, national literary public sphere.

Realism, Melodrama, and the Novelistic Adaptation

Film adaptations of middle-class novels had in many respects the opposite dynamic from the source novels. Whereas the middle-class novels explored sentimental material and humanist themes from within the stylistic form of the realist novel, their adaptations presented Howellsian narratives within a generic template of melodrama. Indeed, one overriding reason that film historians undervalue the influence of middle-class realist literature on Hollywood is that the adaptations made from them appear to be foremost melodramas rather than realist films. For instance, Thomas Schatz's history of 1940s Hollywood gives little attention to the prestige pictures but does offer a brief consideration of *The Human Comedy* as a "woman's picture."[34] Looking back on the output of Hollywood's studio era, films that lie outside of the bounds of more familiar genres (comedies, action and crime films, thrillers, horror and gothic films, and musicals) lack a solid genre category. Accordingly, critics and historians have not used a consistent generic labeling for the literary adaptations of middle-class novels or for the prestige dramas in general. Key qualities about these films merit their inclusion under the rubric of melodrama, whereas in other respects they are not melodramas, at least as many people have understood the genre.

Film adaptations of these books sometimes altered the novels' messages, left out key characters, or changed characterizations. However, in the 1940s, perhaps more than in any other period of the studio years, the adaptations kept to the general ethos of the middle-class novels. As the novels themselves combined humanist themes and social deliberation suitable for a literary public sphere, the films based on them followed suit. The sentimental affect of suffering in these films cannot be adequately explained as generically motivated by melodrama. After all, films and novels were part of a larger cultural formation of humanism. As Karl Schoonover has argued, postwar American culture in particular organized modes of affect in service of foreign policy imperatives associated with the Marshall Plan and Pax Americana. Suffering became a rhetorical buttress for the role of the United States in alleviating postwar poverty and hunger and, on a macro level, addressing the problem of failed states in Western Europe. This global humanism was based in a spectatorship of witnessing suffering by "dramatizing the political stakes of vision and the need for an outside extranational eyewitness."[35] In the case of Hollywood films, humanist aesthetics and Pax Americana themes spanned a range from the child-centered melodramas to canonically realist films.

The films amplified the sentimental elements present in the source novels and moreover shifted tone for two primary reasons. First, there were the challenges that any adaptation of a novel faces: the condensation of events and characters and the refashioning of narrative to match the storytelling modes of Hollywood classicism.[36] Second, the novels did not correspond easily to existing genres that the film industry could market. By emphasizing romance and sentimental narrative elements, studios could find a better genre hook for audiences. *A Tree Grows in Brooklyn* showed some of these challenges. As Bosley Crowther observed after the film's release, "The abbreviation to which the film-makers were inevitably forced has a certain dramatic clarity the novel did not possess. Now the tender and touching devotion between Francie Nolan and her ne'er do well dad . . . is revealed as the focal point in the little girl's meager universe."[37] Elsewhere Crowther praises the film for avoiding the hokum typical of some genres,[38] but here the critic sees adaptation as playing up the pathos of the source material. Although he does not use the term "melodrama," his comments speak to the melodramatic elements that give dramatic form to the adaptation in this film and examples from the 1940s.

Crowther's review also speaks to the gendered dynamic of middle-class realist fiction. Whereas some types of modernist and genre literature were understood discursively to be male literary forms (despite important women novelists), women authors wrote many of the middle-class novels. *A Tree Grows in Brooklyn* was among the most famous of the middle-class novels, and important problem films like *Gentleman's Agreement* and *The Snake Pit* were based on novels written by women. Popular literary realism was not entirely gendered as women's literary culture, since there were many male readers and writers as well, but it did provide a forum in which matters of the official public sphere intersected with the novel of manners and the bildungsroman. Their gentility and their concern with the domestic sphere meant that they were natural source material for Hollywood's melodramas.

Yet to the extent these films are melodramas, they differ considerably from dominant subgenres that film studies has identified in its analysis of melodrama. In contrast to the 1930s maternal melodrama, of which *Stella Dallas* (King Vidor, 1937) is the most cited example, or the 1940s woman's picture, these films lack the emphasis on gender roles. Instead, they focus on male characters or children of either gender, yet are not "male melodramas" or "children's films" as those genre terms are generally understood. Unlike the family melodramas of the 1950s and 1960s, the narratives do not revolve around scenarios of sexual and neurotic repression.[39] The films of Clarence Brown or Sam Wood lack the stylistic excess of Douglas Sirk or Vincente Minnelli.[40] Additionally, the 1940s adaptations differ from the films the film industry considered melodrama, which, as Steve Neale notes, referred in the trade press to action-oriented films, with spectatorial excitement driven by fast-moving narratives and interpersonal conflict.[41] In short, adaptations from the 1940s lack a clear constituency in film studies: not aesthetically excessive or female-centered enough to interest theorists, and not canonical enough to interest adaptation scholars.

Since they lack the contemporary generic label and even the critical recognition as melodramas, these films might even not seem to be melodramas but instead would qualify simply as "dramas." However, not only is "drama" an insufficient genre label (it is often the label critics use to suggest a nongenre film), but these adaptations also differ from other dramatic genres, such as the biopic or historical film. At their core they emphasize sentimental and affective elements that justify their critical treatment as melodramas despite the lack of critical consensus on the term. Ben Singer lists five qualities that serve as a "cluster concept" for defining melodrama: pathos, overwrought emotion, moral polarization, nonclassical narrative structure, and sensationalism. Studio-era Hollywood melodramas typically involved only the first two traits. "In fact," he notes, "many Hollywood melodramas hinged on the absence of the element most accentuated in classic stage melodrama—i.e. moral polarization."[42] Similarly, Lea Jacobs has argued that studio-era melodrama shared with classical stage melodrama the sense of the dramatic "situation" (in which the plotting heightens conflict for emotional effect) but that the nature of the situation shifted from the action-oriented usage to the woman's picture.[43] Even if no one quality unites the different subgenres of melodrama, the 1940s adaptations share with the others heightened elements of pathos and dramatic situations comprising intractable conflict forces beyond the scope of individual agency.

The films may simply qualify as melodramas largely because their narratives center on emotional conflicts and do not have resolutely happy resolution to these conflicts. Syntactically, though, at least four specific generic conventions characterize these 1940s realist melodramas. First, as in the films Lea Jacobs discusses, the 1940s literary adaptations incorporate dramatic situations that elicit pathos through intractable conflict. Second, they combine sentimental and often nostalgic themes with a sense of modernity. Third, the films often include nonclassical narrative structure, especially the episodic structure, to aid both pathos and sentimental themes. Finally, formal choices lend a sense of affective weight to moments of pathos and sentimentality. These films are not excessive in the way theorists have used the term, but directorial and musical choices do shape the melodramatic contours of the narratives.

The film adaptation of *Cass Timberlane* is structured around such melodramatic situations. Not only do major traumatic events (a stillborn child, infidelity, car accident) happen with relative suddenness in the narrative development, the overall pathos of the narrative is of social conflict that is inexorable and situational. Jinny is destined not to fit in with small-town society, Cass is destined not to fit in with big-city life, and Bradd is destined to be unable to act independently. The scholarship on 1930s women's films and maternal melodramas has pointed out how their class politics and gendered ideology work through a relay of identification (especially since the archetypical crisis of the women's picture is the navigation of financial prospects in the marriage market). But *Cass Timberlane* adapts the novel's realist form by placing multiple characters, male and female, in positions of understanding the cause of their situation but unable to change it. The result is a pathos position somewhere between melodramatic fatalism and social determinism.

The Human Comedy also reveals the tension between melodramatic pathos and prestige-drama restraints. Whereas it is not technically a literary adaptation, since William Saroyan wrote the screenplay before the novel version, the impact of Saroyan as literary auteur and the novel's publication prior to the film's release meant that the film's reception was caught up in a comparison of the novel and film. In fact, as much as for Betty Smith's novel, reviews made note of the fidelity to the author's vision.[44] The narrative is idiosyncratic and even more sentimental than the novelistic adaptations. The story is told with voiceover narration from a deceased patriarch (Ray Collins) whose family in fictional small-town Ithaca is adjusting to life during World War II. Like many melodramatic narratives, the novel and film relay the pathos of loss through the perspective of children. The youngest, Ulysses, deals with the absence of the deceased father and his soldier brother serving in active duty. The other son, Homer (Mickey Rooney), delivers telegrams to notify families of the death of soldiers, and much of the narrative focuses on his coming-of-age in the face of mortality. Critics referred to the film as a "tearjerker" or "sentimental" film, and *Motion Picture Daily* remarked that the ending "left a studio preview audience made up of traditional hardboiled newspaper writers alternately on the side of sniffles and tears, this reviewer by no means an exception."[45] *Newsweek* walked the line between praise and criticism: "Not all of the movie makes sense in an—unfortunately—non-Saroyan world. And even those who have proven receptive to Saroyan's stories and plays may find his film occasionally preachy and sentimental to the point of stickiness. It is up to the individual movie-goer to determine what he gets out of 'The Human Comedy.'"[46] James Agee remarked, "Most of my friends detest it. A good many millions of other people, I suspect will like it, as they liked the Andy Hardy films and Rupert Hughes' 'The Old Nest,' whose traditions it returns to more than improves on."[47] Yet despite the clear consensus that the film contained sentimental and

FIGURES 13 AND 14 Location and tonality: *Cass Timberlane* (1947) (left) and *Out of the Fog* (1941) (right).

melodramatic elements, the narrative pushed the episodic nature of the bildungsroman toward an even looser structure. In the context of Hollywood's cultural reputation, such an episodic structure differentiated itself as less genre- and action-oriented and more "realist."

The example of *The Human Comedy* shows that critics did not universally praise the prestige films, even if these films courted critical prestige. During this period, critics were beginning to apply criticisms of Hollywood borrowed from the expectations of literary and theater criticism. Only in some venues—in the *Nation* and the *New Republic*, for instance—did the antimiddlebrow sentiment become the driving habitus of the film critic. Eventually, this impulse would lead to the near-universal castigation of melodrama that remains to this day and was a target of feminist film theory's reclamation of the women's picture. For other critics in the 1940s, though, the melodramatic qualities of the prestige films did not necessarily invalidate them. Taken as a group, critics championed the middle-class novel adaptations as favored prestige films.

Realist Cinematography and Industrial Discourse

Each of the above examples—*The Human Comedy*, *A Tree Grows in Brooklyn*, *Cass Timberlane*, *A Bell for Adano*, and *Kings Row*—shifted from largely realist novels with sentimental overtones to largely melodramatic film adaptations with certain realist exceptions to the genre conventions of excess. However, any account of these films as melodrama must make sense of a strange phenomenon: the film industry frequently viewed the literary adaptations as some of their most realist films. To add to the novels' paradoxical hybrid of realism and sentimentality, Hollywood studios' adaptations compounded the aesthetic mix with the film industry's own changing relation to realism in the 1940s. The adaptations appealed to critics and those inside the film industry on the basis that their realist sensibility elevated them above Hollywood's usual approach. Realism poses a central theoretical and historical problem for 1940s Hollywood. Theoretically, the problem is that film scholars have made a number of claims about realism that vary in their analysis and depart from commonplace notions of what "realism" entails in cinema. For film historians, "realism" is itself a historically specific discourse, since different constituencies of classical

Hollywood had reading formations that were evaluative as much as they were critical, since "realism" was almost inevitably a claim for aesthetic superiority. The contemporary trade discourse and popular critical reception saw "realism" in different terms than the reading formations that were to follow (particularly auteurism and 1970s film theory).

It is indeed surprising how disconnected contemporary understandings of realism were from the canonical critical understandings that have come since. Perhaps the most notable example of this difference is *How Green Was My Valley*. Photographed by Arthur C. Miller, the film won the Academy Award in cinematography for 1941, famously (or infamously) beating out Gregg Toland's work on *Citizen Kane*. The trade magazine *American Cinematographer* championed the film in its pages and used the film as part of a larger case for "realist" deep focus:

> The atmospheric keynote of this story of the Welsh collieries is realism—but it is realism leavened with richly human emotion and character. Bringing it to the screen, Miller makes eloquent use of the modern increased-depth technique. But he does it without lapsing into the brittle artificiality which has so often accompanied the use of this technique. His scenes have depth—often to a surprising degree—but they also have qualities of "good photography" which are all too often lost in attaining unusual depth of field. His scenes have depth, yes: but they also have a lifelike roundness, a soft plasticity of image, and a pleasing gradational range which have all too often been sacrificed in pursuit of depth. If in "Citizen Kane" a new photographic concept was born, in "How Green Was My Valley," it comes of age.[48]

Coming of age is a common metaphor through which Hollywood understood its prestige style of the 1940s, which artists and critics considered a rejection of both the genre-centrism and the glamour-oriented visual style of even the Golden Age of the late 1930s. That most film histories treat *Citizen Kane* as more mature and forward-looking in its visual style only makes more important the need to approach the 1940s reception without auteurist and teleological assumptions of the canon.

More than evaluation is at stake. The *American Cinematographer*'s aesthetic opposition of *Citizen Kane* and *How Green Was My Valley* forms a central part of film historians' account of cinematography in the 1940s. The magazine's review was part of a larger deliberation about the realism of deep focus at the end of 1941 and beginning of 1942. Cinematography in the 1930s had been characterized by a "soft style." Cinematographers tended to shoot in shallow focus and to use lens and lighting diffusion to give the impression of a fuzzy glow. As Barry Salt notes, even as faster film stocks gained popularity in the latter 1930s, cinematographers used them more to reduce the amount of light required for sets than to stop down the aperture to increase depth of field.[49] Gregg Toland's work had demonstrated the aesthetic possibilities of increased depth of field and had elevated it to an expressive element in its own right. 20th Century–Fox cinematographer Charles Clarke complained that the "pendulum has very nearly reached the opposite extreme in its swing; certainly, it would seem difficult for any films to go much farther in the direction of crisp definition and realism than Toland's 'Grapes of Wrath' and 'Citizen Kane.'"[50] Clarke argued that deep focus could be a useful tool for the cinematographer but as an organizing aesthetic got in the way of both the realism and the artistry of cinematography.

The historians of film style David Bordwell and Patrick Keating present a convincing account of how trade discourses of Hollywood cinematographers in the early 1940s reflected and shaped the aesthetic norms of the films.[51] In short, their account maintains that "realism" of the 1920s and 1930s tended to be a functional ideal of unobtrusiveness and motivation. Technological changes and externally imposed norms like those of fine art and portraiture photographic fashions shifted realism to aesthetic qualities that interfered with previous storytelling and star-treatment aims—qualities such as contrast, deep focus, and lack of diffusion. This shift created a crisis of heterodoxy in the trade until aesthetic norms could adapt. Bordwell cites Clarke (and *American Cinematographer*'s stance more generally) as evidence that a trade ideology sought to contain the aesthetic rupture that deep focus created.[52] "That Arthur Miller, not Toland," Bordwell writes, "won the Academy Award for black-and-white cinematography in 1941 and that *Citizen Kane* looks not quite like any later Hollywood film suggest that Toland's extreme style had to be modified to fit classical norms."[53] Patrick Keating adds that Clarke's and others' hostility to Toland came from their sense that the latter did not balance functions expected of classical cinematography. Clarke, Keating notes, sees Toland's work as befitting a "realist" film, since its exaggerated aesthetic is generically motivated, at the same time the cinematographer sees Toland's deep-focus style as distorting "realist" perception.[54] As such, Clarke and *American Cinematographer* seem to occupy the contradictions of a changing discourse, adapting to documentary-realist style and new

FIGURE 15 *The Human Comedy*: the refusal of glamour lighting.

deep-focus capabilities yet clinging to a soon-to-be outmoded definition of "realism" as narrative motivation.

Despite the utility of the historical poetics account, the nuance of prestige realist style gets lost in the focus on classicism as a normative system. Throughout the 1940s, directors and cinematographers developed a realist aesthetic that was more than a mere placeholder between 1930s classicism and postwar docu-realism. Prestige cinematographers like Arthur Miller were neither rule breakers like Toland nor entirely conventionalists. Even an individualist and at times heterodox cinematographer like James Wong Howe worked within the parameters of what *American Cinematographer* championed as realism suited to dramatic storytelling. Keating argues that the late 1930s and the 1940s represented a change in the course of classicism, in which a new rhetoric of realism led cinematographers to develop new styles without altering the underlying classical cinematographic practice.[55] In addition, though, a more specific development characterized the cinematography of the 1940s prestige film: the discourse of a cinematographic realism compatible with what film scholars would now consider melodramatic modes of storytelling. Rather than trying to explain away the paradoxes of the industry's discourse, a fuller historical account can take the trade press's view as an indication of the hybrid aesthetics of these films.

For the 1940s cinematographers and critics, realism was discourse but not merely discourse. "Realism" became a rallying cry by which critics and those in the film industry differentiated prestige filmmaking from its putative opposites. For instance, of all the films of the early 1940s that film historians would identify for their realism, *The Human Comedy* is probably not the first to come to mind, yet for *American Cinematographer* the film was the apotheosis of a new realist turn in American cinema:

> There is not a scene nor an action which does not ring true, to bring to the screen the most sincere and realistic presentation of the real America that we have ever seen.
>
> This applies just as much to Harry Stradling's photography as to the rest of the picture. He contributes enormously to the production: his camera treatment maintains a superb balance between documentary realism and a subtly "different" treatment in lighting and composition which enhance the dramatic values of the story without ever for a moment becoming obviously theatrical.[56]

Similarly, *American Cinematographer* championed *Kings Row*, viewing James Wong Howe's work as "[accentuating] realism" while serving largely functional aims of storytelling.[57] *New Republic* critic Otis Ferguson's review of *Kings Row* shared this sentiment:

> Two of the key families are afflicted by forms of madness; there are murder, suicide, mutilation, sadism (though lightly), and two plans of false commitment to institutions for the insane. It is true that the public will take anything in the way of blood and horror so long as the form is melodrama. But this is not handled for melodrama but for real, seriously and conscientiously.[58]

The notion of trade discourse captures the historically specific constellation of ideas about realism in cinema. The film industry and film critics alike were invested in realism as a positive and normative category and selectively emphasized certain elements over others in their evaluations.

On the other hand, these films do feature realist cinematography in the sense that they appropriated visual styles from still photography and documentary cinema and distinguished themselves from romanticist norms in

Hollywood dramas. The most immediate difference is their overall visual look. Tonality is starker: not only is there a move away from the soft style, the image itself takes on more contrast and definition. This rejection of the soft style is not unique to realist melodramas, but such stylistic choices were important precisely because they worked against the grain of generic motivation and expectation. *The Human Comedy*, for instance, stands out in its difference from the visual style of earlier MGM films. The studio had favored a midgray, pearlescent tonality for its black-and-white films, an effect that, as Barry Salt notes, was created by overexposing and underdeveloping the film stock.[59] *The Human Comedy*'s cinematography, on the other hand, is much darker in tonality, with inky blacks and sharper definition. Much as the film cast Mickey Rooney in a more adult role in a somber, downbeat narrative, the visual style serves as an aesthetically serious alternative to the washed-out high-key look of the Andy Hardy movies.

Although some MGM films would go back to a more muted tonality, MGM continued to favor the starker look for its realist melodramas. *Cass Timberlane* is a good postwar example. The film contains both location and studio shooting, and in both cases the jet-black tone amplifies the realist effect of the cinematography. An early scene frames Cass and Ginnie against the industrial backdrop of the fictional town of Grand Island (figure 13). Compare this with the romanticized, gauzy urban backdrops of an earlier film like *Out of the Fog* (Anatole Litvak, 1940), notably by a director later associated with the problem film cycle and a cinematographer, James Wong Howe, with a reputation for realism (figure 14). Unlike the previous examples where a broad, romanticized use of social types signals only a vaguely social setting, in *Cass Timberlane*, despite the fictionalized setting, the reference is immediately historical: the kind of small-to-medium-size American city that had urbanized and industrialized from the 1920s onward and whose sense of local identity was quickly being subsumed in a national culture by 1940. What the film's narration does not carry over from the novel, the visual register suggests instead.

Film stock and processing changes were partly responsible for the shift in look, but the changing use of diffusion also played a key role. In the soft style of the 1930s, cinematographers used two types of diffusion to soften the image. Lighting diffusion uses reflectors or obstructions to scatter light waves illuminating the subject. Lens diffusion places a covering or partial obstruction in front of the camera, refracting some of the light coming into the camera. Either method or a combination of methods reduces the definition of the photographed subject.[60] The opening scene of *The Human Comedy* is shot with a high-key style that sets the tone of "objective" narration. The aerial photography and a crane shot down to the character of Ulysses (Butch Jenkins) watching a groundhog come out of its hole contrast with the irised superimposition of the deceased narrator. A strong backlight on Ulysses is more striking for its lack of diffusion. Even when cinematographer Harry Stradling aims for a romanticized local-color effect in the shots in which Ulysses wanders along the train tracks, he achieves the look though slight overexposure rather than diffusion.

Another characteristic of the realist melodramas is their repurposing of low-key lighting practice from other genres to explore a wider range of grayscale. Low-key lighting had long served a crucial part of the Hollywood cinematographer's palette, used especially for generic purposes, to lend expressive emphasis to crime, thriller, and horror genres, or for effects lighting with nighttime scenes. By the end of the 1930s, prestige cinematographers like George Barnes (*Once Upon a Honeymoon* [Leo McCarey, 1942]), and Leon Shamroy (*Lillian Russell* [Irving Cummings, 1940]) used aggressively low- and medium-key setups against genre type. In the 1940s the lower-key look became a default for the realist melodrama. Joseph LaShelle's work on *A Bell for Adano* often favors medium-key lighting in interiors, to the point that Major Jappolo's magistrate's office seems to be set in a perpetual twilight. Shamroy's *A Tree Grows in Brooklyn* has a similar downcast look for interior scenes, and even in higher-key scenes the lighting setup emphasizes only portions of the frame. The scene depicting a visit of Francie's aunt Sissy (Joan Blondell) to the Nolan household shows how Shamroy pulls back lighting that ordinarily would be high-key toward medium-key lighting with darker shades of gray. The scene starts out keeping high-key illumination on the actors in the middle of the frame (with medium-key along the margins of the space, adding to a sense of a ramshackle tenement apartment). As Sissy and Katie (Dorothy Maguire) sit in the bedroom, the lighting is starker, based increasingly on a single overhead arc light, and the setup leads to a more somber lighting level overall.

The low-key and medium-key trend accompanied cinematographers' emphasis on narrative motivation for lighting choices. James Wong Howe was particularly noted for this kind of realism since he emphasized the direction and relative intensity of the source light. As Todd Rainsberger notes in his book-length study of Howe's style, "All of the characteristics of Howe's light were, to a large degree, determined by the source of light within the scene. . . . On occasion, Howe took source lighting to its naturalistic extreme by lighting first with everyday household bulbs, then adding his lighting units to intensify the natural effect to allow proper exposure."[61] The cinematographer's strong preference for motivated source lighting led him to clash with directors who preferred more expressive effects not motivated by the scene.[62] Source lighting sometimes entailed the use of practicals, light sources visible within the frame. *Kings Row* features many instances of lamps as the narratively motivated light source within the frame, even as Howe supplements the practical with spot lighting. At other times, the light source is off frame. Although directionality is not strict, it is a guiding principle that provides unexpected shadows or flat illumination. Howe's willingness to accept obscuring shadows, even on the actor's face, means that *Kings Row* departed from classical Hollywood practice without outright violating its conventional rules.

Rainsberger considers *Kings Row* to be Howe's most melodramatic work, with particularly high contrast and dark shadows, but the film can be surprisingly high key in look in parts, often with nearly washed-out grayscale relying on natural light and extensive fill. It combines light diffusion with faster film stock and relatively little lens diffusion. Deep focus becomes a recurring formal device, though it is used in decidedly understated fashion—not like Toland's but more akin to Miller's use of deep focus in *How Green Was My Valley*. Notably, Howe's auteur style derives from the attempt to achieve other ends with motivated source lighting. The first visit Parris Mitchell (Robert Cummings) makes to Dr. Tower (Claude Rains) reveals the line Howe walks between realism and storytelling aims. The scene starts off in a typically low-key shot with directional motivated lighting as Parris walks down the hall toward Tower's office. The remaining shots, from the interior of the office, all use light from the direction of the office window, and in the initial shot a shadow obscures Tower's face. Against the naturalism of the scene, however, the cinematography suggests the gothic undercurrent of the narrative by alternating brighter and higher-key illumination of Cummings with higher contrast shots of Rains. However, rather than doing this with a sudden change in lighting setup (what would generally be called "effects lighting"), Howe keeps a similar "realist" setup and selectively frames and emphasizes within it to achieve genre effects. Among Howe's early 1940s work at Warner Bros., *Kings Row* represents perhaps the fullest subjugation of the realist impulses to the generic storytelling aims of the melodramatic script. Howe may have borrowed from his documentary inspirations in *Air Force*, but in *Kings Row* the stylized and highly planned aesthetic is removed from documentary at some distance.

James Wong Howe and Leon Shamroy were in many ways heterodox, if prestigious, cinematographers within the studio system, but Harry Stradling's work in *The Human Comedy* shows a similar balancing act between the goals of realism and affective storytelling. The scene that introduces Homer's (Mickey Rooney) workplace in the telegraph office is exemplary. The decoupage is fairly typical of a Hollywood A-picture: master shot alternated with a few shot/reverse shot patterns. The look, though, is strikingly different from conventional cinematography. For the long shots, Mickey Rooney is lit simply with strong arc lighting from above, in resistance to normal glamour lighting for stars. However, the lighting is minimal, and much of the set is underlit, including sections where the other two characters, Mr. Spangler (James Craig) and Mr. Grogan (Frank Morgan) sit. Unlike a noir, gothic, or thriller film, the medium-key treatment and underlighting do not serve as a genre cue or as effects lighting. Rather, the lighting signals a difference from more conventionalized set lighting and "nighttime" setting. The characters are occasionally lit with full modeling, but they are just as likely to be obscured or have unflattering light. Moreover, while Stradling lacked Howe's rigorous approach to source lighting, he lights the scene with a naturalism inspired by it: light sources are only partial and are identifiable as such. This approach could serve the ends of realism or achieve melodramatic effects, as in the use of selective lighting to create a halo effect around Homer and Mr. Spangler. (Manny Farber complained about the film's use of halo effects.[63]) The medium shots and medium close-ups keep a directional light on Rooney but with a side direction; the lighting conforms more closely but not perfectly to modeling conventions for figure lighting. The reverse shot of Mr. Grogan covers the character with an even starker shadow.

As with the work by Shamroy and Howe cited above, *The Human Comedy* does not outright flout classical rules or exaggerate stylistic choices. But its aesthetic "balance" does use unconventional practices. These examples show how the cinematography of the realist melodramas departed selectively but significantly from 1930s practice and even the visual norms of contemporary genres of the 1940s. They negotiated the impact of technological change and documentary influence on dramatic storytelling. The aesthetic distinction cut both ways. As historians of style have usefully demonstrated, the industrial discourse relied on a differentiation of prestige realism against the unorthodox and "immature" stylistic bravado of Gregg Toland or, later, the pseudodocumentary films of the postwar years. Even maverick cinematographers like Howe still managed to subjugate realist effects to the emotional needs of the story and the unobtrusive presentation of the diegesis. At the same time, cinematographers praised the prestige realist style because it was, for them, appropriate for the thematic and aesthetic complexity of the contemporary middle-class novel.

The Social Problem Film as Realist Melodrama

As much as adaptation was ubiquitous in classical Hollywood, studios selectively treated certain adaptations as distinctive. The adaptations of middle-class novels fall in between these two critical understandings. On the one hand, while these often best-selling novels formed the basis for a good number of Hollywood productions, they were marked as literary in a way that genre films often were not. Title credits frequently featured book covers or otherwise emphasized the status as adaptation. On the other hand, these dramas are the opposite of what Barbara Klinger has identified as a metagenre of the "celebrity text," films whose fame with popular audiences has grown over time.[64] Either the films themselves are largely forgotten or the fact that they are adaptations is occluded. The former is especially the case with sentimental dramas, whereas the latter applies to the prestige social problem films like *Gentleman's Agreement* and *The Lost Weekend*. Either way, this in-between quality of the middle-class novel adaptation is a source of the wider critical neglect of prestige films.

The adaptation of the middle-class novel was a central genre for such hybrid treatment, and films like *The Human Comedy*, *Kings Row*, and *A Tree Grows in Brooklyn* were part of a broader sensibility in 1940s Hollywood. The adaptation dramas sought to bring a different, "literary" quality to invoke the source material. At times, this source material itself was a mixture of melodramatic and realist styles. Moreover, the 1940s adaptation film frequently translated a naturalist or realist literary style into a cinematic one. Particularly as a strain of American fiction in the first part of the twentieth century presented an objectivist gaze on social relations in the American city or small town, the Hollywood melodrama sought to achieve much of this objectifying stance through its realist visual style. The historical window for this realist-melodramatic hybrid was finite, but the generic treatment helped establish the realist-style direction that prestige films would take in the postwar years.

The genre-wide view of adaptation shows the social problem films' conflicted relationship to documentary realism. As discussed in chapter 3, the 1930s documentary movement influenced the films to encode an objectifying view of the social through formal devices borrowed from documentary; these formal devices comprise the Griersonian text within these films. At the same time, the social problem dramas often differed considerably from the hyperrealist pseudodcumentary or the pulp-modernist film noirs. They created a realist style compatible with more affective moments fitting to the melodrama. Critics hostile to the prestige style would consider it safe in the negative sense, but contemporary critics were more likely to consider it mature, nuanced, or sophisticated. In any case, the filmmakers balanced different discourses of the public sphere by finding an aesthetic vocabulary part documentary and part novelistic adaptation.

The first three scenes of *Gentleman's Agreement* put into relief the dialogue between the Griersonian text and realist melodrama. The film's opening scene exemplifies the visual style and the narration of 1930s and 1940s documentary: grainy, high-contrast fast film stock, a camera pan reminiscent of nonfiction's monstration, and naturalistic blocking. However, the following scenes are more understated. Arthur Miller's cinematography achieves figure modeling and glamour lighting on Gregory Peck but does so in unorthodox ways. He downplays backlighting in favor of careful contrast with the background. Foreground figures are sometimes under-illuminated, while others are lit in flattening light (see figure 1). The house party scene at Mr. Minify's (Albert Dekker) is typical of Miller's emphasis on finely gradated gray scale. The visual style buttresses the film's attempt to depict the settings as social milieu, with realism metonymically standing in for the abstracted social class that the script only suggests.

Some problem films had a similar mix of Griersonian voice and realist melodrama. It was a house style for 20th Century–Fox's problem film cycle. Even Paramount's "grittier" *The Lost Weekend* has its own oscillation between the underworld realism and the novelistic placement of its protagonist in middle-class society. Other social problem films had a different aesthetic—for instance, *Crossfire*'s expressionistic noir style. As a group, though, the social problem films were the most prominent of the postwar prestige films. They drew from the aesthetic template developed by early 1940s melodrama adaptations, but they also fostered something new in the postwar years, a combination of documentary film and the novelistic, of a Habermasian public sphere and vernacular modernism, and of affect and the discourses of sobriety.

Epilogue

I have made the case that the postwar cycle of social problem films not only solidified an inchoate genre but also formed a type of popular sociology bridging the newly emerged field of American sociology with the public sphere aspirations of the studios. Given the growth of the state and the mass public sphere in a period of liberal consensus, Hollywood may have been structurally predisposed to adopt topical subject matter in the context of the entertainment feature. But the process by which Hollywood began to invoke a sense of the social was not a predetermined one. Producers, directors, writers, and cinematographers had to find a cinematic vocabulary to depict the social as an abstract entity. They shifted away from the iconography of the crowd and settled instead on a combination of Griersonian objectivism and affective subjectivism. In the process, Hollywood changed how it approached its prestige films. Realism became an aesthetic focal point by which a new middlebrow sensibility emerged.

The problem film's heyday was in the two decades after World War II, when studio economics and broader public sphere formations aligned. By the late 1960s, the postwar cycle had run its course. Not by happenstance was 1967's *Guess Who's Coming to Dinner* the last prestige problem film of the postwar cycle. Racial politics were shifting rapidly as Black Power and black nationalism vied with more incrementalist civil rights approaches. The liberal consensus that cut across the political party system, public policy, and elite culture had frayed by the late 1960s. The historian James Patterson speaks of a backlash against liberalism. "The reaction," he argues, "as it turned out, was lasting. It affected not only Humphrey in 1968 but also liberals generally thereafter. Polls from the mid-1960s on showed that smaller and smaller percentages of the American people had faith in their elected officials or in the ability of government to do things right."[1] The fate of the political parties in the United States was part of a larger historical crisis in the public sphere, and social thinkers coming from the Frankfurt School tradition grappled with structural political economic problems: Jürgen Habermas spoke of a legitimation crisis in the 1970s, as public sphere institutions broke down, and Claus Offe diagnosed the contradictions of the welfare state, as Keynesian economic policy, at least as postwar fiscal policy makers pursued it, faced crises in the 1970s.[2] These dovetailed with an economic crisis in the Hollywood studio system that felt particularly acute by the end of the 1960s. It would be oversimplification to see the auteur-based Hollywood Renaissance as supplanting studio-era genres across the board. However, the Hollywood auteur films did offer an alternative to the middlebrow prestige film. Throughout the early 1970s, they dominated the Academy Awards and received a disproportionate amount of attention from popular press critics.

The end of the cycle, however, did not mean the end of the social problem film. In many respects (not all), the "Oscar film" as a meta-genre charts the history of the contemporary social problem film. By the latter part of the 1970s, social problem films returned. *Coming Home* (Hal Ashby, 1978), *Kramer vs. Kramer* (Robert Benton, 1979), and *Norma Rae* (Martin Ritt, 1979) could at times be inflected by the auteur style but hewed closer to the postwar model of the prestige film. The 2000s saw a resurgence of social problem content with examples including *Traffic* (Steven Soderberg, 2000), *Million Dollar Baby* (Clint Eastwood, 2004), *Crash* (Paul Haggis, 2005), *Babel* (Alejandro González Iñárritu, 2006), and *Milk* (Gus Van Sant, 2008). Many of these films could also be classified in another genre (the biopic, for instance, or the thriller), and not all prestige films in this vein were received primarily for their topical material. Nonetheless, social problem topicality has been a frequent basis for the claims to the "seriousness" of the prestige films.

Despite the off-and-on return of social problem cycles, though, three major differences separated the problem films of the New Hollywood from the postwar examples. First, the terminology that united industry and critics around a shared genre loosened considerably. Today, popular press critics use the term "social problem film" less often than their counterparts in the two decades after World War II. Dave Kehr's usage is one example of the genre label's appearance:

> For a while social-problem films, shot in sober black and white, continued to dominate the best-film winners ("From Here to Eternity," 1953; "On the Waterfront," 1954; "Marty," 1955), but increasingly the other nominees were devoted to historical or touristic spectacle, filmed in color, wide screen and stereophonic sound—films like "The Robe" (1953), "Three Coins in the Fountain" (1954), and "Love Is a Many-Splendored Thing" (1955), which promised a sweep and scale that home viewing could not provide. . . . By the mid-'70s, the basic elements of an Oscarizable film were fixed in place: literary value, social criticism, grand spectacle and mature content, to be mixed and matched at will.[3]

Because of Kehr's knowledge of film history, his article about the Academy Awards uses the term "social problem film" and connects the postwar cycle to contemporary Hollywood. However, the film reviews themselves, in the *New York Times* or elsewhere, are rare in their description of contemporary "social problem films." The genre appears largely in a historical perspective.

Second, along with the weakened genre, the new social problem films no longer functioned as popular sociology. They could address topical issues and make political protests, but no longer did either academic or popularized sociology impact filmmakers (artists or producers) in any significant way. The shift sprang from the post-1960s fate of sociology in American public life. The sociologist Doug McAdam has argued that the discipline's turn to leftism (a development that has informed his own work) has had the effect of removing sociology from a central role in policy discussion and other applied forums. In contrast to more "pure research" in the field, he contends,

> the fate of the "social problem" tradition has been quite different. Initially, many in the soft left identified with and embraced the "relevance" of the "social problem" approach, granting it a certain intellectual/moral cachet vis-à-vis the "professional project." But this privileged position did not last long. Both [left factions], but especially the Marxists, excoriated the "problems" orientation as blind to broader structural inequities and inherently compromised by its "applied" ties to mainstream institutions and the American state.[4]

Sociology's intellectual critique of social problem sociology matched an institutional break from the field's policy orientation.

Third, the public sphere institutions that held dominance in the postwar years changed in nature. As Gordon Hutner notes, the middle-class novel declined in importance in the 1960s and 1970s.[5] The rise of television changed the stakes of the national mass medium. On the one hand, problem films would examine television itself as constitutive as a problem. *The China Syndrome* (James Bridges, 1979), for instance, uses its news reporter character (Jane Fonda) to add a critique of the mass media to its problem-film interrogation of nuclear power. On the other hand, the critique of the mass public institutions ate away at a common sense of legitimation. Jean Baudrillard writes of the "implosion of the social" in the mass media, created by the hypermediation of the mass public. "There is an obscenity in the functioning and omnipresence of opinion polls as that of publicity," he writes. "Not because they might betray the secret of an opinion, the intimacy of will . . . but because they exhibit this redundancy of the social, this sort of continual voyeurism of the group in relation to itself."[6] The midcentury social problem film had bridged a Durkheimian concept of the social with the invocation of the social as an object of policy intervention, but after the late 1960s this equation had been strained, if not outright refused.

The underlying sea changes brought an end to the particular form of the postwar problem film—its genre orientation, its affective structure, and most of all its status of popular sociology. All the same, the social problem film had an impact on the direction of Hollywood. The realist form of the prestige film gave a model by which filmmakers could adapt hyperrealist visual style into a new synthesis of verisimilar and storytelling aims. Prestige films were instrumental in the broad shift in Hollywood's middlebrow sensibility, from an outward orientation to a distinction based on critical appreciation. While modernism and auteurism overshadow these developments in film histories of American cinema, the problem film had a significant and powerful influence that has since been lost because its vision of the social body has since been eclipsed.

Notes

Introduction

1 Academy awards: *The Lost Weekend*, Best Picture, Director, Screenplay, and Actor, 1946; *The Best Years of Our Lives*, Best Picture, Director, Screenplay, Actor, Supporting Actor, Editing, and Music, 1947; *Gentleman's Agreement*, Best Picture, Director, and Supporting Actress, 1948. Other Academy Award nominations: *Snake Pit*, Best Picture, Director, Screenplay, Actress, and Music, 1949; *Pinky*, Actress, Supporting Actress, 1950.

2 Robert B. Ray, *A Certain Tendency of the Hollywood Cinema, 1930–1980* (Princeton, NJ: Princeton University Press, 1985), 144.

3 Alan Williams, "Is a Radical Genre Criticism Possible?," *Quarterly Review of Film Studies* 9, no. 2 (1984): 121–125; Rick Altman, *Film/Genre* (London: British Film Institute, 1999).

4 Charles Maland, "The Social Problem Film," in *Handbook of American Film Genres*, ed. Wes D. Gehring (New York: Greenwood Press, 1988), 307.

5 Theodor Adorno et al., *The Authoritarian Personality* (New York: Harper, 1950).

6 Michael Tratnor, *Crowd Scenes: Movies and Mass Politics* (New York: Fordham University Press, 2008); Siegfried Kracauer, *The Mass Ornament: Weimar Essays*, trans. and ed. Thomas Y. Levin (Cambridge, MA: Harvard University Press, 1995).

7 United States Department of Labor, Office of Policy Planning and Research, *The Negro Family: The Case for National Action* (Washington, DC: Government Printing Office, 1965).

8 William Ryan, *Blaming the Victim* (New York: Vintage Books, 1976); James T. Patterson, *Freedom Is Not Enough: The Moynihan Report and America's Struggle Over Black Family Life, from LBJ to Obama* (New York: Basic Books, 2010); Susan D. Greenbaum, *Blaming the Poor: The Long Shadow of the Moynihan Report on Cruel Images about Poverty* (New Brunswick, NJ: Rutgers University Press, 2015).

9 See Brian Neve, *Film and Politics in America: A Social Tradition* (London:

Routledge, 1992); and Sarah Kozloff, *The Best Years of Our Lives* (London: British Film Institute, 2011), 56.

10 Peter Roffman and Jim Purdy, *The Hollywood Social Problem Film: Madness, Despair, and Politics from the Depression to the Fifties* (Bloomington: Indiana University Press, 1981).

11 Ellen C. Scott, *Cinema Civil Rights: Regulation, Repression, and Race in the Classical Hollywood Era* (New Brunswick, NJ: Rutgers University Press, 2015).

12 Jürgen Habermas, *Toward a Rational Society: Student Protest, Science, and Politics*, trans. Jeremy J. Shapiro (Boston: Beacon Press, 1971).

13 Charles R. Acland and Haidee Wasson, eds., *Useful Cinema* (Durham, NC: Duke University Press, 2011). See also Dana Polan, *Scenes of Instruction: The Beginnings of the U.S. Study of Film* (Berkeley: University of California Press, 1997).

14 Karl Schoonover, *Brutal Vision: The Neorealist Body in Postwar Italian Cinema* (Minneapolis: University of Minnesota Press, 2012).

15 Susan Ohmer, *George Gallup in Hollywood* (New York: Columbia University Press, 2006).

16 Bill Nichols, *Representing Reality* (Bloomington: Indiana University Press, 1991), 6.

17 Mark Betz, "Art, Exploitation, Underground," in *Defining Cult Movies: The Cultural Politics of Oppositional Taste*, ed. Mark Jancovich et al. (Manchester: University of Manchester Press, 2003), 202–222; Schoonover, *Brutal Vision.*

18 Miriam Bratu Hansen, "Vernacular Modernism," in *World Cinemas, Transnational Perspectives*, ed. Nataša Ďurovičа and Kathleen Newman (New York: Routledge, 2010), 294. Her earlier formulation is in "The Mass Production of the Senses: Classical Cinema as Vernacular Modernism," *Modernism/Modernity* 6, no. 2 (1999): 59–77.

19 Some of this discussion, including the example of *The Snake Pit*, emerged from a conversation with Ellen Scott and the students in her seminar on the social problem film.

20 Thomas M. Pryor, "Dr. Litvak and the 'Pit,'" *New York Times*, November 7, 1948.

21 Leslie Fishbein, "*The Snake Pit* (1948): The Sexist Nature of Sanity," *American Quarterly* 31, no. 5 (Winter 1979): 665. I would like to thank Ellen Scott for directing me to Fishbein's essay.

22 John Hill, "The British 'Social Problem' Film: *Violent Playground* and *Sapphire*," *Screen* 26, no. 1 (1985): 35.

23 Maland, "Social Problem Film."

24 Lee Rainwater, ed., *Social Problems and Public Policy* (Chicago: Aldine, 1971); Howard Becker, *Outsiders* (New York: Free Press of Glencoe, 1963); Erving Goffman, *Asylums: Essays on the Social Situation of Mental Patients and Other Inmates* (Garden City, NY: Anchor Books, 1961).

25 Howard Becker, ed., *Social Problems: A Modern Approach* (New York: Wiley, 1966), 7.

26 Jacques Donzelot, *L'invention du social: Essai sur le déclin des passions politiques* (Paris: Fayard, 1984).

27 Gilles Deleuze, "Foreword: The Rise of the Social," in Jacques Donzelot, *The Policing of Families*, trans. Robert Hurley (New York: Pantheon Books, 1979), ix.

28 Lee Grieveson, *Policing Cinema: Movies and Censorship in Early Twentieth-Century America* (Berkeley: University of California Press, 2004).

29 William Uricchio and Roberta E. Pearson, *Reframing Culture: The Case of the Vitagraph Quality Films* (Princeton, NJ: Princeton University Press, 1993); Miriam

Bratu Hansen, "Early Cinema, Late Cinema: Transformations of the Public Sphere," *Screen* 34, no. 3 (Autumn 1993): 197–210.

30 Scott, *Cinema Civil Rights.*

31 Edward Buscombe, "Notes on Columbia Picture Company, 1926–1941," *Screen* 16, no. 3 (Autumn 1975): 18.

32 Alan Brinkley, *The End of Reform: New Deal Liberalism in Recession and War* (New York: Alfred A. Knopf, 1995).

33 Godfrey Hodgson, *America in Our Time* (New York: Vintage Books, 1976).

34 Claus Offe, *Contradictions of the Welfare State*, ed. John Keane (Cambridge, MA: MIT Press, 1985), 194.

35 Hodgson, *America in Our Time*; see also Sanford M. Jacoby, *Modern Manors: Welfare Capitalism since the New Deal* (Princeton, NJ: Princeton University Press, 1997).

36 See Frank Krutnik et al., eds., *"Un-American" Hollywood: Politics and Film in the Blacklist Era* (New Brunswick, NJ: Rutgers University Press, 2007); Tony Williams, "1947: Movies and the Enemy Within," in *American Cinema of the 1940s: Themes and Variations*, ed. Wheeler Winston Dixon (New Brunswick, NJ: Rutgers University Press, 2006); and Jon Lewis, "'We Do Not Ask You to Condone This': How the Blacklist Saved Hollywood," *Cinema Journal* 39, no. 2 (Winter 2000): 3–30.

37 Langdon-Teclaw, "The Progressive Producer in the Studio System," in Krutnik et al., *"Un-American" Hollywood*, 166.

38 Robert Griffith, "Forging America's Postwar Order: Domestic Politics and Political Economy in the Age of Truman," in *The Truman Presidency*, ed. Michael J. Lacey (Cambridge: Cambridge University Press, 1989), 57–88.

39 Thom Andersen, "Red Hollywood," in *Literature and the Visual Arts in Contemporary Society*, ed. Suzanne Ferguson and Barbara Groseclose (Columbus: Ohio State University Press, 1985), 141–196. See also Charles J. Maland, "*Film Gris:* Crime, Critique, and Cold War Culture in 1951," *Film Criticism* 23 (Spring 2002): 1–26.

40 See Neve, *Film and Politics in America*; and Langdon-Teclaw, "Progressive Producer," 152–168.

41 Thomas Schatz, *Boom and Bust: The American Cinema in the 1940s,* vol. 6 of *History of the American Cinema*, ed. Charles Harpole (Berkeley: University of California Press, 1997), 383; Jennifer Langdon, *Caught in the Crossfire: Adrian Scott and the Politics of Americanism in 1940s Hollywood* (New York: Columbia University Press, 2008).

42 Roffman and Purdy, *Hollywood Social Problem Film*; Russell Campbell, "The Ideology of the Social Consciousness Movie: Three Films of Darryl F. Zanuck," *Quarterly Review of Film Studies* 3, no. 1 (1978): 49–71.

43 These approaches sometimes resist the term "popular science" to begin with. See, for example, James A. Secord, "Knowledge in Transit," *Isis* 95 (2004): 654–672.

44 Peter Broks, *Understanding Popular Science* (Maidenhead, England: Open University Press, 2006); Constance Penley, *NASA/TREK: Popular Science and Sex in America* (London: Verso, 1997).

45 See Marcel Lafollette, *Science on American Television: A History* (Chicago: University of Chicago Press, 2013), 6.

46 Bruce V. Lewenstein, "Popularization," in *Reader's Guide to the History of Science*, ed. Arne Hessenbruch (London: Fitzroy Dearborn, 2000), 586–587. See also Richard Whitley, "Knowledge Producers and Knowledge Acquirers," in *Expository*

Science: Forms and Functions of Popularisation, ed. Terry Shinn and Richard Whitley (Dordrecht: D. Reidel, 1985), 3–29.

47 Roger Cooter and Stephen Pumfrey, "Separate Spheres and Public Places: Reflections on the History of Science Popularization and Science in Popular Culture," *History of Science* 32 (September 1994): 249.

48 The first graduate program in sociology was established in 1892, and the first part of the twentieth century saw the steady development of the discipline. Chapter 2 discusses the history of American sociology in more detail.

49 John Guillory, "The Ordeal of Middlebrow Culture," *Transition* 67 (1995): 87.

50 Andrew Sarris, *The American Cinema: Directors and Directions, 1929–1968* (New York: Simon & Schuster, 1973), 260.

51 Gordon Hutner, *What America Read: Taste, Class, and the Novel, 1920–1960* (Chapel Hill: University of North Carolina Press, 2009), 7.

52 Russell Lynes, "Highbrow, Lowbrow, Middlebrow," *Harper's Magazine*, December 1, 1949; Dwight Macdonald, "Masscult & Midcult," *Partisan Review* 27, no. 2 (1960): 203–233.

53 C. Wright Mills, *White Collar: The American Middle Classes* (New York: Oxford University Press, 1956).

54 For the most straightforward discussion of Bourdieu's notion of fields, see Pierre Bourdieu and Loïc Wacquant, *An Invitation to Reflexive Sociology* (Chicago: University of Chicago Press, 1992). For an applied field analysis, see Pierre Bourdieu, *State Nobility: Elite Schools in the Field of Power* (Palo Alto, CA: Stanford University Press, 1998).

55 Pierre Bourdieu, *The Rules of Art: Genesis and Structure of the Literary Field*, trans. Susan Emanuel (Stanford, CA: Stanford University Press, 1996); Pierre Bourdieu, *In Other Words: Essays Toward a Reflexive Sociology* (Palo Alto, CA: Stanford University Press, 1990).

56 Hodgson, *America in Our Time*; Offe, *Contradictions of the Welfare State*.

57 Hutner, *What America Read*.

Chapter 1 Two Modes of Prestige Film

1 David Thomson, *A Biographical Dictionary of Film*, 3rd ed. (New York: Alfred A. Knopf, 1994), 832.

2 Brian Taves, "The B Film: Hollywood's Other Half," in *Grand Design: Hollywood as a Modern Business Enterprise, 1930–1939*, ed. Tino Balio (Berkeley: University of California Press, 1993), 332.

3 Erik Barnouw, *Tube of Plenty: The Evolution of American Television*, 2nd rev. ed. (New York: Oxford University Press, 1990), 161.

4 Balio, *Grand Design*, 179–180.

5 Michael Conant, *Antitrust in the Motion Picture Industry: Economic and Legal Analysis* (Berkeley: University of California Press, 1960), 107–112.

6 Taves, "B Film," 313.

7 Robert W. Chambers, "The Double Feature as a Sales Problem," *Harvard Business Review* 16, no. 4 (Winter 1938): 226–236. *Variety* complained of a "vicious circle"

keeping double features entrenched as industry practice. Mike Wear, "Growth of Double Bills," *Variety*, January 3, 1937, 12.

8 Thomas Schatz, *Boom and Bust: The American Cinema in the 1940s*, vol. 6 of *History of the American Cinema*, ed. Charles Harpole (Berkeley: University of California Press, 1997), 152.

9 "Dualers' Dearth of B's in 1950," *Variety*, November 16, 1949, 7; "Certain Secondary Houses in a Spot Because of Dearth of A's," *Variety*, June 29, 1949, 6.

10 Schatz, *Boom and Bust*, 172, 331.

11 Ibid., 330–331; "Top-Drawer Industry Leaders Accept Staggering Production Costs but Fear No B.O. Dip," *Variety*, January 8, 1947, 5. In *Boom and Bust*, Schatz points to the 1947 loss of the British exhibition market as a major factor in studio planning for 1948.

12 Aubrey Solomon, *Twentieth Century–Fox: A Corporate and Financial History* (Metuchen, NJ: Scarecrow Press, 1988), 66. All Fox production costs and domestic receipts cited are from ibid., 242–244.

13 Schatz, *Boom and Bust*, 332.

14 The correspondence held in the Stanley Kramer Collection is a good sample of the admiration, organized and spontaneous, that these members of the cultural elite afforded Kramer for his problem films. Stanley Kramer Collection, Charles E. Young Library Special Collections, University of California, Los Angeles.

15 Betty Lasky, *RKO: The Biggest Little Major of Them All* (Englewood Cliffs, NJ: Prentice-Hall, 1984), 196–197.

16 "When's a 'B' film Not a 'B'?," *Variety*, February 4, 1948, 7.

17 "Hughes Wants No 'Messages' in Pix; viz. *Green Hair*," *Variety*, August 4, 1948, 1.

18 Darryl Zanuck, memo, February 1, 1949, Box 2420.2, 20th Century–Fox Script Archive, Special Collections for Cinema and Television, Doheny Library, University of Southern California.

19 Schatz, *Boom and Bust*, 178–188.

20 Thom Andersen, "Red Hollywood," in *Literature and the Visual Arts in Contemporary Society*, ed. Suzanne Ferguson and Barbara Groseclose (Columbus: Ohio State University Press, 1985), 141–196; Charles J. Maland, "*Film Gris:* Crime, Critique, and Cold War Culture in 1951," *Film Criticism* 23 (Spring 2002): 1–26.

21 "FC's Fee Gamble on *Boundaries* Pays Off Solidly," *Variety*, November 23, 1949, 3; "*Boundaries, Wanted* Cause Film Classics to Revise Budget Ideas," *Variety*, July 27, 1949, 9.

22 Dennis Bingham, "'I Do Want to Live!': Female Voices, Male Discourse, and Hollywood Biopics," *Cinema Journal* 38, no. 3 (1999): 8.

23 C. Wright Mills, *White Collar: The American Middle Classes* (New York: Oxford University Press, 1956), 239.

24 Pierre Bourdieu, with Luc Boltanski et al., *Photography: A Middle-brow Art* (Stanford, CA: Stanford University Press, 1990), 95–96.

25 David Bordwell, *On the History of Film Style* (Cambridge, MA: Harvard University Press, 1997), 44.

26 "A Democratic Art," *Nation*, August 28, 1913, 193. I am indebted to Lawrence Levine for the pointer. Lawrence Levine, *Highbrow/Lowbrow: The Emergence of Cultural Hierarchy in America* (Cambridge, MA: Harvard University Press, 1994), 231.

27 Richard Watts Jr., "A Dying Art Offers a Masterpiece," *New York Herald Tribune*, March 31, 1929.

28 For histories of how cultural legitimization fed into the rise of academic film studies, see Dana Polan, *Scenes of Instruction: The Beginnings of the U.S. Study of Film* (Berkeley: University of California Press, 1997); and Lee Grieveson and Haidee Wasson, eds., *Inventing Film Studies* (Durham, NC: Duke University Press, 2008).
29 Haidee Wasson, *Museum Movies: The Museum of Modern Art and the Birth of Art Cinema* (Berkeley: University of California Press, 2005); Raymond J. Haberski Jr., *It's Only a Movie! Films and Critics in American Culture* (Lexington: University of Kentucky Press, 2001).
30 Pierre Bourdieu, *Distinction: A Social Critique of the Judgment of Taste*, trans. Richard Nice (Cambridge, MA: Harvard University Press, 1984), 47.
31 Lauren Rabinowitz, "The American Avant-Garde," in Schatz, *Boom and Bust*, 459.
32 Joan Shelley Rubin, *The Making of Middlebrow Culture* (Chapel Hill: University of North Carolina Press, 1992), 295.
33 Marianne Conroy, "'No Sin in Lookin' Prosperous': Gender, Race, and the Class Formations of Middlebrow Taste in *Imitation of Life*," in *The Hidden Formation: Cinema and the Question of Class*, ed. Rick Berg and David James (Minneapolis: University of Minnesota Press, 1996), 119.
34 Janice Radway, *A Feeling for Books: The Book-of-the-Month Club, Literary Taste, and Middle-Class Desire* (Chapel Hill: University of North Carolina Press, 1997); Conroy, "No Sin in Lookin' Prosperous"; Mills, *White Collar.*
35 Bourdieu, *Distinction*, 311.
36 Ibid., 359.
37 Ibid., 362.
38 Ibid., 351.
39 Robert B. Ray, *A Certain Tendency of the Hollywood Cinema, 1930–1980* (Princeton, NJ: Princeton University Press, 1985), 141.
40 Pierre Bourdieu, *Practical Reason: On the Theory of Action* (Stanford, CA: Stanford University Press, 1998), 9.
41 Lea Jacobs, "The B Film and Problem of Cultural Distinction," *Screen* 33, no. 1 (1992): 1–13.
42 Barbara Wilinksy, *Sure Seaters: The Emergence of Art House Cinema* (Minneapolis: University of Minnesota Press, 2001), 38.
43 Review of *Crossfire*, *Newsweek*, July 28, 1947, 84.
44 Robert Hatch, review of *The Snake Pit*, *New Republic*, November 8, 1948, 28–29.
45 Review of *The Boy with Green Hair*, *Time*, January 10, 1949, 84.
46 Jerry Wald, "1946 in Review," *Variety*, January 8, 1947, 5.
47 John McCarten, review of *All The King's Men*, *New Yorker*, November 12, 1949, 101.
48 Review of *Crossfire* and *Gentleman's Agreement*, *Saturday Review of Literature*, December 6, 1947, 69–70.
49 Review of *The Snake Pit*, *Saturday Review of Literature*, November 27, 1948, 28–30.
50 Bosley Crowther, review of *The Snake Pit*, *New York Times*, November 5, 1948.
51 Review of *Pinky*, *Time*, October 9, 1945, 96; Review of *The Best Years of Our Lives*, *Time*, November 25, 1946, 103.
52 Review of *The Best Years of Our Lives*, *Newsweek*, November 25, 1946, 104; Review of *Lost Boundaries*, *Newsweek*, July 4, 1949, 72; Review of *Home of the Brave*, *Newsweek*, May 16, 1949, 86.
53 Review of *The Best Years of Our Lives*, *Commonweal*, December 13, 1946, 230.
54 Review of *The Lawless*, *Time*, July 3, 1950, 76.

55 Bosley Crowther, review of *The Lost Weekend*, *New York Times*, December 3, 1945.
56 Robert Warshow, "The Movie Camera and the American," in *The Immediate Experience: Movies, Comics, Theatre & Other Aspects of Popular Culture*, intro. Lionel Trilling (New York: Atheneum, 1975), 180.
57 Bosley Crowther, review of *Gentleman's Agreement*, *New York Times*, November 12, 1947; Bosley Crowther, review of *Pinky*, *New York Times*, September 30, 1949.
58 Frank Eugene Beaver, *Bosley Crowther: Social Critic of the Film, 1940–1967* (New York: Arno Press, 1974), 36.
59 See, for example, review of *Gentleman's Agreement*, *Life*, December 1, 1947, 82.
60 Philip Dunne, memo to Darryl Zanuck, April 19, 1948, Philip Dunne Collection, Doheny Library, University of Southern California.
61 Darryl Zanuck, memo, February 1, 1949, Box 2420.2, 20th Century–Fox script archive.
62 Darryl Zanuck, story conference memo, December 2, 1946, Box 2364.2, 20th Century–Fox script archive. Elsewhere, Zanuck ponders *Night and the City*'s Academy Award chances in his discussion of *No Way Out*'s approach. Memo on final script, June 7, 1949, Box 2420.9, 20th Century–Fox script archive.
63 1949 advertising budget, 20th Century–Fox, Charles Schlaifer Collection, Margaret Herrick Library, Beverly Hills, CA.
64 George Thomas, internal UA publicity memo, Collection 161, Box 18, Stanley Kramer Collection.
65 For instance, see Jürgen Habermas, *Legitimation Crisis* (Boston: Beacon Press, 1972).

Chapter 2 Hollywood as Popular Sociology

1 Review of *Gentleman's Agreement*, *New Yorker*, November 15, 1947, 117; Bosley Crowther, review of *Gentleman's Agreement*, *New York Times*, November 12, 1947; Review of *Crossfire*, *Commonweal*, August 1, 1947, 386.
2 Much of this discussion draws on Craig Calhoun, ed., *Sociology in America: A History* (Chicago: University of Chicago Press, 2007). See especially Calhoun's introduction.
3 Jacob Riis, *How the Other Half Lives: Studies among the Tenements of New York* (1901; repr., New York: Dover, 1971); Jane Addams, *Hull-House Maps and Papers: A Presentation of Nationalities and Wages in a Congested District of Chicago* (New York: T. Crowell, 1895). Of these Progressive surveys, Craig Calhoun remarks, "Surveys did not connote systematic sampling but rather a rationally organized overview, not unlike the work of a land surveyor. . . . Surveys were often designed as much to prove the need for action to political and other powers as to gain greater precision in scientific understanding." Calhoun, *Sociology in America*, 12.
4 Lee Grieveson, *Policing Cinema: Movies and Censorship in Early Twentieth-Century America* (Berkeley: University of California Press, 2004), 67.
5 Kay Sloan, "A Cinema in Search of Itself: Ideology of the Social Problem Film during the Silent Era," *Cineaste* 14, no. 2 (1985): 34.
6 There is debate among sociologists and historians of sociology over what exactly characterized the Chicago school. Andrew Abbott remarks, "The Chicago school

was one thing to those who participated in it, another thing to its immediate inheritors at Chicago, and various other things to later writers." Andrew Abbott, *Department and Discipline: Chicago Sociology at One Hundred* (Chicago: University of Chicago Press, 1999), 5. Such caveats are useful, but for the purposes here, even the interpretation that later sociologists had of the Chicago school reinforced a broader discursive shift into how "society" was conceived in midcentury America.

7 Harvey Warren Zorbaugh, *Gold Coast and the Slum: A Sociological Study of Chicago's Near North Side* (Chicago: University of Chicago Press, 1929).

8 Robert E. Park, Ernest W. Burgess, and Roderick D. McKenzie, *The City*, intro. Morris Janowitz (Chicago: University of Chicago Press, 1967); Robert E. Park, "The Urban Community as a Spatial Pattern and a Moral Order," in *On Social Control and Collective Behavior*, ed. and intro. Ralph H. Turner (Chicago: University of Chicago Press, 1967), 55–68.

9 Harvey W. Zorbaugh, "The Shadow of the Skyscraper," in *The Social Fabric of the Metropolis*, ed. James F. Short Jr. (Chicago: University of Chicago Press, 1971), 9.

10 Richard Maltby, "Why Boys Go Wrong: Gangsters, Hoodlums, and the Natural History of Delinquent Careers," in *Mob Culture: Hidden Histories of the American Gangster Film*, ed. Lee Grieveson, Esther Sonnet, and Peter Stanfield (New Brunswick, NJ: Rutgers University Press, 2005), 47.

11 Production Code Administration, letter from James Wingate to Joseph Breen, August 6, 1937, Special Collections, Margaret Herrick Library, Beverly Hills, CA.

12 Production Code Administration, telegram from Joseph Breen to Paul Koretz, October 28, 1937, Special Collections, Margaret Herrick Library, Beverly Hills, CA.

13 Calhoun, "Introduction," in *Sociology in America*, 34.

14 Stephen Park Turner and Jonathan H. Turner, *The Impossible Science: An Institutional Analysis of American Sociology* (Newbury Park, CA: Sage, 1990), 90–92.

15 Ibid., 123.

16 Emile Durkheim, *Suicide: A Study in Sociology*, trans. John A. Spaulding and George Simpson, ed. George Simpson (New York: Free Press, 1951), 46.

17 Ibid.

18 Talcott Parsons, *The Social System* (Glencoe, IL: Free Press, 1951); Robert Merton, "Paradigm for Functional Analysis in Sociology," in *On Social Structure and Science* (Chicago: University of Chicago Press, 1996), 65–86, esp. 70–71.

19 Talcott Parsons, *On Institutions and Social Evolution: Selected Writings*, ed. and intro. Leon H. Mayhew (Chicago: University of Chicago Press, 1982).

20 Emile Durkheim, *Division of Labor in Society*, trans. W. D. Halls (New York: Free Press, 1997). Lest one jumps to the conclusion that Durkheim is trying to make a natural science out of social science, in the manner of the positivists or Social Darwinists, it should be noted that Durkheim pointed out ways in which social solidarity differed from the organic division of labor. The analogy simply provides a model to think about functions of interdependence. See Anthony Giddens, *Capitalism and Modern Social Theory: An Analysis of the Writings of Marx, Durkheim, and Max Weber* (Cambridge: Cambridge University Press, 1973), for a useful explication of Durkheim's work, including its relation to Marx.

21 Ferdinand Tönnies, *Community and Society* (1887; repr., East Lansing: Michigan State University Press, 1957).

22 Parsons, *On Institutions and Social Evolution*.

23 Andrew Abbott and James T. Sparrow make this case in "Hot War, Cold War: The

Structures of Sociological Action, 1940–1955," in Calhoun, *Sociology in America*, 308. See also Dennis Smith, *The Chicago School: A Liberal Critique of Capitalism* (New York: St. Martin's Press, 1988), 145.

24 Durkheim, *Suicide.*

25 Durkheim, *Division of Labor in Society.*

26 Michael Burawoy, "Introduction: The Resurgence of Marxism in American Sociology," *American Journal of Sociology* 88 (1988): S1–S30. For an account of the post-1960s left critique of functionalism, see Craig Calhoun and Jonathan VanAntwerpen, "Orthodoxy, Heterodoxy, and Hierarchy: 'Mainstream' Sociology and Its Challengers," in Calhoun, *Sociology in America*, 367–410.

27 Howard W. Odum, *American Sociology: The Story of Sociology in the United States through 1950* (New York: Longmans, Green, 1951), 281.

28 Edwin Sutherland, interview with Colin Goff and Gilbert Geis, "Edwin H. Sutherland: The Development of Differential Association Theory," in *The Origins of American Criminology*, ed. Francis T. Cullen et al., vol. 16 of *Advances in Criminological Theory* (New Brunswick, NJ: Transaction Publishers, 2011), 45.

29 Frank Tannenbaum, *Crime and the Community* (Boston: Ginn, 1938).

30 James F. Short Jr., with Lorine A. Hughes, "Criminology, Criminologists, and the Sociological Enterprise," in Calhoun, *Sociology in America*, 605–638.

31 Charles Maland, "The Social Problem Film," in *Handbook of American Film Genres*, ed. Wes D. Gehring (New York: Greenwood Press, 1988), 305–329.

32 Thomas Doherty, *Pre-Code Hollywood: Sex, Immorality, and Insurrection in American Cinema; 1930–1934* (New York: Columbia University Press, 1999), 50.

33 Abbott and Sparrow, "Hot War, Cold War," 301–302.

34 Gunnar Myrdal, with Richard Sterner and Arnold Rose, *An American Dilemma: The Negro Problem and Modern Democracy* (New York: Harper and Row, 1944); Theodor Adorno et al., *The Authoritarian Personality* (New York: Harper, 1950); Samuel A. Stouffer et al., *The American Soldier: Adjustment during Army Life* (Princeton, NJ: Princeton University Press, 1949).

35 This history comes from Martin Jay, *The Dialectical Imagination: A History of the Frankfurt School and the Institute of Social Research 1923–1950* (Boston: Little, Brown, 1973). *Studies in Prejudice* remained unpublished but informed later Institute works, including *The Authoritarian Personality.*

36 Jay, *Dialectical Imagination*, 221–222.

37 Jürgen Habermas, *Structural Transformation of the Public Sphere: An Inquiry into a Category of Bourgeois Society*, trans. Thomas Burger (Cambridge, MA: MIT Press, 1989).

38 Ellen C. Scott, *Cinema Civil Rights: Regulation, Repression, and Race in the Classical Hollywood Era* (New Brunswick, NJ: Rutgers University Press, 2015).

39 David Southern, *Gunnar Myrdal and Black-White Relations: The Use and Abuse of "An American Dilemma," 1944–1969* (Baton Rouge: Louisiana State University Press, 1987).

40 Howard Winant, "The Dark Side of the Force: One Hundred Years of the Sociology of Race," in Calhoun, *Sociology in America*, 535–571.

41 Ibid., 561.

42 Myrdal, *American Dilemma*, 1050.

43 Fred H. Matthews, *Quest for an American Sociology: Robert E. Park and the Chicago School* (Montreal: McGill-Queens University Press, 1977), 188. For further analysis

of the diverging views of Park and Myrdal, see R. Fred Wacker, "An American Dilemma: The Racial Theories of Robert E. Park and Gunnar Myrdal," *Phylon* 37, no. 2 (Summer 1976): 117–125.

44 Talcott Parsons, "Introduction: Why 'Freedom Now,' Not Yesterday?," in *The Negro American*, ed. Talcott Parsons and Kenneth B. Clark (Boston: Beacon Press, 1967), xxvii.

45 Scott, *Cinema Civil Rights*, 120.

46 Philip Dunne, "Approach to Racism," *New York Times*, May 1, 1949.

47 Michael Abel, memo to Darryl Zanuck, conference, *Pinky*, November 17, 1948, Box 2391.12, 20th Century–Fox Special Collection, Special Collections for Cinema and Television, Doheny Library, University of Southern California.

48 Myrdal, *American Dilemma*, 969.

49 Darryl Zanuck, story conference memo, *Pinky*, November 17, 1948, Box 2391.11, 20th Century–Fox Special Collection.

50 Myrdal, *American Dilemma*, 688.

51 Ibid., esp. chs. 1 and 45.

52 Noel Polk, "Man in the Middle: Faulkner and the Southern White Moderate," in *Children of the Dark House: Text and Context in Faulkner* (Jackson: University Press of Mississippi, 1996), 219–241.

53 Gordon Hutner, *What America Read: Taste, Class, and the Novel, 1920–1960* (Chapel Hill: University of North Carolina Press, 2009), 245.

54 Descriptions are based on the screenplay transcription of these trailers. MGM Script Collection, Box 5300, Doheny Library, University of Southern California.

55 See, for instance, Ellen Scott's reading of Zanuck's race problem films as brutalizing spectacles in *Cinema Civil Rights*; or Michele Wallace, "Race, Genre, and Psychoanalysis in Forties Film: *Home of the Brave* and *The Quiet One*," in *Black American Cinema*, ed. Manthia Diawara (New York: Routledge, 1993), 257–271.

56 See the essays collected in Lucy Fischer, ed., *Imitation of Life* (New Brunswick NJ: Rutgers University Press, 1991).

57 Kenneth B. Clark and Mamie P. Clark, "Racial Identification and Preference among Negro Children," in *Readings in Social Psychology*, ed. Theodore M. Newcomb and Eugene L. Hartley (New York: Holt, Reinhart, and Winston, 1947), 169–178. Credit to Sasha Torres for initially pointing me to the connection between *Imitation of Life* and the Clark study.

58 *Brown v. Board of Education of Topeka,* 347 U.S. 483 (1954), footnote 11.

59 Review of *The Lost Weekend*, *Variety*, August 15, 1945.

60 Crowther, review of *Gentleman's Agreement*.

61 Siegfried Kracauer, "Those Movies with a Message," *Harper's*, June 1948, 568.

62 Robert Warshow, "The Anatomy of Falsehood," in *The Immediate Experience: Movies, Comics, Theatre and Other Aspects of Popular Culture*, intro. Lionel Trilling (New York: Atheneum, 1975), 158.

63 Russell Campbell, "The Ideology of the Social Consciousness Movie: Three Films of Darryl F. Zanuck," *Quarterly Review of Film Studies* 3, no. 1 (1978): 49–71; Peter Roffman and Jim Purdy, *The Hollywood Social Problem Film: Madness, Despair, and Politics from the Depression to the Fifties* (Bloomington: Indiana University Press, 1981); Brian Neve, *Film and Politics in America: A Social Tradition* (London: Routledge, 1992).

64 C. Wright Mills, *The Power Elite* (New York: Oxford University Press, 1956). See

also his critique of grand theory and abstract empiricism in *The Sociological Imagination* (New York: Oxford University Press, 1959).

65 Anthony M. Platt, *The Child Savers: The Invention of Delinquency* (Chicago: University of Chicago Press, 1969).

Chapter 3 Hollywood and the Public Sphere

1 For this formulation of Capra's signature genre, see Charles Maland, "Frank Capra at Columbia: Necessity and Invention," in *Columbia Pictures: Portrait of a Studio*, ed. Bernard Dick (Lexington: University of Kentucky Press, 1992), 71–88.

2 Jürgen Habermas, *Structural Transformation of the Public Sphere: An Inquiry into a Category of Bourgeois Society*, trans. Thomas Burger (Cambridge, MA: MIT Press, 1989).

3 See, for instance, Nancy Fraser, "Rethinking the Public Sphere," in *The Phantom Public Sphere*, ed. Bruce Robbins (Minneapolis: University of Minnesota Press, 1993), 6.

4 Walter Lippmann, *The Phantom Public* (New York: Harcourt, Brace, 1925); C. Wright Mills, *The Power Elite* (New York: Oxford University Press, 1956), especially ch. 13, "The Mass Society."

5 Habermas, *Structural Transformation*; Mills, *Power Elite*; Walter Lippmann, *The Phantom Public* (New York: Harcourt, Brace, 1925).

6 See Claus Offe, *Contradictions of the Welfare State*, ed. John Keane (Cambridge, MA: MIT Press, 1985), 194.

7 Stuart Ewen, *PR! A Social History of Spin* (New York: Basic Books, 1996).

8 Rex Harlow, "A Timeline of Public Relations Development," *Public Relations Review* 6 (Fall 1980): 3–13; Scott M. Cutlip, *The Unseen Power: Public Relations, a History* (Hillsdale, NJ: L. Erlbaum, 1994), 529.

9 The historian Susan Herbst notes that polling became professionalized by the mid-1930s, but that difficulties in sampling meant a cautious and gradual adoption of scientific polling for political legitimation. Susan Herbst, *Numbered Voices: How Opinion Polling Has Shaped American Politics* (Chicago: University of Chicago Press, 1993), 83–110.

10 Sarah E. Igo, *The Averaged American: Surveys, Citizens, and the Making of a Mass Public* (Cambridge, MA: Harvard University Press, 2007), 5.

11 Charles Wolfe, "Authors, Audiences, and Endings," in *Meet John Doe*, ed. Charles Wolfe (New Brunswick, NJ: Rutgers University Press, 1989), 27.

12 For a broader reading of crowds in Hollywood cinema, see Michael Tratner, *Crowd Scenes: Movies and Mass Politics* (New York: Fordham University Press, 2008).

13 V. Penelope Pelizzon and Nancy M. West, *Tabloid, Inc.: Crimes, Newspapers, Narratives* (Columbus: Ohio State University Press, 2010).

14 Thanks to Chris Robé for suggesting I look more closely at this film in connection to the public sphere.

15 Leonard Ray Teel, *The Public Press, 1900–1945: The History of American Journalism* (Westport, CT: Praeger, 2006). See also Richard Ohmann, *Selling Culture: Magazines, Markets, and Class at the Turn of the Century* (London: Verso, 1996), for

an argument for the centrality of the national magazine in American middle-class identity.

16 Pelizzon and West, *Tabloid Inc.*, 89.

17 Matthew Erlich, *Journalism in the Movies* (Urbana: University of Illinois Press, 2004).

18 John Grierson, *Grierson on Documentary*, ed. Forsyth Hardy (New York: Praeger, 1971), 207. For more on Grierson's intellectual underpinnings, see Paul Swann, *The British Documentary Film Movement, 1926–1946* (Cambridge: Cambridge University Press, 1989).

19 John Grierson, "First Principles of Documentary," in Hardy, *Grierson on Documentary*, 145–156.

20 Brian Winston, *Claiming the Real: The Griersonian Documentary and Its Legitimations* (London: British Film Institute, 1995); Jonathan Kahana, *Intelligence Work: The Politics of American Documentary* (New York: Columbia University Press, 2008); Joshua Malitsky, *Post-Revolution Nonfiction Film: Building the Soviet and Cuban Nations* (Bloomington: Indiana University Press, 2013).

21 Erik Barnouw, *Documentary: A History of the Nonfiction Film* (New York: Oxford University Press, 1974); Jack Ellis and Betsy McLane, *A New History of Documentary Film* (New York: Continuum Books, 2005).

22 Barnouw, *Documentary*, 121–122.

23 John Grierson, "Pictures without Theaters," *Nation*, January 13, 1945, 37–39; "America's Most Vital Medium: The Documentary Film," *Library Journal* (May 1, 1946): 630–634.

24 For instance, Joris Ivens, "Documentary Films," *American Cinematographer*, July 1942, 298–299, 332; James Wong Howe, "Documentary and Hollywood," *American Cinematographer*, January 1944, 10, 32.

25 As an index of this change, see Manny Farber, "Memorandum for Hollywood," *New Republic*, October 5, 1942, 414–415.

26 Thomas Doherty, "Documenting the 1940s," in Thomas Schatz, *Boom and Bust: The American Cinema in the 1940s* (Berkeley: University of California Press, 1997), 397–421.

27 Jesse Lerner, "Introduction: Troubling Taxonomies," in *F Is for Phony: Fake Documentary and Truth's Undoing*, ed. Alexandra Juhasz and Jesse Lerner (Minneapolis: University of Minnesota Press, 2006), 19.

28 Robert B. Ray, *A Certain Tendency of the Hollywood Cinema, 1930–1980* (Princeton, NJ: Princeton University Press, 1985); Dana Polan, *Power and Paranoia: History, Narrative, and the American Cinema, 1940–1950* (New York: Columbia University Press, 1986).

29 André Gaudreault, "Narration and Monstration in the Cinema," trans. Paul Attallah and Tom Gunning, *Journal of Film and Video* 39, no. 2 (1987): 29–36; Tom Gunning, *D. W. Griffith and the Origins of American Narrative Film: The Early Years at Biograph* (Urbana: University of Illinois Press, 1991).

30 David Bordwell, "The Classical Hollywood Style: 1917–1960," in David Bordwell, Janet Staiger, and Kristin Thompson, *The Classical Hollywood Cinema: Film Style and Mode of Production to 1960* (New York: Columbia University Press), 79.

31 Lee Grieveson, *Policing Cinema: Movies and Censorship in Early Twentieth-Century America* (Berkeley: University of California Press, 2004).

32 Habermas, *Structural Transformation*, 242–243.

33 Paul F. Lazersfeld and Herbert Menzel, "Mass Media and Personal Influence," in *The Science of Human Communication*, ed. Wilbur Schramm (New York: Basic Books, 1963), 95.

34 L. E. Raths and F. N. Trigger, "Public Opinion and *Crossfire*," *Journal of Educational Sociology* 21 (February 1948): 345–368; Irwin C. Rosen, "Effect of the Motion Picture 'Gentleman's Agreement' on Attitudes toward Jews," *Journal of Psychology* 26 (October 1948): 525–536; Mildred J. Wiese and Stewart G. Colt, "A Study of Children's Attitudes and the Influence of a Commercial Motion Picture," *Journal of Psychology* 21 (January 1946): 151–171; Russell Middleton, "Ethnic Prejudice and Susceptibility to Persuasion," *American Sociological Review* 25, no. 5 (October 1960): 679–686.

35 J. E. Hulett Jr., "Estimating the Net Effect of a Commercial Motion Picture upon the Trend of Local Public Opinion," *American Sociological Review* 14 (August 1949): 263.

36 Review of *Pinky*, *Time*, October 9, 1945, 96.

37 Review of *The Lost Weekend*, *Newsweek*, December 10, 1945, 112; Review of *The Best Years of Our Lives*, *Life*, December 16, 1946, 71.

38 *Saturday Review of Literature*, December 6, 1947.

39 Review of *The Snake Pit*, *Life*, November 13, 1948.

40 Thomas M. Pryor, "Dr. Litvak and the 'Pit,'" *New York Times*, November 7, 1948.

41 Philip Dunne, "Approach to Racism: Scenarist of 'Pinky' Explains How Film Will Treat Subject of Negro Prejudice," *New York Times*, May 1, 1949.

42 James Agee, review of *Crossfire*, *Nation*, August 2, 1947, 129.

43 Michael Abel, memo to Darryl Zanuck, conference, *Pinky*, November 17, 1948, Box 2391.12, 20th Century–Fox Special Collection. Discussed in chapter 2.

44 Report on *Gentleman's Agreement* campaign, November 10, 1947, Charles Schlaifer Collection, Margaret Herrick Library, Beverly Hills, CA. See also a letter from Darryl Zanuck to Laura Hobson dated November 15, 1947, in the same collection.

45 Charles Schlaifer, Memo to Spiras Skouros, November 2[illegible], 1947, Charles Schlaifer Collection.

46 See, for instance, C. Wright Mills, "Mass Media and Public Opinion," in *Power, Politics, and People; The Collected Essays of C. Wright Mills*, ed. and intro. Irving Louis Horowitz (New York: Oxford University Press, 1963), 577–599.

Chapter 4 A Genre Out of Cycles

1 Peter Roffman and Jim Purdy, *The Hollywood Social Problem Film: Madness, Despair, and Politics from the Depression to the Fifties* (Bloomington: Indiana University Press, 1981).

2 Kay Sloan, *The Loud Silents: Origins of the Social Problem Film* (Urbana: University of Illinois Press, 1988).

3 Sarah Kozloff, "The Social-Problem Film," in *An Introduction to Film Genres*, ed. Lester Friedman et al. (New York: W. W. Norton, 2013), 447.

4 Rick Altman, "A Semantic/Syntactic Approach to Film Genre," in *Film Genre Reader II*, ed. Barry Keith Grant (Austin: University of Texas Press, 1995), 27.

5 Steve Neale, "Questions of Genre," in Grant, *Film Genre Reader II*, 166.

6 Steve Neale, *Genre and Hollywood* (London: Routledge, 2000), 9.
7 Amanda Ann Klein, *American Film Cycles: Reframing Genres, Screening Social Problems, and Defining Subcultures* (Austin: University of Texas Press, 2011), 6.
8 See Sloan, *Loud Silents.*
9 Lee Grieveson, *Policing Cinema: Movies and Censorship in Early Twentieth-Century America* (Berkeley: University of California Press, 2004).
10 Roffman and Purdy, *Hollywood Social Problem Film*, 305.
11 Tino Balio, *Grand Design: Hollywood as a Modern Business Enterprise, 1930–1939* (Berkeley: University of California Press, 1993), 281.
12 Jackie Byars, *All That Hollywood Allows: Re-reading Gender in 1950s Melodrama* (Chapel Hill: University of North Carolina Press, 1991), 112–131.
13 For a reading of how *I Want to Live!* both draws on and differs from the social problem film genre, see Dennis Bingham, "'I Do Want to Live!': Female Voices, Male Discourse, and Hollywood Biopics," *Cinema Journal* 38, no. 3 (1999): 2–26.
14 Thomas Schatz, *Hollywood Genres: Formulas, Filmmaking, and the Studio System* (New York: McGraw-Hill, 1981); Alan Williams, "Is a Radical Genre Criticism Possible?," *Quarterly Review of Film Studies* 9, no. 2 (1984): 123.
15 All Zanuck memos and story conferences quoted here are contained in the 20th Century–Fox Archive and Philip Dunne Collections, Special Collections in Cinema and Television, Doheny Library, University of Southern California.
16 Thomas Doherty, *Pre-Code Hollywood: Sex, Immorality, and Insurrection in American Cinema, 1930–1934* (New York: Columbia University Press, 1999), 162. Doherty cites RKO's *Hell's Highway* as the first in a convict film cycle, before *I Am a Fugitive from a Chain Gang.*
17 Russell Campbell, "The Ideology of the Social Consciousness Movie: Three Films of Darryl F. Zanuck," *Quarterly Review of Film Studies* 3, no. 1 (1978): 49–71. The summary here is a quote, a favorable one, from Michael Ciment, *Kazan on Kazan* (New York: Viking, 1974), 62.
18 Rudy Behlmer, ed., *Inside Warner Bros. (1935–1951)* (New York: Viking Press, 1985), 44–45.
19 Rick Altman, *Film/Genre* (London: British Film Institute, 1999), 47.
20 "Jack Warner Burns at Cycles," *Variety*, October 3, 1932, 4.
21 Altman, *Film/Genre*, 47.
22 Darryl F. Zanuck, story conference, *Pinky*, November 17, 1948, Box 2391.12, 20th Century–Fox Special Collection, Doheny Library, University of Southern California.
23 Zanuck, memo, February 1, 1949, Box 2420.2, 20th Century–Fox Special Collection.
24 Zanuck, conference notes on first draft, *Island in the Sun*, October 25, 1955, Box 3006.2, 20th Century–Fox Special Collection.
25 De Rochemont did in fact produce one of the cycle's films in pseudodocumentary fashion: *Lost Boundaries.* Meanwhile, Zanuck tried hard to distance *Pinky* from that very genre: "We should find ways and means of keeping it, from beginning to end, the personal story of Pinky. . . . Seeing it in terms of the adventures of a girl they will accept it much more readily than if we tried to give it to them in terms of THE MARCH OF TIME." Zanuck, conference on first draft, *Pinky*, May 26, 1948, Box 2391.3, 20th Century–Fox Special Collection.

26 Zanuck, memo, *No Way Out*, February 1, 1949, Box 2420.2, 20th Century–Fox Special Collection.
27 Philip Dunne, memo to Darryl F. Zanuck, April 19, 1949, Philip Dunne Collection, Doheny Library, University of Southern California.
28 Zanuck, memo, *No Way Out*, February 1, 1949, Box 2420.2, 20th Century–Fox Special Collection.
29 Zanuck, conference on preliminary script, *No Way Out*, June 20, 1949, Box 2420.7, 20th Century–Fox Special Collection.
30 Zanuck, conference, *Pinky*, November 17, 1948, Box 2391.12, 20th Century–Fox Special Collection.
31 Zanuck, memo to Dudley Nichols, November 1, 1949, Philip Dunne Collection. Emphasis in original.
32 Zanuck, memo, *No Way Out*, February 1, 1949, Box 2420.2, 20th Century–Fox Special Collection.
33 Zanuck, conference notes on first draft, *Island in the Sun*, October 25, 1955, Box 3006.2, 20th Century–Fox Special Collection.
34 Reviews in *Variety: Cabin in the Cotton*, October 4, 1932; *I Am a Fugitive from a Chain Gang*, November 11, 1932; *Wild Boys of the Road* and *Our Daily Bread*, October 3, 1934; *Black Fury*, April 11, 1935; *Bordertown*, January 21, 1935; *Legion of Terror*, November 2, 1934; *They Won't Forget*, June 30, 1937; and *Dead End*, August 4, 1937.
35 Picture Grosses, *Variety*, October 3, 1932, 9.
36 Review of *Black Legion*, *Variety*, January 20, 1937.
37 Review of *Black Fury*, *Variety*, April 18, 1935.
38 Review of *Fury*, *Variety*, June 10, 1936.
39 Steve Neale, "Melo Talk: On the Meaning and Use of the Term 'Melodrama' in the American Trade Press," *Velvet Light Trap* 32 (1993): 66–89.
40 Review of *Legion of Terror*, *Variety*, November 12, 1936.
41 "Hughes Wants No 'Messages' in Pix; viz. *Green Hair*," *Variety*, August 4, 1948, 1.
42 "*Agreement* 20th-Fox's Top Grosser This Year, $3,900,000," *Variety*, December 22, 1948, 3.
43 "*Snake Pit* Strong in Smaller Cities, Allaying Fox Fears," *Variety*, January 12, 1949, 5.
44 "*Snake Pit* Seen No Problem After All," *Variety*, January 19, 1949, 7.
45 "'Pinky' Message Pic, Zanuck's '49 Film," *Variety*, January 26, 1949, 26.
46 "Kramer's Negro Theme Pic May Outrace Both 20th and de Rochemont," *Variety*, March 2, 1949, 3.
47 "'Message' Pix Must Have Quality; Negro-Themes B.O., Red Cycle Sags," *Variety*, October 10, 1949, 1.
48 Reviews in *Variety: Pinky*, October 5, 1949; *Intruder in the Dust*, October 12, 1949; and *Right Cross*, August 16, 1950.
49 *Annual Report to Motion Picture Producers and Distributors of America*, by Will H. Hays, president (New York: privately printed, 1933–46), 2, 14.
50 Production Code Administration, internal memo, October 15, 1934, Special Collections, Margaret Herrick Library, Beverly Hills, CA.
51 Ibid.
52 Production Code Administration, internal memo Hays to Breen, April 30, 1937, Special Collections, Margaret Herrick Library, Beverly Hills, CA.
53 Neale, "Melo Talk." The literature on melodrama as a film genre is extensive, but for a more recent example of a textual genre approach, see Mary Ann Doane, "Pathos

and Pathology: The Cinema of Todd Haynes," *Camera Obscura*, no. 57 (2004): 1–20.

54 Altman's notion of syntax and semantics is not exactly the same thing as Thomas Schatz's distinction between structure and iconography, but the terms do have a high degree of overlap and identify much of the same phenomena. Schatz, *Hollywood Genres.*

55 Kozloff, "Social-Problem Film," 459.

Chapter 5 Realist Melodrama

1 Review of *The Lost Weekend*, *Newsweek*, December 10, 1945, 112.

2 James Wong Howe, "The Documentary Technique in Hollywood," *American Cinematographer*, January 1944.

3 Lisa Dombrowski, "Postwar Hollywood," in *Cinematography*, ed. Patrick Keating (New Brunswick, NJ: Rutgers University Press, 2014), 61.

4 Robert B. Ray, *A Certain Tendency of the Hollywood Cinema, 1930–1980* (Princeton, NJ: Princeton University Press, 1985), 138–139.

5 Peter Roffman and Jim Purdy, *The Hollywood Social Problem Film: Madness, Despair, and Politics from the Depression to the Fifties* (Bloomington: Indiana University Press, 1981), ix.

6 Richard Maltby, "Post-classical Historiographies and Consolidated Entertainment," in *Contemporary Hollywood Cinema*, ed. Steve Neale and Murray Smith (London: Routledge, 1998), 40.

7 Janice Radway, *A Feeling for Books: The Book-of-the-Month Club, Literary Taste, and Middle-Class Desire* (Chapel Hill: University of North Carolina Press, 1997).

8 Gordon Hutner, *What America Read: Taste, Class, and the Novel, 1920–1960* (Chapel Hill: University of North Carolina Press, 2009), 7.

9 Laura Z. Hobson, *Gentleman's Agreement* (New York: Simon and Schuster, 1947), 13.

10 Bill Nichols, *Representing Reality* (Bloomington: Indiana University Press, 1991), 6.

11 Jeanne Allen, "*Now Voyager* as Women's Film," in *Now Voyager*, ed. Jeanne Allen (Madison: University of Wisconsin Press, 1984), 17.

12 Hutner, *What America Read*, 1.

13 Andrew Lawson, *Downwardly Mobile: The Changing Fortunes of American Realism* (Oxford: Oxford University Press, 2012). Lawson's argument is indicative of the historical gap: it makes a new historical reading of late nineteenth-century American realist novels against the economic malaise of the middle classes yet skips to the 1970s and 1980s in its historical coda.

14 Jürgen Habermas, *Structural Transformation of the Public Sphere: An Inquiry into a Category of Bourgeois Society*, trans. Thomas Burger (Cambridge, MA: MIT Press, 1989), 50.

15 Hutner, *What America Read*, 4.

16 John Hersey, *A Bell for Adano* (New York: Alfred A. Knopf, 1944), v–vi.

17 Karl Schoonover, *Brutal Vision: The Neorealist Body in Postwar Italian Cinema* (Minneapolis: University of Minnesota Press, 2012).

18 C. Wright Mills, *White Collar: The American Middle Classes* (New York: Oxford University Press, 1956).

19 Brian Neve, *Film and Politics in America: A Social Tradition* (London: Routledge, 1992).

20 Michael Szalay, *New Deal Modernism: American Literature and the Invention of the Welfare State* (Durham, NC: Duke University Press, 2000).

21 "Top Grossers of 1947," *Variety*, January 7, 1948, 63; "Top Grossers of 1948," *Variety*, January 5, 1949, 46.

22 Frederick J. Hofmann, *The Modern Novel in America* (Chicago: Henry Regnery, 1951); Evan Brier, *A Novel Marketplace: Mass Culture, the Book Trade, and Postwar American Fiction* (Philadelphia: University of Pennsylvania Press, 2010).

23 There may be exceptions to this tendency, but the overwhelming constitution of a "Realist and Naturalist period" as a subfield in American literary studies confines realism to canonical figures, generally up to the 1920s at the latest.

24 For a notable account of American realism, see Donald Pizer, *Realism and Naturalism in Nineteenth-Century American Literature*, rev. ed. (Carbondale: Southern Illinois University Press, 1984). Pizer's study contests much of Howells's theory but overall accepts the agenda and the canon of the American realist novel.

25 Hutner, *What America Read.*

26 Janet Holmgren McKay, *Narration and Discourse in American Realistic Fiction* (Philadelphia: University of Pennsylvania Press, 1983), 92–94; William Dean Howells, "Novel-Writing and Novel-Reading: An Impersonal Explanation," in *Howells and James: A Double Billing*, ed. William Gibson (New York: New York Public Library, 1958), 22.

27 Hersey, *Bell for Adano*, 172–173.

28 Colin MacCabe, "Realism and Cinema: Some Brechtian Theses," *Screen* 15, no. 2 (1974): 7–27.

29 John T. Flanagan, "A Long Way to Gopher Prairie: Sinclair Lewis's Apprenticeship," in *Critical Essays on Sinclair Lewis*, ed. Martin Bucco (Boston: G. K. Hall, 1986), 83.

30 Sinclair Lewis, *Cass Timberlane* (New York: Random House, 1945), 24.

31 Lea Jacobs, *The Decline of Sentiment: American Film in the 1920s* (Berkeley: University of California Press, 2009).

32 Some of the difference undoubtedly arises from the difference between American and European class structure.

33 Betty Smith, *A Tree Grows in Brooklyn* (New York, Harper, 1947), 424. In-text citations will be given for further quotations.

34 Thomas Schatz, *Boom and Bust: The American Cinema in the 1940s,* vol. 6 of *History of the American Cinema*, ed. Charles Harpole (Berkeley: University of California Press, 1997), 192.

35 Schoonover, *Brutal Vision*, xiv.

36 See Robert Stam, "Beyond Fidelity: The Dialogics of Adaptation," in *Film Adaptation*, ed. James Naremore (New Brunswick, NJ: Rutgers University Press, 2000), 54–76.

37 Bosley Crowther, "'A Tree' Flourishes on Film," *New York Times*, March 4, 1945.

38 Bosley Crowther, "The Screen in Review," *New York Times*, March 1, 1945.

39 Thomas Elsaesser, "Tales of Sound and Fury: Observations on the Family Melodrama," in *Home Is Where the Heart Is: Studies in Melodrama and the Woman's Film*, ed. Christine Gledhill (London: BFI Publishing, 1987), 43–69; Thomas

Schatz, *Hollywood Genres: Formulas, Filmmaking, and the Studio System* (New York: McGraw-Hill, 1981).

40 Geoffrey Nowell-Smith, "Minnelli and Melodrama," in Gledhill, *Home Is Where the Heart Is*, 70–74. See also the essays collected in Lucy Fischer, ed., *Imitation of Life* (New Brunswick NJ: Rutgers University Press, 1991).

41 Steve Neale, "Melo Talk: On the Meaning and Use of the Term 'Melodrama' in the American Trade Press," *Velvet Light Trap* 32 (1993): 66–89.

42 Ben Singer, *Melodrama and Modernity: Early Sensational Cinema and Its Contexts* (New York: Columbia University Press, 2001), 53.

43 Lea Jacobs, "The Woman's Picture and the Poetics of Melodrama," *Camera Obscura* no. 31 (1991): 121–147.

44 James Agee, review of *The Human Comedy*, *Nation*, March 20, 1943, 426.

45 Ibid.; Review of *The Human Comedy*, *Motion Picture Daily*, February 26, 1943, 6.

46 "Saroyan, Rooney, and Butch," *Newsweek*, March 15, 1943, 80.

47 Agee, review of *The Human Comedy*.

48 Review of *How Green Was My Valley*, *American Cinematographer*, February 1942, 66.

49 Barry Salt, *Film Style and Technology: History and Analysis*, 3rd ed. (London: Starword Press, 2009), 215–216.

50 Charles G. Clarke, "How Desirable Is Extreme Focal Depth?," *American Cinematographer*, January 1942, 14.

51 David Bordwell, "Deep Focus Cinematography," in David Bordwell, Janet Staiger, and Kristin Thompson, *The Classical Hollywood Cinema: Film Style and Mode of Production to 1960* (New York: Columbia University Press); Patrick Keating, *Hollywood Lighting from the Silent Era to Film Noir* (New York: Columbia University Press, 2010), 341–352.

52 Walter Blanchard, "Aces of the Camera XVI: Arthur Miller, A.S.C.," *American Cinematographer*, April 1942, 158.

53 Bordwell, "Deep-Focus Cinematography," 349.

54 Keating, *Hollywood Lighting*, 237.

55 Ibid., 243.

56 Review of *The Human Comedy*, *American Cinematographer*, March 1943, 95.

57 Review of *Kings Row*, *American Cinematographer*, April 1942, 161.

58 Otis Ferguson, review of *Kings Row*, *New Republic*, February 18, 1942, 237.

59 Salt, *Film Style and Technology*.

60 For a primer of cinematographic equipment, see John Alton, *Painting with Light* (Berkeley: University of California Press, 1995); Keating, *Hollywood Lighting*.

61 Todd Rainsberger, *James Wong Howe: Cinematographer* (San Diego, CA: A. S. Barnes, 1981), 78–79.

62 Ibid.

63 Manny Farber, "The Too Beautiful People," *New Republic*, March 15, 1943, 347.

64 Barbara Klinger, "Mutations or Mutilations?: Reissues of Classic Hollywood Films," conference keynote, 21st Screen Studies Conference, University of Glasgow, July 2011.

Epilogue

1 James T. Patterson, *Grand Expectations: The United States, 1945–1974*, vol. 10 of *Oxford History of the United States* (Oxford: Oxford University Press, 1997), 708.

2 Jürgen Habermas, *Legitimation Crisis* (Boston: Beacon Press, 1972); Claus Offe, *Contradictions of the Welfare State*, ed. John Keane (Cambridge, MA: MIT Press, 1985).

3 Dave Kehr, "Big, Important Picture? Sure. But Is It Best?," *New York Times*, January 4, 2009.

4 Doug McAdam, "From Relevance to Irrelevance: The Curious Impact of the Sixties on Public Sociology," in *Sociology in America: A History*, ed. Craig Calhoun (Chicago: University of Chicago Press, 2007), 411–426.

5 Gordon Hutner, *What America Read: Taste, Class, and the Novel, 1920–1960* (Chapel Hill: University of North Carolina Press, 2009), 333–334.

6 Jean Baudrillard, "The Masses: The Implosion of the Social in the Media," in *Jean Baudrillard: Selected Writings*, ed. and intro. Mark Poster (Stanford, CA: Stanford University Press, 1988), 210.

Index

Page numbers followed by an f *refer to figures (stills); those followed by a* t *refer to tables.*

About the Author

CHRIS CAGLE is an associate professor of film and media arts at Temple University in Philadelphia. His research interests include classical Hollywood, cinematography, contemporary documentary, and social theory. He has published essays in *Cinema Journal*, *Screen*, and *Quarterly Review of Film and Video*, and in a number of edited volumes, including, most recently, *Cinematography*, edited by Patrick Keating.